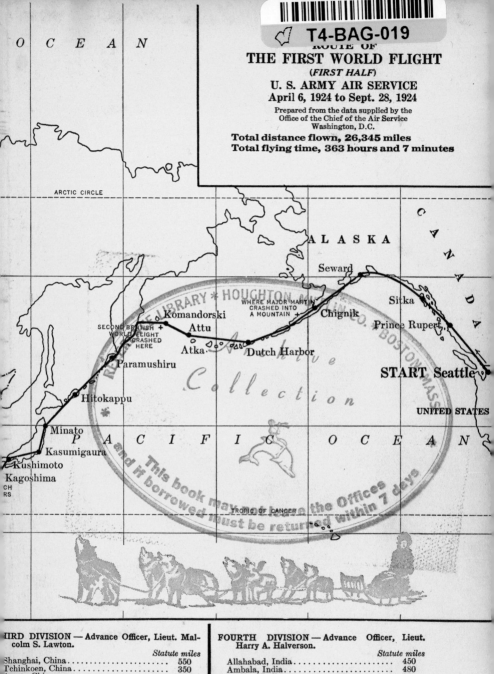

ROUTE OF
THE FIRST WORLD FLIGHT
(*FIRST HALF*)
U. S. ARMY AIR SERVICE
April 6, 1924 to Sept. 28, 1924

Prepared from the data supplied by the
Office of the Chief of the Air Service
Washington, D.C.

Total distance flown, 26,345 miles
Total flying time, 363 hours and 7 minutes

O C E A N

ARCTIC CIRCLE

A L A S K A

C A N A D A

Seward

Sitka

WHERE MAJOR MARTIN
CRASHED INTO
A MOUNTAIN

Komandorski

Chignik

Prince Rupert

SECOND BRITISH
WORLD FLIGHT
CRASHED
HERE

Attu

Atka

Dutch Harbor

START Seattle

Paramushiru

UNITED STATES

Hitokappu

Minato

P A C I F I C   O C E A N

Kasumigaura

Kushimoto

Kagoshima

CH
RS

TROPIC OF CANCER

THIRD DIVISION — Advance Officer, Lieut. Malcolm S. Lawton.	Statute miles
Shanghai, China	550
Tchinkoen, China	350
Amoy, China	250
Hongkong, China	310
Haiphong, French Indo-China	495
Tourane, French Indo-China	410
Saigon, French Indo-China	540
Bangkok, Siam	585
Rangoon, Burma	495
Akyab, Burma	480
Calcutta, India	445
	4910

FOURTH DIVISION — Advance Officer, Lieut. Harry A. Halverson.	Statute miles
Allahabad, India	450
Ambala, India	480
Multan, India	360
Karachi, India	455
Chahbar, Persia	410
Bandar Abbas, Persia	365
Bushire, Persia	390
Bagdad, Mesopotamia	530
Aleppo, Syria	450
Constantinople, Turkey	560
	4450

THE FIRST WORLD FLIGHT

FROM ARCTIC TO TROPIC ON MAN'S FIRST FLIGHT ROUND THE WORLD

THE FIRST
WORLD FLIGHT

Being the personal narratives of

LOWELL SMITH   ERIK NELSON   LEIGH WADE
LESLIE ARNOLD   HENRY OGDEN   JOHN HARDING

Written by
LOWELL THOMAS

Illustrated

BOSTON AND NEW YORK
HOUGHTON MIFFLIN COMPANY
The Riverside Press Cambridge
1925

The Riverside Press
CAMBRIDGE · MASSACHUSETTS
PRINTED IN THE U.S.A.

TO ALL MEN OF THE AIR
TO THOSE
WHO HAVE GONE BEFORE US
AND WHO MADE OUR JOURNEY POSSIBLE
TO THOSE
WHO ARE FLYING TO-DAY, AND
TO THOSE
WHO WILL FOLLOW US THROUGH THE SKIES
IN THE DAYS THAT ARE TO COME
WE DEDICATE THIS STORY OF OUR EXPERIENCES
ON THE FIRST ROUND THE
WORLD FLIGHT

CONTENTS

CONTENTS

CONTENTS

ILLUSTRATIONS

ILLUSTRATIONS

ILLUSTRATIONS xiii

ILLUSTRATIONS

FOREWORD BY THE FLIERS

As we look back in memory over the days and nights of our long flight around the world, the pleasantest memories are of the delightful people we met. To all who cheered us on our way and to the millions of our countrymen who welcomed us on our return, we wish that we could express our personal appreciation. But words are inadequate.

There are so many to whom we would like to express our thanks that it would take a separate book to include them all. But first, we owe a debt of gratitude that we can never repay to our Chief of Air Service, General Mason M. Patrick, and the members of his staff, who selected us for this enterprise of carrying our country's flag around the earth.

Then there is Donald Douglas, the genius who designed and built the aerial cruisers in which we made the flight. We also feel a deep sense of gratitude toward the members of his staff, a sterling corps of American workmen, and the men who designed and the mechanics who built our Liberty motors.

Next come our colleagues of the Air Service, many of whom we refer to by name in our story. There are also those who helped us during the flight: the advance officers who laid out our supply depots, the Bureau of Fisheries, the United States Coast Guard Service, members of the State Department, representatives of the Standard Oil Company in many parts of the world; and finally, the officers and men of the United States Navy who threw themselves just as enthusiastically into coöperating with us as they could have done if it had been a Naval Air Service undertaking.

We hope that all who open this book may get at least a part of the enjoyment from reading it that we have had in recalling our adventures. Flying, not writing, is our specialty. So, with the help of Mr. Lowell Thomas, the traveler and explorer who has devoted his life to visiting the countries across which we flew, and with the authorization of our Government, we have here recorded the most memorable things that befell us on our flight.

During the time that Mr. Lowell Thomas was flying with us for thousands of miles, in an accompanying plane, we were passing through the busiest days of our lives. How he managed to assemble the details in a connected and readable form will always be a mystery to us. But the book is written as we would have written it had we been able, and we extend our sympathy and our thanks to the writer.

Without the pictures that appear in this volume the record of our Flight would indeed be incomplete. Although many were taken from the cockpit of the *New Orleans* by Lieutenant Harding, and many others have been supplied by Mr. Lowell Thomas and his photographic assistant Mr. Harry Chase, we are also deeply indebted to a host of friends in all parts of the world who have sent us hundreds of pictures taken by themselves or by professional photographers at the various stops which we made in Asia, Europe, Iceland, Greenland, and North America. Among the many to whom we are indebted we wish to make special acknowledgment of the pictures sent to us by Pacific & Atlantic Photos Inc., International Newsreel, Underwood & Underwood, The New York Times and Wide World Photos, Harris & Ewing of Washington, Kadel & Herbert, the Photographic Section of the Royal Air Force stationed in Baghdad, Asahigraph of Tokyo, London News Agency Photos Limited, the Engineering Division of the U.S. Army Air Service, World Flight advance officers Lieut. Clayton Bissell and Lieut. Le Claire Schultz, Asahel Curtis of Seattle, and Messrs. H. A. Erickson of San Diego, Hamilton Maxwell of New York, and Frank Jacobs of Seattle.

Last and chief of those to whom we would offer our gratitude and love, are our mothers, who sent us away with a smile and welcomed us home with tears.

MEN WHO MADE THE WORLD FLIGHT POSSIBLE

Members of the World Flight Committee and Advance Officers. In center: Lieut. Robert J. Brown, Jr., Chairman of Committee. Clockwise, beginning at top (12 o'clock): Lieut. H. A. Halverson, Advance Officer in Southern Asia; Lieut. Clayton Bissell, Advance Officer in both Alaska and Greenland; Lieut. LeClaire D. Schultze, Advance Officer in Greenland; Capt. Lorenzo L. Snow, Foreign Relations Member of Committee; Capt. William Volandt, Finance Member of Committee; Lieut. Clifford C. Nutt, Advance Officer in Japan; Capt. Burdette S. Wright, Advance Officer in the United States; Lieut. M. S. Lawton, Advance Officer along the China Coast; Lieut. Clarence E. Crumrine, Advance Officer in Iceland.

LIEUTENANT ST. CLAIR STREETT, COMMANDER OF THE GREAT
FLIGHT FROM NEW YORK TO NOME, ALASKA, AND RETURN

He was in charge of much of the organization work in connection with the
World Flight, and the success of the latter was due in no small part to his
genius and enthusiasm *plus* his capacity for handling details.

Our flight is over and our story told. We are now bidding *au revoir* to each other, so this may be our last opportunity of speaking collectively as the so-called 'six world fliers.' But we like to think that this United States Army Air Service flight, in which it was our privilege to play a part, is just one more step in advancing the history of civilization. And we hope that it will contribute thereto by impressing you with the boundless possibilities of aerial transport. Some day — soon perhaps — we shall look back and smile at the difficulties we encountered, for we are now entering upon a new era, in which travel by air will be as commonplace as travel by covered wagon for our forefathers.

INTRODUCTION BY GENERAL PATRICK

On September 28, 1924, two airplanes landed at Seattle, Washington, thus completing the first flight around the world. These planes and the men they carried had flown 26,345 miles, their actual flying time being about 363 hours. They had experienced all varieties of climate from the cold, the snow and ice of Arctic regions to the tropical heat of India.

These World Fliers have frequently been called the Magellans of the Air. They have now completed a modest record of their achievement. In this they contrast with the great mariner who first sailed around the world, for we are told that 'no record of his exploits was left by Magellan himself.'

The story of this, the first flight around the world, is evidence of the skill and courage of those who were sent forth upon this mission. It also evidences the fact that the airplanes in which they flew were worthy products of the designers and of the manufacturers who were responsible for their building. They were the best planes of their type which could have been produced anywhere at the time when they were constructed. But when, in future years these planes are viewed in the National Museum, people will no doubt wonder, contrasting them with the air liners then in use, that men could be found who were bold enough to undertake so hazardous an air voyage in such small and fragile craft, just as to-day, when viewing the

Leviathans which ply the ocean, we contrast them with the cockleshells in which Columbus ventured forth on the unknown and uncharted seas.

Of what these World Fliers did, we may well be proud, and I commend their story to our people who have always admired those who are willing to venture into new fields, to show themselves to be men, undaunted by dangers, resourceful and unafraid.

MASON M. PATRICK

Major-General, A.S.

Chief of Air Service

THE FIRST WORLD FLIGHT

THE FIRST WORLD FLIGHT

CHAPTER I

THE NARRATOR'S TRIBUTE

WHEN the Muse of History takes up her pen to chronicle the achievements of our era, in the clear blue above them all she will write the names of the explorers and navigators who venture forth into the unknown to pioneer the way. Those restless ones, God's chosen sons, who go forth to win or die, have the greatest claim of all to immortality, for it is they who keep aflame that spirit of adventure by which the world progresses.

Before the dawn of history, when the first explorers went out from Central Asia, there were men of daring and vision ready to prepare the way for the early migrations of the human race. Since then the generations of mankind have never lacked for inspiration. Every nation that has played an important part in history has had its great navigators. Phœnician captains of four thousand years ago ventured in their frail triremes across the North Atlantic to the then unknown British Isles and sailed eastward to the tin mines of Malay. In the service of the Pharaohs were the Ethiopian navigators who offered up their prayers to Isis and Osiris and then fared forth to circumnavigate the continent of Africa. King Solomon, we recall, sent his Nabatæan galleys to the fabled mines of Ophir and the frankincense shores of tropic Malabar for ivory, apes, and peacocks. Since the time of Ulysses, the young men of Greece have sailed to every corner of the earth. This same spirit of adventure added many a thrilling page to the glory of Carthage and of Rome. Nor in all the chronicles of the past has there been a more enthralling

chapter than the record of the voyages of those bold sea-
rovers, Eric the Red and Leif the Lucky, who were the first
to visit Iceland, Greenland, and the Labrador.

Spain had her Columbus and her Magellan; Portugal
her Vasco da Gama and her Affonso Albuquerque; Holland
her Hudson and her Tasman. Great Britain owes her empire to her long line of sea-captains such as Raleigh, Drake,
and Frobisher. And now to this gallant company America
has added the names of the six lieutenants of the United
States Army Air Service, who were the first men to fly
through the air around this terrestrial sphere.

These young Americans went across the world with the
light heart of youth, but the 'courage of a day that knows
not death.' They had the shrewdness of men who had won
their way as boys in the rough-and-tumble of the market-
place; they had the grit of the pioneer stock from which
they came, the loyalty to high ideals, the skill to achieve
and the strength to endure which were needful to their
task. These things they had, for they were chosen out of
many. They had also a splendid backing in the thoroughness with which the flight was planned. And they had luck.
Gainsay it who will, luck was theirs.

In one respect especially these boys are typical of this
day and age. From childhood, their toys were not swords
or soldiers, but clocks and engines. To-day their ambitions
are not concerned with the old tools of conflict, but with
the new, delightful, and dangerous arms of peace. They
are of the race that shall forge new powers to carry us
where the spirit wills, from horizon to horizon, perhaps
from star to star.

This story of the first flight around the world was related to me by the boys themselves in the days when we
lived and flew together, after they had returned to American soil. It is told as they told it to me, hurriedly, laugh-
ingly, in trains and hotels, while their minds were filled
with quite other matters than pioneering an air-path across
Arctic storms, Siamese jungles, Arabian deserts, and the
friendless North Atlantic. But to any one who knows

what danger means, or has ever flown, their story is glorious and gallant.

Let me not dim the luster of their achievement with superlatives: glorious and gallant these boys are, but their voyage was successful because it was well planned by General Patrick, because the ships and engines were right, and because the pilots and mechanics are of America's wonderful best. No need to paint them as supermen. They are young Americans who had a fine chance and took it and made good. History will give them a place among the great adventurers.

Magellan's journey around the world opened up the sea-routes and civilization of to-day: the voyage of which these pages tell is the forerunner of a commerce that shall bring the nations closer still and of aerial enterprises so vast that they stretch beyond living sight.

CHAPTER II

THE GENESIS OF THE ADVENTURE

JUST who originated the idea of the World Flight will never be known. But General Patrick, Chief of the Air Service; General William Mitchell, his Chief of Staff; and Lieutenants Erik Nelson, Robert J. Brown, Jr., St. Clair Streett, and C. E. Crumrine were among the first to become so interested in the project that they translated enthusiasm into action. To them belongs the chief honor for its organization.

It had been long the ambition of aviators of all lands to be the first to circumnavigate the world by air. Especially was this true after the World War. British, French, Italian, Portuguese, and Argentine airmen were either attempting the World Flight, or planning for it, when General Patrick announced America's intention of entering the race.

Once General Patrick and his associates had decided that the attempt was to be made, they called up every resource of the Government and set about their task with characteristic thoroughness.

To ensure success, they believed that there were three essential factors to consider:

First, not only to have an aerial cruiser capable of making the flight, but to have a fleet of them, so that at least one would stand a good chance of making the circuit.

Second, not only to have supply bases wherever they might be needed, but also to get the coöperation of other branches of the Service, including the Army, Navy, Diplomatic Corps, Bureau of Fisheries, and Coast Guard Services, and to get the help of American private concerns engaged in business in foreign lands — thus eliminating just as many elements of risk as possible from an undertaking that was sure to be fraught with danger at every turn. For instance, the complete destruction of one of the escort planes in Oregon, Major Martin's crash into a mountain in the Aleutian Islands, and the sinking of Wade's cruiser, the *Boston*, give us a hint of the hazards involved.

Third, and of equal importance, was the task of picking the ablest airmen in the country, men who combined skill with stamina and grit.

Quietly but enthusiastically, a group of officers at headquarters in Washington began to gather together all the maps that might conceivably be of any use, data regarding landing-fields throughout the world, information as to climatic conditions from the Arctic Circle to the Equator, as well as every other odd bit of information that might be of the slightest value in attempting this most ambitious adventure.

The supply activities in connection with the Flight were worked out by property maintenance and cost compilation, in greater detail than had ever been attempted before. Spare parts for planes and engines, a fairly complete outfit of tools, small quantities of standard utility parts, and material, such as tubing, shock-absorber cord, plywood, and items other than spare parts, were sent to each station on the route of the Flight. The spare parts and tools were packed in specially constructed boxes designed at the Fairfield (Ohio) dépôt and built in the repair shops. The boxes themselves were constructed of ash, spruce, and plywood so that they might be used for the furnishing of wood for emergency repairs. Carpenter tools for working up the wood were sent in the tool chests. Tubing and other items which could not readily be bent were packed with the propellers in lengths of six feet or more. The weight, cubic contents, and dimensions of every article were carefully considered, about four hundred and eighty separate items being sent to each station, so arranged that the Fliers could find spare parts or repair material even in the dark.

Among other matters attended to, the Air Service had to get the consent of the twenty-two foreign governments over whose possessions the American air cruisers hoped to fly. Nor was this permission always easily obtained.

The original World Flight Committee in Washington was made up of Captain W. D. Volandt, and Lieutenants Robert J. Brown, Jr., St. Clair Streett, Erik Nelson, and Clarence E. Crumrine. Brown was the chairman, and all agree, who had anything to do with the World Flight, that no one is more entitled to credit than he for the success of the great adventure. Lieutenant Lowell Smith and his companions have won undying fame, but Brown and Streett, as well as the advance officers, of whom we shall hear more later, are entitled to more praise than they will ever receive from the public. But the pilots whom they helped select, and for whose welfare they worked night and day, never tire of praising the efficient World Flight organization which coördinated the various branches of the Government so that America's airmen enjoyed facilities that no other country had provided for its World Fliers.

A study of climatic conditions convinced Brown and Streett that the safest way to fly around the world would be in the opposite direction to that which had been taken by the aviators of all other countries. By flying West instead of East, the American aviators were able to get through Alaska before the fog closed down completely, to get from Japan to China ahead of the typhoon season, to miss the monsoons in Burma and India, and then to cross the North Atlantic before the Arctic winter came.

Lieutenant Erik Nelson is one of the ablest practical engineers in the American Air Service. Moreover, he is known to be as fine a pilot as he is an engineer. Out at Santa Monica, in California, there was a persistent young American named Donald Douglas, who had designed a seaplane for the Navy several years before, a plane that had proved successful both for land and sea flying. It had so impressed Nelson that, while on an inspection trip on the West Coast, he visited the Douglas factory and asked Mr. Douglas to lay out a design for an airplane to fly around the world, to be built according to United States Army Air Service specifications. This design was submitted to General Patrick in Washington, who approved it on August 1st and authorized Nelson to proceed to the Douglas Company to supervise the construction of an experimental world cruiser. Douglas provided the theoretical knowledge and Nelson the practical criticisms. The two fought long and often, but their respect for each other has outlived all their heated disputes and ripened into a firm friendship.

Each plane measured fifty feet from wing tip to wing tip and thirty-eight feet from propeller to rudder. Each could carry four hundred and sixty-five gallons of gasoline, thirty gallons of oil, and five gallons of reserve water. Empty, it weighed nearly three tons, and loaded, with crew of pilot and mechanic, over four tons.

The chief instruments on the dashboard are the tachometer, recording the revolutions per minute at which the engine crank-shaft turns the propeller, the air-speed indicator, engine ignition switches, ampère-meter, volt-meter, oil-pressure gauge, gasoline-pressure gauge, altimeter, an ordinary airplane compass, a new earth-inductor compass, a bank-and-turn indicator comprising two small gyroscopes for flying in fog, an automatic ignition cut-out switch, six gasoline control valves; also altitude controls to change the proportions of gasoline and air fed to the engine at varying heights, and an engine primer for starting in cold weather.

The pilot sits in a roomy cockpit directly behind a 450-horse-power, twelve-cylinder Liberty engine, on an aluminum bucket seat. He has a wheel in his hand like an automobile's, but set at a steeper slant to his body; the rotary motions of the wheel operate a vertical wing surface in the tail assembly, steering the ship to right or left, as also does the rudder bar at his feet, while the 'driving-post' on which the wheel is mounted (known in an airplane as the 'stick') can be moved to or from the body, thereby operating the ailerons (the hinged horizontal sections of wings and tail) which cause the plane to move upward or downward.

The assistant pilot, or mechanic, sits in the rear cockpit. Behind and beneath him in the tapering fuselage is a roomy baggage and tool compartment. Both cockpits are of identical size and contain the same controls so that the plane may be navigated by either occupant. Small transparent shields! protect the pilot and mechanic from the powerful air stream of the ship in motion.

Once the habit of flying is formed, it is rarely lost. The sense of power and well-being which comes from the pure air and the wide sweep of vision on every side bring a new delight to human experience. With the world at his feet, out in the untrammeled sky, with well-tuned engine singing a pæan of praise to the Creator of birds and men and Liberty-'twelves,' a pilot will sing for sheer joy of life. But in fog and storm, the Flier's task is one of the loneliest and most terrible that man may meet before the face of Nature, for, when the horizon is invisible, then balance and direction are lost save for puny, and as yet imperfect, gyroscopes.

On earth we do not realize how dependent we are on horizons and gravity for our stability, but many a storm-blinded pilot has learned the lesson to his cost. Stated broadly, the reason is simple, although the underlying causes would lead us, as underlying causes always do, into the borderland of the Unknown. The airplane, of course, moves in all three dimensions known to us, forward, sideways, up-and-down, and at constantly varying speeds and constantly changing combinations of the three directions; hence the action of the spirit-level, which on earth is obedient only to gravity and shows us correctly whether or not we are on an even keel, is confused in the air by the action of centrifugal and other forces. These forces also distract the compass, in its effort to nose itself toward magnetic north. On emerging from a fog it is not only possible, but a common occurrence, for a pilot to find himself whirling toward the earth in a spin when he had thought he was holding a straight and level course. This very thing happened to the *New Orleans* when flying over the Atlantic.

Energy, first cause of Creation, is in a particular sense the upholder of airplanes, for without motion they cannot function. It is the forward drive of the engine which causes the atmosphere to press on the cambered surface of the wings resulting in the upward pressure that sustains flight. When the engine stops, the airplane can maintain its life in the air only by gliding downward, eventually coming to earth. Hence motion is life to these creatures of man's fashioning, as it is in a deeper sense to man himself.

The strain on nerve and sinew — endless tension of every faculty — which long-distance flight still entails, is an ordeal that only the fittest and youngest of men can undergo. With blind weather ahead, hurtling into nothingness at ninety miles an hour, snow slashing their eyes, ice numbing their hands, air pockets and eddies swinging their ships giddily God-knows-where — is there a man whose pulse does not quicken in admiration for the pilots of the World Flight? Those who have flown for pleasure or for business — and have therefore shared in some small way in man's latest and greatest triumph over Nature — will realize the stress under which they lived during the storms they met across the earth.

To return to our Douglas Cruisers. The trial airplane was completed on time. After about two hours of preliminary flying tests, it was flown across the continent to Dayton, Ohio, where further tests were conducted to determine if it had the necessary qualifications for the World Flight. Several changes were made, that later on were incorporated in the final four airplanes that were built. It was in Dayton that General Patrick inspected this model, and, after flying in it, remarked that he only wished he was 'young enough to go on this great undertaking.'

After the tests were completed at McCook Field, the airplane was flown to Langley Field, Hampton, Virginia, where the landing-gear was removed and pontoons installed. Further tests were conducted as a seaplane to de-

termine if the plane could get off with sufficient load to
make the required distances on the various legs of the flight.
All these tests proved satisfactory, and Lieutenant Ernest
Dichman, of McCook Field, was tireless in his work on the
performance charts.

Up to this time, Nelson had no idea that he was going to
be selected to take part in the flight. In fact, he was quite
sure that he would not be, because he had already taken
part in more than his share of great flights and it was the
policy of the Air Service to divide such honors among as
many of the ablest pilots in the Service as possible.

The General had asked all the officers commanding the
various aviation centers in the United States to recommend
pilots. By this time everybody in the Air Service knew
about the flight and hundreds of men volunteered.

There were scores of pilots in the Service who met
General Patrick's requirements of character, courage, and
initiative, so it was not an easy task to single out any one in
particular. However, a decision had to be made, and five
Lieutenants were finally selected, three to pilot the Douglas
Cruisers, and two to serve as alternates in case one of the
others fell ill before the expedition left American soil. In
addition to these five, it was decided to select some officer
of higher rank, to take command and to pilot the Flagship.
The men chosen, as all the world knows, were Major
Frederick L. Martin, and Lieutenants Lowell H. Smith,
Leigh Wade, and Erik H. Nelson. Lieutenants Leslie P.
Arnold and LeClaire Schultze were the alternates. Martin,
Smith, Wade, and Nelson were each to have the privilege of
choosing a companion to act as mechanician and junior
pilot.

The pilots and alternates were notified to proceed to
Langley Field, at Hampton, Virginia, a few days before
Christmas, 1923, and the orders came as a complete sur-
prise to all of them.

Upon arrival at Langley Field, they went through a six
weeks' special course in all the subjects that General
Patrick and his associates thought might be useful to men

DONALD DOUGLAS, THE ENGINEER WHO BUILT THE PLANES IN
WHICH MAN FIRST CIRCUMNAVIGATED THE WORLD BY AIR

THE ORIGINAL PERSONNEL OF THE FLIGHT

Left to right: — Major Martin, Lieutenants Smith, Wade, Harding, and Nelson, and Sergeants Harvey, Turner, and Ogden.

LEIGH WADE WITH HIS MASCOTS, JIGGS AND MAGGIE

JACK AND ERIK HOLDING BOZO AND DODO

READY FOR THE START

Left to right: Sergeant Turner, Sergeant Ogden, Lieutenant Arnold, Lieutenant Wade, Lieutenant Smith, Major Martin, Sergeant Harvey. Lieutenants Nelson and Harding were absent when this picture was taken.

setting out on such an undertaking — subjects such as the study of wind velocity, the origin and behavior of storms, the climate of the countries they would pass over, aerial navigation, and enough medical and surgical knowledge to pull them out of minor mishaps in case of a forced landing in some region remote from civilization.

The leading meteorological expert of the American Army, Major Blair, gave them a special course of lectures on the subject of weather forecasting, to which he has devoted his life. Mr. Bradley Jones, one of the world's foremost authorities on aerial navigation, gave them a brief course in navigation and marine law. Major Noblett, of the Air Service medical staff, lectured to the Fliers regarding the uses of the drugs which he had placed in their first-aid kits, and advised them regarding the sorts of food to avoid in the tropics, and cognate matters.

A portion of each day was spent in the air, to familiarize themselves with the plane, making various tests, and working out navigation problems. Both pilots and mechanics also devoted several hours each day to calisthenics, medicine-ball, tennis, basket-ball, and road work. The boys went about their physical training as though they belonged to a football squad, or were training for the Olympic Games.

Ten mechanics had been detailed to Langley Field to work on the first Douglas Cruiser, and before the six weeks were over, Major Martin had chosen Sergeant Alva Harvey as his companion, Lowell Smith had picked out Technical Sergeant Arthur Turner, Leigh Wade's choice had fallen on Staff Sergeant Henry Ogden, and Erik Nelson had selected Jack Harding, who had worked under him for several years in Dayton.

At the end of February, pilots and mechanics were ordered to proceed to California, there to remain at the Douglas plant in Santa Monica, watching the building of the planes, so that each man would be thoroughly familiar with every detail of construction. By the middle of March, 1924, the first three were finished, so Martin, Smith, and

Wade flew them down to Rockwell Field, San Diego, to adjust the compasses on the special turntable there.

By this time everybody in Southern California was enthusiastic over the flight and the boys were deluged with social invitations. But they accepted very few, as their work and training would not permit it. Some functions, however, they did attend, such as a luncheon tendered by the Optimists' Club of Los Angeles, an aviation ball at the Biltmore, and another ball and reception held at the Ambassador Hotel, where the manager took eight stuffed monkeys down from the imitation palm trees and presented them to the Fliers, asking each to take one as a mascot. Martin and Harvey named their mascots 'Jiggs' and 'Maggie.' Smith and Arnold took 'Felix' and 'Petie' in the *Chicago*. Wade and Ogden named their monkeys 'Mutt' and 'Jeff,' while Erik and Jack called theirs 'Dodo' and 'Bozo.'

Although several lasting friendships resulted from these functions, the airmen accepted the preliminary honors with reluctance and diffidence and as a tribute to the Air Service rather than to themselves. The people of Los Angeles, of course, were keen to lionize them because every one knew full well that the boys were about to start on a journey which might take them, not around the world, but to that bourne from which no traveler returns.

The aviators themselves were troubled by no such forebodings, however. A great adventure was before them: their motto — 'Let's go!'

CHAPTER III

THE FLIGHT FROM LOS ANGELES TO SEATTLE

CLOVER FIELD, Santa Monica, fifteen miles from Los Angeles, had been selected as the official starting-point for the flight. Seven A.M. March 17, 1924, was 'zero hour,' but they were held up by fog and it was nine-thirty before they finally taxied across the field. Hundreds of people had been there since long before daylight, waiting in the cold to see the start.

A scout pilot had reported that flying conditions were unfavorable, but, despite the thick weather, Smith assured Martin that he could lead them through to Sacramento. The Major assented, for Smith had flown up and down the coast so often that he knew every pass in the mountains.

Pilots and mechanics jumped into their cockpits and with a mighty roar the great Cruisers started on the World Flight. Plane Number 1, piloted by Major Martin, with Sergeant Harvey as mechanic, was the first to leave the ground. Next came Lieutenant Lowell Smith, with Sergeant Turner, followed by Lieutenant Leigh Wade with Sergeant Ogden.

Lieutenant Nelson's plane had been completed only the day before, and was due at San Diego to have the compass 'swung' and a new motor installed. So he and Lieutenant Harding were ordered to follow the next day and catch up with the others in Seattle.

Behind the World Cruisers, led by Smith, came ten escort planes, carrying photographers and newspaper men. As they headed toward the mountains, the fog was so dense and so low that it forced them down between the narrow walls of the canyons. The worst stretch was through the Tehachapi Pass, a little over halfway between Santa Monica and Bakersfield. But the danger was soon over. Coming out of the northern end of the pass, they left the fog behind and plunged into the bright sunshine of the San Joaquin Valley. A moment later they were looking down on thousands of oil derricks in the vicinity of Bakersfield.

Still farther to the right, disappearing to the southeast, were the yellow sands of the Mojave Desert.

The rest of the flight to Sacramento was made in gorgeous weather, and was uneventful, except that Major Martin had a forced landing which delayed him for thirty minutes.

An enthusiastic crowd bade the Fliers welcome when they taxied across Mather Field. Sacramento had once been Smith's headquarters and all his old friends were out to wish him luck. Through the Chamber of Commerce, the Sacramento descendants of the Forty-Niners presented each of the World Fliers with a horseshoe, a rabbit's foot, and a four-leaf clover. And before they had flown very far along the Alaskan coast, they needed all their mascots, but benefited by none.

Since the World War the majority of aviators have been superstitious. Leigh Wade, for instance, knocks on wood half a dozen times a day, hates to see three cigarettes lit off the same match, and had a row with Ogden on one occasion when the latter walked under a ladder on a ship in the North Atlantic. Erik, on the other hand, scoffs at all superstitions but one — the one that seems to be universal among airmen — that a tragedy is likely to occur if you carry flowers in your plane.

Next morning the Fliers took off from Sacramento and headed north to Eugene over the Bret Harte country, 'Poker Flat,' and the placer gold-fields of Central California. Soon Wade's engine started to sputter and balk, and he was forced down on the outskirts of Cottonwood, California, a little town near the headwaters of the Sacramento River. Loss of water, resulting from a drain-cock that had vibrated open, had started the trouble. In landing, Wade tore off his tail skid, but, with the help of the pilots and mechanics of the escort planes, he and his companion, Ogden, quickly made the necessary repairs, refilled the radiator, took off

again, and dived down to the landing-field at Eugene
hardly forty minutes behind Martin and Smith.

Eugene is a second home for Smith; he had made his
headquarters there during the years when he commanded
the forest fire squadron that patrolled the skies over Oregon and Washington.

With the cheers of their Eugene friends nearly drowning
the roar of the Liberties, they took off early next morning
and pushed on toward Portland. Here they were visiting
a city as beautiful as any they were to see on their way
round the world, but a city, like so many others in this
country, that had failed to awaken to the possibilities of
aviation. Strange though it may seem, there was no place
for them to land in Portland and they had to fly across the
Columbia River to Vancouver, Washington. Of course,
Portland will some day forget her roses long enough to see
her opportunities in the skies and to realize that airplanes
will bring her within a few minutes of the ocean.

Their next flight was to Seattle, the city that hopes to
make itself the airport of the West. For an hour they flew
above the Columbia and its tributaries. Far below were
great log jams, lumber mills, and miles of virgin timber.

A hundred miles north of Portland they ran head on into
heavy rain and fog that forced them down into a canyon.
Denser and denser grew the weather. Playing leap-frog
with trees under such conditions is all right for those who
want to climb the 'golden stairs,' but they had a twenty-
seven-thousand-mile journey ahead of them and had
decided that discretion was to be the better part of valor.
So they turned back to Portland.

So far the planes that had escorted them from Santa
Monica were still with them — all but two. One had
dropped out. The other had crashed in the mountains
over the Cascades which the World Flight had just successfully passed.

They spent one night in Portland, and then despite a
heavy fog took off for Seattle. Climbing above the fog, they
flew along in a cloud realm far above the world of men with

nothing to guide them but the snow-capped summits of
St. Helena, Adams, and Rainier. It was gorgeous flying
weather up there above that rolling cloud continent, and
they flew for hundreds of miles across the forests of
Washington without seeing a sign of the earth beneath
until they plunged through the fog again and landed near
Seattle on the shores of Puget Sound at Sand Point Flying-
Field, which had been designated as the official termination
point of the World Flight.

But what of Nelson and Harding?

When the World Fliers left Santa Monica on Saint
Patrick's Day, March 17, 1924, Nelson and Harding were
busily engaged completing the work on their plane at San
Diego. Next day they flew back to Santa Monica, and at
dawn on the 19th of March started on their long journey.

They had planned on getting as far as Portland the first
day. But the clear weather lasted for only six hundred
miles, and, just after they passed Mount Shasta and the
mountains where one of the escort planes had crashed, a
blinding rain obliged them to spiral down and spend the
night at Eugene. However, they had made a non-stop
flight of eight hundred miles, which, next to the hop of
eight hundred and thirty miles from Reykjavik, Iceland,
to Fredericsdal, Greenland, was to be the longest jump of
the World Flight.

Next day, when they passed over Vancouver Flying-
Field on the outskirts of Portland, they saw that Major
Martin and the others had already gone on, so they kept
straight ahead and landed in Seattle just a half-hour after
the other planes.

Although the flight certainly started from Santa Monica,
it was decreed in Washington that the flights from Clover
Field down to San Diego and return and then up the coast
to Puget Sound should be regarded as tests. The Fliers had
not yet assembled their personal equipment, and there
were also a number of finishing touches to be added.
Covers had to be made for the engines and cockpits,

propellers had to be changed, spare parts packed into the smallest space possible, personal equipment cut to an absolute minimum, metal parts greased to prevent corrosion, and wheels replaced with pontoons.

All this took nearly three weeks' hard work on the planes at Sand Point Field, and every night the boys worked on their maps at the Seattle College Club, where they lived.

In the planes were rifles for killing game in case of a forced landing and a supply of hooks and lines. Each man had an automatic pistol and each ship carried a Véry pistol with which to fire off red, white, and green signal lights. Then there were two Thermos bottles filled with concentrated food for each man, and a small supply of chocolate and malted-milk tablets. Major Martin and Sergeant Harvey were to make good use of theirs in Alaska, while Smith and Arnold were to find use for their Véry pistol in the jungles of French Indo-China.

Each plane had its first-aid kit filled with medicines and bandages; there were canvas message bags, and, in addition to a few spare parts and rolls of maps, each Cruiser carried a sixty-pound ship's anchor with one hundred and fifty feet of rope.

Every article was weighed and listed because the Cruisers could not get off the water if the gross weight exceeded four tons and two hundred pounds. Thus, over and above the weight of each Cruiser and crew there was a bare three-hundred-pound margin for spare parts, guns, emergency rations, photographic equipment, personal effects, and the sixty-pound anchor. Each man, therefore, limited himself to two changes of underwear, an eleven-pound fur-lined flying-suit, special fur-lined gloves, two flannel shirts, two pairs of breeches, two pairs of long wool stockings, the one pair of hunting-boots that he wore, a cap, handkerchiefs, a waterproof match-box, a safety razor, and toothbrush. Parachutes, which had been included in the original list of equipment, were discarded owing to their weight of twenty-odd pounds, and because much of the flight was to be over the sea. Life preservers were also discarded owing to their weight and the space occupied by them.

Prior to the final departure came the ceremony of christening the Cruisers. General Patrick had issued instructions that the beverages used should be in accordance with the 'spirit of the times,' and that the planes should be named after four important cities of the country. So the *New Orleans* received a special bottle taken from where the Mississippi flows into the Gulf of Mexico, while the *Boston* was christened with brine that the citizens of the Hub had drawn from the Atlantic. A non-refillable stoup of *aqua pura* was taken from Lake Michigan for the *Chicago*, and the Flagship *Seattle* was, of course, christened with the water of Lake Washington, on whose shores the ceremony took place.

To Mrs. David Whitcomb, Jr., wife of the President of the local Chamber of Commerce, went the honor of baptizing Major Martin's Cruiser *Seattle*. The wife of Captain Car Connell, of the United States Army Air Service, broke the flask from Lake Michigan over the *Chicago*. The *Boston* and *New Orleans* were christened by the wives of Major M. F. Harmon and Lieutenant T. J. Koenig, both of the Army Air Service.

It was while in Seattle that the only change in the personnel of the World Flight was made. Lieutenant Leslie Arnold, one of the alternate pilots, was invited by Lieutenant Lowell Smith to take the place of his mechanic, Sergeant Turner. Although Arnold was a pilot rather than a mechanical expert, Smith decided to be his own mechanician. And in a way the selection of Arnold was most fortunate, for he excelled in some of the things that were rather out of Smith's line. For instance, after Major Martin's crash, when Smith took command, the task of making official calls in foreign lands fell to him, and likewise the difficult duty of responding at banquets. While Smith is a man of few words, 'Les' Arnold can speak almost as well as he can fly, and was therefore able to relieve

MAJOR FREDERICK L. MARTIN

CHRISTENING THE CHICAGO WITH A BOTTLE OF LAKE MICHIGAN H₂O, EXTRA
WET, VINTAGE OF 1924

his Commander of considerable responsibility by taking the 'control stick' on numerous oratorical flights.

Arnold also was the only member of the World Flight to keep a complete log of the trip. He often wrote it up while Smith was flying the plane, as they went sailing across oceans and remote countries. Then again he would work on it while sitting on a pontoon in a tropic lagoon, or at night while his companions slept on the floor of some trader's shack in Alaska.

'No man was ever more astonished than I when I found that I was to go along,' says Arnold. 'For months, I had been assigned to the World Flight, but merely as an alternate pilot. I never dreamed that there was the remotest chance of my actually going, because I thought that none of the pilots were likely to fall ill. The idea of my riding in the mechanician's seat had never even dawned on me because I never was an expert engineer. But one afternoon Lowell called me aside and asked me would I like to make the trip.

'"Sure, I'll fly to Mars if you say so," said I, not thinking for a moment that he could be in earnest.

'"Will you work like the devil?" he asked.

'"Sure, I'll work like a whole flock of devils," I replied, still thinking he could only be joking.

'"How long will it take you to get ready?"

'"I'm ready now," I said. "Let's go."

'Lowell to many people is an enigma. They don't quite know how to take him because he usually wears a poker face. But I noticed that he was even quieter than usual.

'"Not serious about this, are you?" I said.

'He nodded.

'"But what's the matter with Turner?"

'"I've decided that he is not going," said Smith; and with that he left me — in a daze.

'"It's too good to be true. Surely, I'll wake up in a minute and find that I am dreaming," I kept saying to myself over and over again.

'Later, I found that poor Turner's health was the cause.

He had developed lung trouble, and Smith had decided that it would be a mistake to take him when it was doubtful if he could even survive the flight to Alaska.'

From March 22d until April 6th, the Fliers remained in Seattle going over their planes, changing motors, tightening wires, taking off the wheels and putting on pontoons, and rearranging the compartments in which they were to carry their spare parts, tools, food, and personal effects.

In Seattle, just as in Los Angeles, they were overwhelmed with hospitality. Committees were constantly attempting to lure them away from their work. But Sand Point Flying-Field was too far from the city to enable them to combine work and pleasure, so they omitted the latter.

At last the eventful morning came and everything was in readiness. Seattle had been chosen as the official starting-point because from here on north no airplane had ever flown.

But before we take our seats in the cockpits of the Douglas Cruisers, it is only right that we should be given the opportunity of making the personal acquaintance of these circumnavigators who have added so much to the prestige of their country.

CHAPTER IV

SMITH AND ARNOLD, CREW OF THE *CHICAGO*

THE life of Major Martin and his mechanic Sergeant Harvey cannot be told here. Major Martin is a man who would have been well suited to represent his country in foreign lands had he not met with his sad accident in the North Pacific. But as he and Harvey only took part in the first 'jump,' we will not transgress on the limits of the story of the World Flight by including details of their careers.

Of the others there is much to tell. Each of the young Argonauts had tried his hand at many tasks before setting out on the Round-the-World Flight. Of the six, five are of as pure American stock as can be found on this continent. One traces his ancestry to the Pilgrim Fathers, another has Daniel Boone as a forbear. Two come of fine old Southern families. The fifth is a descendant of the sea-captains of the Connecticut Coast who commanded the tea-clippers and whaling-schooners in the days when America's merchant fleet was conspicuous on every sea.

Only one of the six is a naturalized American, and he, appropriately enough, is a descendant of the Vikings.

Three of the six ran away from home when they were youngsters and did everything from sailing round the world before the mast to serving under Pancho Villa, the rebel-bandit of Mexico.

After the *Seattle* had crashed and fallen, a twisted mass of wreckage amidst the mountains of the Alaskan Peninsula, Lieutenant Lowell Smith was placed in command of the expedition.

Although Smith's father and mother are Californians by adoption, their relatives on both sides of the family were among the pioneers who fought the Indians and cut little clearings out of the virgin forest of Kentucky. His great-grandfather was a stalwart backwoodsman who wore a coonskin cap, carried a long-barreled flintlock, wore a horn of powder at his belt, and was the father of seventeen children. Coming from such stock it is not surprising that 'Silent Smith' has been successful.

He was born on October 8, 1892, at Santa Barbara, California, the son of an ordained minister who can operate a lathe as well as preach the Gospel. Lowell derives his mechanical aptitude from his father and his silent disposition plus other qualities from his mother. It is on his mother's side that he is descended from Daniel Boone.

He is the second of a family of four children, and as a child, Lowell lived first in Santa Barbara, then in North Yakima and Spokane, Washington, and later on in San Fernando, California, where the Reverend Jasper G. Smith alternated between the pulpit and mechanical and electrical engineering.

His mother confesses that as a child he could never sit still for more than two minutes at a time. She left him at home with a friend on one occasion while she went out to make some calls. Upon her return the friend complained that Lowell had simply 'run her ragged.' He had gone out to the garden, pulled up most of the flowers and then replanted them according to his own ideas. Then he had turned the hose on the house as well as onto the next-door neighbor's. Never inclined to be boisterous in his play, he was nevertheless about the most mischievous lad in the neighborhood. Baseball and tinkering with engines were his chief pastimes, while Sunday School and girls were his pet aversions. However, he has recovered somewhat from his timidity regarding the latter.

After attending high school at San Fernando, also a business college, he suddenly broke away from school and went off into the Mohave Desert where he spent six months overhauling and then operating a pumping plant. From there he went to Los Angeles and became a mechanic in an automobile repair shop, but gave this up to join

Villa's army in Mexico. He found the bandit-general a fascinating character, an idealist fighting to free his fellow peons from bondage. Villa's army, according to Lowell Smith, had the finest *esprit de corps* that he has ever seen. The air service consisted of three planes piloted by three soldiers of fortune. Smith became the engineering officer of this flight; but when one plane collided with an adobe hut and the second was riddled with bullets and the third nose-dived into the ground, the air service melted away, so Smith came north and got a job on the 'Whittier' and 'Betty O'Neal' silver mines, at Battle Mountain, Nevada.

In 1917, the moment America entered the World War, he boarded the first train for San Francisco, 'wangled' his way into the Air Service, took a special course in aeronautics at the University of California, and was assigned first to Rockwell Field, near San Diego, and then to Kelly Field, Texas, the largest flying-school in the world. He showed such a natural aptitude for flying that for a long time the authorities would not let him go to France, but kept him as an instructor, and for the last three months he acted as officer in charge of flying. When he eventually did manage to get overseas, he arrived too late to take an active part in the war; however, several of his students became ' aces.'

Returning to America, he was assigned as Engineering Officer at Rockwell Field and later to the aerial fire patrol in the Pacific Northwest, in command of the 91st Squadron, where in the dry season fierce fires sweep swaths through the forests of California, Oregon, and Washington. Day after day Smith and his squadron of over twenty planes cruised up and down the backbone of the Cascades where it was but seldom that they would pass over a field big enough to land. Only once during the four years that he led the aerial fire patrol did a member of his squadron have a forced landing in the mountains, and then there were no fatalities. In the course of each fire season he and his sky-riders spotted on an average of six hundred fires and flashed the news by radio to the rangers. He is proud of the fact — and rightly — that during all his years of service he has never lost an airplane.

Under his leadership this patrol saved the Government millions of dollars' worth of the most valuable timber in America. This work also gave Smith important training in cross-country flying, a training that later assisted him to accomplish the really marvelous feat of navigation in leading his Cruisers around the globe without ever getting off the course.

In 1919, he was assigned to take part in the Trans-Continental Speed, Reliability, and Endurance Contest from San Francisco to New York and return. On this flight he broke one record when he reached Chicago as the first person ever to arrive in the Windy City from San Francisco by air. He was third at New York and first to return to San Francisco. There were seventy pilots entered in the contest, and he won a larger number of prizes than any of the other contestants.

It was in 1923 that he conceived the idea of attempting to refuel an airplane in midair. As everybody knows, it is a dangerous business for two airplanes to fly close to each other when sliding through the air at from seventy to one hundred and thirty miles an hour. Many experts said it would be hopeless to try to keep two planes together long enough for gas and oil to be transferred from one to the other. But as usual Smith had thought the matter out. After a few experiments he and his friend, Lieutenant John Paul Richter, remained aloft in their De Haviland airplane all through the day from dawn to dark, all through that night and right on through the second day. Never once during all this time did either of them have a moment's chance to sleep. They were fed, watered, oiled, and gasolined by means of a hose lowered from another plane. The first time they attempted to make contact with the hose, Richter accidentally knocked open the valve as he caught the dangling nozzle and got a gasoline shower bath. But luck was with them, for not a drop landed on the red-hot exhaust manifolds, else they would have gone up in flames.

Sixteen different times was contact established between their De Haviland and the refueling plane, from fifty to a hundred gallons of gasoline being transferred each time.

During this flight they established sixteen world records for distance, speed, and duration. During the thirty-seven hours and fifteen minutes they remained in the air, traveling at an average speed of 88.5 miles an hour, they actually covered twice the distance of the non-stop trans-Atlantic flight of Alcock and Brown.

Shortly after this, Smith and Richter gained more fame on their 'dawn to dusk' flight from Canada to the Mexican Border. This also was a non-stop, refueling affair. For twelve hours they sat in their cockpits as they flew twelve hundred and eighty miles over Washington, Oregon, and California at an average speed of better than one hundred miles an hour. Supply-planes met them at Eugene and Sacramento and refilled their gas tanks at the rate of fifty gallons a minute. The full moon was just going down behind the mountains of British Columbia when they started the flight, and, as they approached the desert of Northern Mexico, the moon again cast a brilliant light over the flying-field at San Diego. This historic flight proved that fleets of airplanes can cross any part of the United States at high speed to meet a possible invasion, without the delay of descending for supplies.

Another interesting episode in Smith's career, prior to the World Flight, was in 1922, when he set out with a squadron of planes from San Diego in search of Colonel Marshall and Lieutenant Webber who had mysteriously disappeared while flying above the desert en route to Huhua, Arizona, and whose charred remains were eventually found in the Cuyamaca Mountains. One of Smith's objectives on this desert flight was the hut of an old Indian guide. Nothing much was known about the Indian except that he lived 'somewhere about one hundred and ten miles southwest of Nogales.' With the vaguest possible description of the country to guide him, Smith led the way from Nogales across barren mountains and desert valleys

off to the uninhabited southwest. There was neither railroad, river, town, nor other landmark to guide him, yet at
the end of an hour and a half, Smith's plane made a sudden
dive and when the airmen following him looked over the
edges of their cockpits, far below, they saw the shack of the
Indian guide. Rarely in the history of cross-country flying
has there been a feat to equal this, except such episodes of
the World Flight as when Smith led his squadron through
fog, rain, and snow across uncharted seas around the world.
Smith was a Captain in the Army Air Service until the re-
organization of the Army in 1921, and held many responsible positions, at times having more than one thousand men
under his command; he also had had over two thousand
hours' actual piloting before the World Flight.

Lowell Smith is a tall, dark-complexioned, good-looking
young man with a determined mouth. His gray eyes suggest shrewdness and reserve power. About his lips there
lurks a whimsical smile. He is sensitive and quiet, quick to
think, but slow to speak. On all matters pertaining to
aerial navigation his fellow airmen knew that they could
rely absolutely upon his judgment. And to men engaged
in such an enterprise nothing is more precious than im-
plicit faith in one's leader.

History tells us that Daniel Boone, in addition to being
a great hunter and an intrepid explorer, was 'mild-
mannered, quiet, and unassuming.' So is Smith.

One night, shortly after the completion of the Round-
the-World Flight, Mayor Rolph, of San Francisco, was
introducing Lieutenant Lowell Smith and his fellow airmen to an audience of ten thousand people in the Munici-
pal Auditorium. Another five hundred thousand were
'listening in' on the air. All were eager to hear an address
from the lips of the man who had commanded the American
airplanes. Smith replied to the Mayor's oration in four
sentences:

'Friends, we are overwhelmed by San Francisco's hospitality. But I must confess that I have returned home
to discover that there is something even more difficult than

THE FIRST TIME IN HISTORY THAT A PLANE WAS EVER REFUELED IN MID-AIR

LIEUTENANT LOWELL H. SMITH

LIEUTENANT LESLIE P. ARNOLD

THE FLAG-PLANE SEATTLE GETTING READY TO TAKE OFF FOR ALASKA

Major Martin kneeling and Sergeant Harvey standing on the fuselage.

flying around the world, and that is making a speech. On our flight I often owed much — at times everything — to the other five officers who accompanied me, and especially to the man who flew with me in the *Chicago*, and now I am going to ask him to say something for the Flight. Ladies and gentlemen, allow me to present Lieutenant Leslie Arnold.'

Whereupon a smart young aviator stepped forward and, without a moment's hesitation and without groping for a single word, delivered a fifteen-minute address to that vast audience in a clear and ringing voice.

'How did he get that way?' asked one of the leading film directors of America who happened to be standing near the historian of the World Flight.

'That's easy,' was the answer. 'Before "Les" Arnold carved out his niche in the Hall of Fame he acted in a stock company.'

'That explains it!' said the Hollywood director. 'Any man who has been an actor in "stock" must be resourceful enough to *walk* around the world if necessary, or address a young ladies' seminary. I know, for I've been in "stock" myself.'

Like the other World Fliers, 'Les' Arnold has played many parts in his time. He was born August 28, 1894, at New Haven, Connecticut, the son of Frank Arnold, a railroad man, of Colonial stock. Among his ancestors were men who manned the ships that carried the fame of New Bedford, New Haven, and New London from the Coromandel Coast to South Georgia. His family moved from New Haven to New London when he was a youngster. As a youth he was bubbling over with high spirits and was always either being expelled from school or being taken back on probation. The last words that 'Les' recalls having heard from his high-school principal were: 'Arnold, my hand just itches to get at you.' But, when he landed in Boston on the last lap of the Round-the-World Flight, among the hundreds of telegrams and letters of congratulation that poured in was a message from that same high-school principal.

In his school days he took a prominent part in sports and built up the splendid physique that enabled him to stand the strain of flying around the world and the emergency feat of pumping gasoline by hand for four hours on the long jump from Greenland to Labrador, when the engine pump failed and when the *Chicago* was in danger of sharing the fate of the *Boston.*

In school, football was his favorite sport, basket-ball and baseball next. For several months one summer vacation he hired out as a lineman, 'digging holes and juggling telephone poles.' The last summer before graduation he toured New England 'in stock' with 'The Associated Players,' playing the part of one of Monty Brewster's spendthrift chums in 'Brewster's Millions' and filling the rôle of thug in 'The House of a Thousand Candles.'

After finishing high school, he drove about the country selling pianos to farmer's wives all one summer. In the fall he became a tobacco salesman. His job was to visit the grocery stores of 'Main Street,' taking orders for 'Horseshoe plug cut,' cheroots and 'Scrap.' Later that fall he was employed by a firm that specialized in building submarines, and for four years he studied the various phases of that work and in making many trial trips on newly finished submarines; he remained at this until he joined the Air Service in 1917. His ground school training in aero-mechanics, machine-gunnery, aero-dynamics, and other branches of aviation were obtained at Princeton, and he then qualified as a pilot at Waco, Texas, where he chafed at the idea of remaining in America as an instructor and went to 'A.W.O.L.' so often and made himself such a general nuisance that his superior officers sent him to France to get rid of him.

Like Leigh Wade, and most of the other pursuit pilots sent to Europe, he went straight to the great training center at Issoudun, arriving just at the time when the flower of American youth was being rushed through their tests at such speed that many had the finishing touch put to their flying careers without ever reaching the Front.

Just as he arrived at the Front, the Armistice was signed. For a month he went around France, salvaging planes and ferrying them back to the central air dépôt at Romorantin. One afternoon, five minutes after he had 'taken off' in a Breguet plane, the machine burst into flames as a result of faulty ignition. He pointed her nose down, and when she struck the ground he jumped out and watched her go up in smoke.

Christmas found him with the First Aero Squadron in Germany. He spent several months with the American Army of Occupation cruising above the Rhine between Cologne and Mainz. Until hostilities actually ceased, like nearly every other American airman, he had thrown himself heart and soul into the business of war. But once the fighting was over, he was delighted when orders came for his return.

Back in America, he was ordered to do exhibition flying at county fairs in the Middle West and South, in order to stimulate interest in aviation. He would go from one fair to another, and soon got acquainted with the snake-charmers, sleight-of-hand performers, dog-faced boys, and other side-shows that followed the same itinerary.

It was at Dresden, Tennessee, that he had one of the narrowest escapes of his flying career. The field was too short and much too muddy for safety. But the local committee begged him not to disappoint the crowds and he promised to go up, albeit against his better judgment. At the end of the field were some tall trees and a cliff two hundred feet high. Owing to the mud on the field, he couldn't get up enough speed in 'taking off' to enable him to turn before reaching the cliff. The plane stalled, and, in order to avoid crashing into the trees, Arnold shoved his control stick forward and nose-dived two hundred feet into the roof of one of the main buildings, where the prize poultry was housed. The roof gave way gently and broke the shock, but the nose of the plane went right on through until it rested on the floor of the second story, in the midst of a flurry of white Wyandottes and Buff Orpingtons. Arnold unwrapped a few boards from around his neck and climbed out unhurt. In fact, the only person injured was a woman in a building across the street who was so frightened that she jumped out of a first-story window. Arnold telegraphed for another plane and next day went on with his exhibitions.

In the winter of 1921, General William Mitchell, then Assistant Chief of the Air Service, stirred up considerable excitement when he told a Congressional committee that airplanes could sink battleships. Much doubt was expressed at this statement, so the Air Service arranged a joint maneuver with the Navy near Newport News. Arnold, Wade, Nelson, and a number of other Army aviators took up five planes, and in a very short time dispatched a destroyer, a submarine, a cruiser, and a battleship. The latter was a modern heavily armored German battleship, the *Osterfriesland*. Congressmen, Senators, and American as well as foreign military and naval experts were present. Instead of dropping bombs directly on the battleship, Arnold and his colleagues put them in the water right alongside, believing that they could wreck the more vulnerable part of the ship below the water-line. The bombs were made of 'T.N.T.' and weighed two thousand pounds each. Five of them were dropped near the battleship and she keeled over and disappeared under the waves in twenty-seven minutes.

Later, Arnold spent a number of months ferrying Martin bombers from Ohio to Washington. One day, just as he was about to 'take off' from McCook Field, Dayton, a smartly dressed civilian, carrying two big suitcases, approached him.

'At first I thought this tourist had made a mistake,' says Arnold, 'and had confused my Martin bomber with one of those saloon-planes *de luxe* that cross from London to Paris. But when he reached me, he dropped his suitcase, hitched up his trousers, grinned, and said: "I've got every-body's permission to ride along to Washington in this 'bus but yours. How about it?" And that was my introduction to one of the men with whom I was to fly round the world. It was Jack Harding from Tennessee.'

CHAPTER V

WADE AND OGDEN, CREW OF THE *BOSTON*

JUST south of Kalamazoo is Cassopolis. Hitherto the latter has been completely overwhelmed by the international notoriety of the former's strange name. But henceforth Cassopolis will have a place in history, for it is the home of a young man whose name will be associated with those of the great navigators of all time. As Arthur Brisbane says, 'History will forever record, if only in two lines, the dates and names connected with the first human flight around the world.' Among these was Lieutenant Leigh Wade, of Cassopolis.

Leigh has flown nearly every contrivance, both safe and unsafe, that was ever designed to leave the ground, and was one of the chief test pilots of the United States Army Air Service. He had had more thrills in his short career, before he set out to girdle the earth, than a hundred average men have in their lives.

On his mother's side Leigh's ancestors crossed on the *Mayflower*, and were of the old English aristocracy. His father's parents and relatives were Canadians. Leigh was born on a farm three miles from Cassopolis, Michigan, on the 2d of February, 1897, attended the traditional little red country schoolhouse, and then got his first taste of town life when he went to high school. Mathematics was the only study that interested him, but whatever enthusiasm he may have lacked in his classes he more than made up for in sports.

His first adventure was inspired by moonlight and a fair maiden. Leigh met and wooed the young lady on a lake near Cassopolis one still and silver night of summer. But instead of accepting his suggestion to elope with him to Kalamazoo, the young lady, who hailed from the 'bad-lands' of Dakota, called Leigh a tenderfoot and dared him to go West and do a man's work on a Dakota ranch. So Leigh caught the next train. Once there, he liked Dakota so well that he entirely forgot the maid whom he had met in the moonlight and turned his face forward toward adventure.

He joined the First North Dakota Infantry of the National Guard and went with this organization to the Mexican Border, to help General Pershing corral the elusive Pancho Villa, in whose air force Lowell Smith had been serving.

As soon as Uncle Sam lined up with the Allies in the World War, Leigh volunteered for the Air Service and trained with the Royal Air Force at Toronto. Until then he had never been in an airplane, but he learned to fly as naturally as a young bird. After instructing in Texas for a short while, he was ordered to France, made a splendid record as an instructor on *Nieuports* at Issoudun, and later was one of two pilots selected to introduce acrobatic instruction in looping, side-slips, Immelmann turns, vertical banks, tail-spins, nose-dives, and the other refinements of aerial combat.

Not long afterward he was ordered to Paris to test the planes that the United States were buying from the French. He held this position until the Armistice. Before returning to America, he spent months picking up airplanes left here and there all over France, and flying them to the main dépôt at Romorantin, near Tours. He also would go up to the frontier and fly back the planes that the Germans were surrendering to the Allies. So by the time he had been ordered home, he had flown everything in Europe that had wings.

Upon arrival in America, he was appointed as an experimental test pilot at McCook Field, Dayton, Ohio, where he continued flying planes of all types. He also did a great deal of altitude work and established a record of 27,120 feet with a multi-motored plane. In making this flight he froze his face severely.

One day Leigh went up to try out a new pursuit plane.

At about twenty-five hundred feet, while doing a nose-dive to test the ailerons, the latter locked and wouldn't budge. The plane dived toward the earth at twice the pace of gravity. He was aimed at the spot where one of his friends had crashed a year before. 'I was surely going to hit it,' said Leigh, 'and make another grease-spot just like poor Mac.' But about twenty feet from the ground, by sheer strength on the controls he pulled her out of the dive, flattened out, and landed safely.

Two weeks later, Lieutenant Harold Harris, another test pilot, was up in the same plane when the ailerons locked again. The plane shivered and shook and started to fly to pieces in midair. Harris jumped, and was the first man in the Air Service to save his life by descending in a parachute.

On another occasion, Leigh was testing out a propeller when it flew to pieces. He was flying over a speed course at an altitude of only ten feet and the propeller as it broke tore out the entire front of the engine. But Wade slid his ship into a grass field at over one hundred and twenty miles an hour, and, after hopping over several fences and a ditch, he still managed to keep her right-side up.

Another time, when flying at an altitude of two thousand feet, a crank-shaft broke and ripped the engine apart, causing it to catch fire. With flames creeping nearer and nearer to his cockpit, Leigh made a fair landing, shouted to some farmers standing near by to form a bucket brigade, and succeeded in putting out the blaze. When the fire was extinguished, he was so black that a farmer's wife thought him a colored aviator and was astonished to find that the Ethiopian changed his skin with soap and water.

Such incidents are all in the day's work of the test pilot. What an age is this! What heroes we are privileged to entertain, so often unawares! Leigh Wade did not imagine he would be selected for the greatest honor his country could give him. But if ever man deserved such recognition, it was this clean-living, hard-working young dare-devil.

LIEUTENANT LEIGH WADE

LIEUTENANT HENRY H. OGDEN AND HIS PET RACCOON

Sergeant — later Lieutenant — Henry Ogden was Leigh Wade's mechanic on the World Flight. 'Trouble-Shooting Henry' is the name by which Lieutenant Ogden is sometimes known to his fellows in the Air Service. For short, they call him 'Hank' or 'Houdini.' A 'trouble-shooter' is a doctor of engines. Whenever a motor develops a cough, staggers, altitude sickness, or any other ailment, a 'trouble-shooter' like Ogden diagnoses the patient and performs an operation or an autopsy.

'Hank' declares emphatically that there is nothing interesting or romantic about himself, or anything that he ever did, up to the time when he was picked out to fly around the world by Lieutenant Wade. But Henry, who is so shy and modest, has done everything from punching cows in the delta country along the Mississippi to wing-walking and leaping from plane to plane in midair.

He has a Southern accent thicker than molasses in January. Born on a plantation about as far south as it is possible to get in these United States, Henry Horatio Ogden spent his youth playing with pickaninnies on his father's cotton plantation between Baton Rouge and Natchez.

The plantation owners around Woodville specialize in cotton, beans, and cattle, and in the midst of this country, E. P. Ogden, a descendant of the early Colonists, controls four plantations and a cotton-gin, where his son, Henry of this story, acquired his first knowledge of engines as he tinkered with the machines that extracted the seeds and packed his father's cotton bales.

After Henry had finished high school at Woodville, he attended business college in New Orleans, and he is the youngest of the World Fliers, having been born on September 13, 1900. When America entered the World War, he was only seventeen; so he was not allowed to join the Army until 1919, entering the Air Service repair dépôt at Montgomery, Alabama, in the summer of that year. Up to that time he had never even seen an airplane.

After a six weeks' course in the construction of airplane motors, during which he frequently studied all night, he showed such aptitude for mechanics that he was made an instructor. Five months after he had enlisted, he passed an examination that raised him to the rank of staff sergeant. In the summer of 1921, he was transferred to Ellington Field, Houston, Texas; and later to Selfridge Field, Detroit.

During his time in the Air Service, he has spent his leisure either experimenting with aero engines in his own private shop or flying about the country in commercial airplanes owned by his friends. It was during his off hours that he started amusing himself by jumping from plane to plane in midair for excitement.

The pilots of the World Flight had already been selected, and each had tentatively chosen a second man to accompany him as mechanical expert. 'But there were six more of us who had been called to Langley Field to help in the preliminaries,' says Lieutenant Ogden. 'There we worked for some weeks on the first Douglas Cruiser, changing pontoons and propellers in order to find out which type would be the best for the trip. The six of us who were extras figured that we had no chance of getting in on the great flight. However, to our delight Major Martin drove up to the hangar one day and announced that none of the mechanics had been definitely accepted and that an examination would be held in a week. He said that the men who gave the best account of themselves in the examination would be chosen. So I started studying and working as I had never worked before in my life. Lieutenants Lowell Smith and Erik Nelson gave us our test. The examination was oral, and the following day it was announced that the mechanics chosen were Jack Harding, Alva Harvey, Arthur Turner, and myself.

'That was the happiest moment of my life! The fact that at first I was skeptical about the feasibility of the undertaking did not damp my enthusiasm. I knew that aviators of other countries had been attempting to fly around the world for several years. I knew that every expedition had been a failure. However, after I discovered how elaborate were the arrangements made by our Air Service, and after sizing up the pilots with whom we were to fly and the planes we were to use, I concluded that our chances of success were considerably greater than I had at first imagined.

'As I look back on it now, it seems like a dream, from which I may wake to find that I never was in the Air Service and that I am still manicuring cows along the Mississippi.'

CHAPTER VI

THE FLYING VIKING AND SMILING JACK

ERIK NELSON, pilot of the *New Orleans*, comes of a line of seafarers. While Smith got his instinct of a homing pigeon and his bump of location from Daniel Boone, Erik inherited his love of adventure from the fierce old Norse sea-rovers who sailed the North Atlantic and discovered the mainland of North America centuries before the voyages of Columbus or the Cabots.

Born on the 12th of June, 1888, in the city of Stockholm, he was the son of Erik Nelson, a Swedish engineer. Like Smith, he too inherited his mechanical genius from his father. As a youngster he was ambitious enough not to be satisfied with the usual eight hours a day in the Stockholm public schools, and for several years also took night courses in a technical institute where he learned the rudiments of mechanics. When summer came, he gave free rein to the other side of his nature — the Viking side — and put even more enthusiasm into swimming, sailing boats, and climbing about the rigging of sailing ships than he had devoted to his books.

His father took him for long walks. They were fast friends, and together hunted wild flowers, pressed them carefully, and later classified them according to their Latin nomenclature. Together with this practical botany, Nelson senior passed on to his son much knowledge of engineering, which gave him the foundation that was later to result in his being selected as the engineering officer of the World Flight.

'It isn't so much what you do. It's how you do it,' admonished his father. That has been Erik's motto ever since.

After completing public school, young Erik spent a summer as a sailor on a Swedish training ship in the Gulf of Finland. He took to the sea like a seal. At the age of sixteen, the lure of it became resistless, and, giving up all thought of following engineering as a profession, he packed his carpetbag, slipped away, and, like his ancestors, went out across the world to see what he could find.

As a sailor on a Swedish barque of a thousand tons he visited England and then crossed the Atlantic to Guadeloupe. From the lumber ports on the Gulf, where his barque took on timber for Montevideo, he voyaged up and down the coast of South America. It was on these trips that he first visited the United States, eventually reaching Sweden by way of Russia after a two-year cruise. Erik was a full-fledged sailor now, but it had been a tough experience. As the youngster of the crew, in addition to his regular routine of swabbing decks, making and mending sails, and wrestling cargo, the 'old-timers' made him catch *bonito* for the mess when off watch and spend the rest of his waking hours washing dishes in the galley.

In the odd moments, however, that we can all make for ourselves if the will be there, Erik applied himself to mastering English. His first cruise convinced him that, although his knowledge of Swedish, German, and French might be useful for social purposes on the poop deck, if he ever wanted to succeed in this new world of ships and commerce, he must learn English. In the absence of schoolbooks, he took an intensive course in the translation of articles from magazines. On top of this the bo's'n gave him an extension education in expletives whenever their tiny barque happened to be becalmed near the Equator.

Shortly after returning to Stockholm from his first voyage, he felt the call of the sea again and spent several more years before the mast on English ships, making two trips around the world. Having been paid off in Germany from a four-master barque and hearing that sailors were well paid for working on racing yachts in America, Erik took passage from Hamburg in the spring of 1909. He was not yet twenty-one when he arrived at Hoboken. Although his first job on this side was as a rigger in the shipyard at Greenwich, Connecticut, he soon got the place he wanted on a yacht, and spent the summer racing for a New York millionaire. When fall came, he had to hunt for some other way of earning a living and wandered aimlessly about the streets of New York for some days until a job was offered him as a Swedish rubber and swimming instructor in Fleischmann's Turkish bath on Forty-Second Street. In ten days the heat had reduced him by twelve pounds, so he 'quit' and got his next job in Grand Opera. Lina Cavallieri, of 'Merry Widow' fame, was being starred as 'Salome' by Oscar Hammerstein. Erik became a Roman Centurion with sword and shield and shiny helmet, on guard in the banqueting-hall while Salome danced the dance of the seven veils.

Noting that Mr. Hammerstein made no feverish attempt to sign him up for a long career in opera, Erik walked the sidewalks of New York until A. T. Demarist & Co., importers of foreign automobiles, took him on as a handy man and general roustabout. Here he stayed until the spring of 1911, and acquired his first experience with motors.

The summer of 1911 he spent at the Indian Harbor Yacht Club at Greenwich, Connecticut, in charge of the launches and the garage. Fall saw him back in New York, where he tried his luck at various jobs, working on and off for the Lancia Company until the summer of 1914, when he took a job as captain of a seventy-five-foot motor yacht. That fall, he and his cousin Bill went South to Miami with the birds and started a small automobile repair shop. Erik wound up the winter as mechanic for an aviator who gave exhibition flights. The season was poor, the aviator went broke, and did not pay Erik his last month's salary. Both he and his cousin Bill being broke, they bummed their way back to New York arriving there with twenty-two cents between them. From then on, his mind was on flying. Part of the time he would work for the Lancia Company; then for the Curtiss Aeroplane Company, whenever a job was to be had, dreaming of the day when he too would be a flier. After driving a car across the continent in 1916, he tried to enlist in the Esquadrille Lafayette, but failed to be chosen and went to work for the Curtiss Aeroplane Company in Buffalo. By now he was a recognized expert in building and testing engines. The following February both Bill and Erik tried to enlist in the United States Air Service, but were rejected, despite their experience. In July of 1917, Erik crossed into Canada and tried to get into the Royal Air Force, but was turned down on account of his age. Then he tried the Royal Air Force recruiting offices in New York, and also made a second attempt to get into the air with Uncle Sam's Army. Both attempts failed. But in October, 1917, he finally managed to squirm into the American Air Service, took his ground school training at Cornell, and became a bombing pilot in Texas. Meanwhile Bill, impatient to get overseas, had sailed for France with the Artillery.

In January, 1919, Erik flew a plane over the Grand Canyon of the Colorado and enabled a photographer to take aerial pictures of it for the first time. This four-thousand-mile trip was known as the flight from the Gulf to the Pacific and return, and was the beginning of extensive cross-country flying in America. In the late summer of 1919, Erik, with a squadron of four planes, visited thirty-two different cities, crossed nearly every State, and flew a total of seven thousand miles doing recruiting work. He not only was the chief engineering officer on this flight, but he piloted his own plane, and came back with a fine record for the whole squadron of never having had a forced landing.

The following spring, the Air Service decided to attempt one of the most difficult flights in the history of aviation. It was to be from Mitchel Field, Long Island, to Nome, Alaska, and back to New York. Lieutenant St. Clair Streett, one of the ablest aviators in America, and the man who did much of the thankless work behind the scenes in connection with the World Flight, was the commander of this New York to Nome expedition. Erik Nelson was his chief engineering officer.

Erik pulled all the planes through that great Atlantic
to Arctic flight without a single engine failure.

On the return from Nome, Lieutenant Streett, in landing on the soft field at Hazelton, British Columbia, got
one of the wheels stuck in the soft ground. Erik, who was
riding in the rear cockpit, had slid down on the tail of the
plane to keep it from going over on its back. However,
this was not sufficient; the plane went up on its nose and
Erik was catapulted through the air for about twenty-
five feet. Every one expected to find him badly hurt, but
he wasn't, and was able to repair the damaged landing-
gear so that the next hop south would not have to be
delayed.

Naturally, Lieutenant Nelson won the admiration of his
fellow airmen on this flight. Later, he was sent as a pilot
on the San Antonio to Porto Rico flight and increased the
good reputation he had already earned as a pilot and engineer.

The only one of the six World Fliers who was not born
in this country, Erik combines the best qualities of virile
America with the poise of the Old World. Daring as you
would expect him to be, he also has two other useful
qualities: pertinacity and common sense. As for vision
and imagination, his ancestors who roamed the Atlantic
could have been no more generously endowed. Erik is
one of those individuals who can dream and make his
dreams come true. He was one of the first to propose that
American aviators be sent around the world. Later it was
he who supervised the construction of the World cruisers.
It was natural and fitting, therefore, that he should have
been the pilot of one of the two planes that completed the
World Flight without mishap.

We have already seen how Lieutenant Leslie Arnold
made the acquaintance of 'Smiling Jack.' When Arnold
'took off' from Dayton, he thought his passenger was a
civilian. But an incident occurred on the way that opened
Arnold's eyes. While flying over West Virginia, thirty

LIEUTENANT ERIK H. NELSON

LIEUTENANT JOHN HARDING, JR.

miles west of Moundsville, one of his engines started to
sputter. To Arnold's amazement, the passenger crawled
out of his cockpit and began to tinker with the engine in
midair, so that it kept running until a landing could be
made at Moundsville.

Here mechanics inspected the machine and informed
Lieutenant Arnold that it would be necessary to stop overnight in order to give the motor a complete overhauling.
'Beg pardon, Lieutenant,' interposed John Harding, 'but
if you like, I'll fix her so that you can push on to Washington in a half-hour.' So saying he pulled on a pair of overalls and got busy. In less than thirty minutes the engine
was in order and the flight resumed.

Instead of being an ordinary civilian, Jack turned out to
be a man who had served two terms of enlistment in the Air
Service as Master Signal Electrician and Airplane Mechanician and was still employed as an airplane motor expert
at Aviation Headquarters in Dayton.

The son of John Harding and Mrs. Roberta C. Harding,
of Nashville, Tennessee, was born on the 2d of June, 1896.
All his ancestors on both sides of the family came from
England. The Hardings were among the first families of
Virginia to migrate West to the blue-grass country of
Tennessee. 'Belle Meade,' the famous Harding plantation
of five thousand acres near Nashville, was owned by four
generations of John Hardings and was one of the most
famous estates in the South in slavery days.

After the Civil War, the Hardings, together with nearly
all of their neighbors, encountered vicissitudes. Parts of
'Belle Meade' had to be sold, and to-day the sons of the
New South, in 'plus fours,' chase golf balls in the blue
grass where the Harding ancestors hunted buffalo.

Lieutenant John Harding, Jr., is the son of an inventor
and chemical engineer. His mother, a charming Southerner whose family came from Virginia, says that her Jack
always wanted to know what made the wheels go round
and preferred tinkering with alarm clocks to listening to
fairy stories. Before he was ten, he had filled the woodshed

with wheels and dynamos. Instead of buying candy with
money earned doing 'chores,' he would invest it in copper
wire and batteries. Always he dreamed of the day when he
could build engines better than any one else.

The severest thrashing Jack ever received was when he
disassembled his mother's sewing machine and scattered
it all over the room just when she was in a hurry to put the
finishing touches to a tea-gown needed that afternoon.
Jack's father thought that this was carrying the eccentri-
city of genius too far and did not stay his hand, although
his offspring offered to put the machine together again
in perfect order, and did in fact do so after his 'licking.'

After finishing grade school in the country, he went off
to Webb Preparatory School, at Belle Buckle, Tennessee,
the most conservative academy south of the Mason-Dixon
Line. There were no dormitories at Webb and the boys
lived in private homes in the village. Upon arrival they
were obliged to sign a pledge promising never to go out
after dark.

Webb produces very self-reliant young men. And young
Jack Harding, who worked his way through the school
cutting wood for the classroom stoves, probably received
as fine a training as this country affords.

Three summers, during his school days, he spent working
as a locksmith, opening doors and trunks for careless people
who had lost their keys. Later, he went to work in a
garage at Nashville and earned enough money to help him
through a course in mechanical engineering at Vanderbilt
University, where he remained for two years. Following
this, he took a special three months' course in engineering
at the University of Tennessee in Knoxville, and then
went north to Detroit, where he became a road-tester for
the Chalmers Motor Car Company. From there he
migrated to the Dodge plant, where for months he juggled
with one-hundred-and-fifty-pound engines and developed
the brawny arms and shoulders that stood him in such
good stead when fighting the fury of Arctic winds off the
Alaskan coast.

In August, 1917, just as Jack was about to return home to resume his university work with the funds that he had earned in Detroit, America entered the War and he immediately enlisted in the Air Service as a private. Uncle Sam, however, did not take advantage of his mechanical genius, but sent Jack to Fort Oglethorpe and put him on kitchen police duty for months, later transferring him to Kelly Field, San Antonio, Texas, where after several more months of scouring pots and pans he lost his temper with a cook and fought him. As a consequence, he was transferred to digging work, where again Fate was fitting his physique for the hardships of the Round-the-World Flight.

Jack did everything he could to get into the air as a pilot. Eventually his officers found out that he was better at repairing their staff cars than at digging trenches, and he was sent to the Aviation Mechanics' Training School in St. Paul, Minnesota. Here he made such an excellent impression that he was transferred to Wilbur Wright Field, Dayton, as a sergeant, and later raised to the rating of Master Signal Electrician and Aviation Mechanician.

His first great flight was in 1919, and came about by his having attracted the notice of Lieutenant Ernest E. Harmon by repairing the engine of a Martin bomber for him which had defied the skill of other mechanics. Just as happened on a similar occasion with Arnold, so now Jack succeeded in a few minutes — with a spin of the propeller he started it off with a crash and a roar that swept him on to fame. Lieutenant 'Tiny' Harmon made a mental note of him as a mechanic worth remembering; a month later, when he needed a man to help him on 'The-Round-the-Rim Flight,' he asked for permission to take Harding as his mechanic. The feat was attempted by a single Martin bomber under the command of Colonel R. H. Hartz, and piloted by 'Tiny' Harmon. The bomber flew from Washington, D.C., to Maine, then straight west across the continent to Puget Sound, on down the Pacific Coast from Canada to Mexico, and back to Washington by way of the Gulf States, Florida, and the Carolinas. It was the first time that the United States had ever been circumnavigated by air, and Jack was a made man.

When his first period of Army Service ended in 1920, he reënlisted for another year and served most of the time at Bolling Field, Washington, D.C., and at McCook Field, Dayton, Ohio. It was at the latter aerodrome that he became intimately acquainted with Erik Nelson, who later selected him for the Flight. When his second enlistment was up, he retained his position with the Air Service as a civilian expert mechanic under the title of Assistant Chief of Airplane and Engine Maintenance.

Although he had always been a mechanic and for some time had been a Lieutenant in the Air Service Reserve, he had never been given an opportunity of realizing his dream of becoming a full-fledged pilot. But before starting on the World Flight he had a record of over five hundred hours in the air as a mechanic.

In addition to his celebrated smile which has gained him the nickname of 'Smiling Jack,' he has another physical peculiarity. While one of his eyes is blue, the other is brown. Jack is absent-minded where girls are concerned — once he returned to Nashville for a visit and found himself sitting in a hammock with a lovely young Southern girl — who murmured sweet nothings and slipped her hand into his.

'Sure — great —' Jack answered. 'If I could just figure out — cylinders — magneto — dynamo —'

Whereupon the débutante snatched her hand away. And that was as far as 'Smiling Jack' got with courtship — until he had flown around the world.

CHAPTER VII

THE START

In spite of the fact that Sand Point Flying-Field was away out on Lake Washington, many miles from Seattle, hundreds of cars arrived soon after dawn to see the official start of the Flight.

The weather on the morning of April 4th was too foggy to fly, so the start was postponed. Next morning all the Fliers' friends were there again to bid them good-bye. Major Martin was the first to open his throttle, but, in trying to get off, broke his propeller and smashed a hole in one of his pontoons. Apparently the Major's plane was overloaded so some of his and Harvey's personal effects were discarded. But the Flight was again postponed, for it took the rest of the day and all that night to make repairs.

Two hours before dawn on the morning of April 6th, the Fliers were at their planes and ready to start for the third time. To their surprise there was almost as large a crowd as on the previous mornings — this enthusiasm on the part of their Seattle friends impressed the boys greatly.

Major Martin was the first to leave the water. Then Smith and Arnold, and then Nelson and Harding. Wade had trouble and was left behind. The tail of his ship seemed too heavy. So, opening the tool compartment of the *Boston*, he and Ogden threw out their rifle, an eleven-pound anchor, their extra boots, and other odds and ends, rearranged the angle of their stabilizer, and then got off without further trouble.

'As I look down on Lake Washington and Seattle,' wrote Arnold in his diary, 'and see them growing smaller and smaller behind us, I keep wondering what all those people far below us in the streets are thinking. One of Jack's friends last night told him that we might as well crook our toe in a trigger and get over with it! The betting

in Seattle is that not more than one plane will get around.
Of course we don't agree. Nevertheless, I wonder just how
many of us will get all the way round.

'Of course, we all have confidence in ourselves or we
wouldn't be here and — which is just as important — we
have faith in our Douglas Cruisers and Liberty motors,
confidence in our Air Service, and complete trust in the
staff doing our advance work.

'A number of other planes have been following us for
about thirty miles, but now, after coming up one by one,
dipping their wings and giving us the salute of the air,
they have all turned back and disappeared into the haze.
Visibility is only fair this morning. But above the haze
that half veils the earth tower snow-capped Rainier, the
peaks of the Olympic Peninsula, and the Canadian
Rockies. The summit of Rainier stands out as clear as
crystal. No wonder the Indians called that monarch
"Tahoma," "the mountain that was God."

'Instead of turning out over the Straits of Juan de
Fuca, the gate through which steamers pass on their way
to the Far East, we are heading north along the coast of
Washington. Major Martin is leading. A moment ago he
left the formation just long enough to swing out over
Bellingham and wave farewell to the friends in his old
home town.

'Now we are swinging to the left and flying above the
Strait of Georgia which separates Vancouver Island from
the mainland of British Columbia. The city of Victoria
has just disappeared on our left and out there through the
struts of our right wing are the skyscrapers of Vancouver.

'Our last American friend has just bid us *bon voyage*. Old
Mount Rainier is no longer visible. We are flying through
a fog-bank now and the mountain that has been watching
us for nearly a hundred miles, long after we reached Canada,
has passed out of view. But there was something almost
spiritual about that mountain. I saw Lowell glance back
over his shoulder at it several times, and I am sure the
memory of its grandeur will inspire us all the way around

the world. This undertaking somehow makes you feel the presence of the Ruler of the Universe as you have never felt it before.

'I wonder just how long it will be until we shall see old Mount Rainier again? Surely no more fitting spot for the start of a flight around the world could be found than at the base of such a mountain.

'Now we are passing through a haze like the smoke from a forest fire.'

At this point Arnold found other things to think about, but he resumes his narrative next day:

'We soon discovered that this haze was the forerunner of a fog which gradually grew thicker and thicker, forcing us to fly lower and lower until we were soon flying only a few feet above the water.

'Over little inlets and passages and between islands, we flew. The land on both sides was heavily wooded right down to the shore. Imagine what a commotion the roar of our Liberty engines must be creating up here in these primeval forests where ordinarily everything is so still!

'The region through which we are passing [the Inside Passage] looks utterly uninhabited. But I suppose there are plenty of representatives of the animal kingdom watching us. I wonder what the bears think of us! Once in a while we pass a cottage or two in a clearing. Twice we have seen people paddling canoes — Indians, I suppose. Occasionally the fog breaks for a moment and we catch a glimpse of a waterfall or a rugged forest-covered mountain.

'We have just passed over Discovery and Johnstone Straits, where part of the time we were nearly skimming the water to keep under the fog. In several places where we passed between islands the sea rushed and boiled like a mill-race. Near the upper end of Johnstone Strait we came out of the fog into the clear air and narrowly avoided crashing into an excursion steamer. If we were surprised — and, believe me, we were — I wonder what folks on that steamer thought when they saw a fleet of giant planes come swooping toward them out of the fog. As we swerved and went bellowing by, the passengers waved, and we waved back. It certainly does cheer you up to see people and be able to wave to them when you are flying over a strange region.'

As a result of all the trouble that Wade and Ogden had in getting the *Boston* off the water at Seattle, they had to make this entire flight from Puget Sound to Prince Rupert alone. But on they came through all the fog, rain, and snow. In groping their way over Johnstone Strait, flying just off the water, they, too, narrowly avoided running into ships. Twice they saw masts looming up just in time to 'kick rudder' and zoom to one side.

'Just before we passed into Queen Charlotte Sound,' writes Arnold, 'the ceiling lifted to five hundred feet, and although we had run into a rainstorm, we could see the Indian settlement at Alert Bay, on the east coast of Vancouver Island.

'Plunging on through drenching rain, and rounding Cape Caution, we saw the great swells rolling in from thousands of miles across the Pacific. Fully forty or fifty feet high those cold gray waves looked to me as I leaned over the edge of the cockpit. Hurling themselves against the rocky cliffs of Cape Caution, the great rollers burst into a shower of spume and spindrift that shot hundreds of feet into the air.

'It would have been fun to watch the old waves pounding against Cape Caution, but I wondered what would happen if we had to flop down in the middle of those angry seas. You can land in fairly rough water, but never in such wild, angry seas as these were. This was about the most vicious stretch of water that any of us, excepting Erik, had ever seen, and even our Viking got a thrill out of it.

'Rounding Calver Island, we swung to the right and again sought the shelter of the "Inside Passage." From then on there wasn't a clear stretch of water all the way to Prince Rupert. Sometimes we were flying through driving rain, sometimes through fleecy snow, again

BIDDING FAREWELL TO OLD MOUNT RAINIER

ADVANCE OFFICER CLAYTON BISSELL BEACHING SUPPLIES FOR THE FLIERS IN ALASKA

through sheets of sleet, and twice through squalls of hail that pelted the fuselage and wings like a flock of machine-gun bullets all striking at once.

'After groping our way over Bella Bella, Milbank Sound, Aristazable Island, Estevan and Napean Sounds, Petrel and Ogden Channels, and Malacca Passage, we reached Prince Rupert in a driving snowstorm at 4.55 in the afternoon, and came down into a refuge entirely surrounded by high wooded hills, called Seal Cove.

'Blinded by a snowstorm, Major Martin and Sergeant Harvey nearly ended their flight right then and there. The *Seattle* side-slipped, fell thirty feet, and dug the left pontoon into the sea. Imagine four tons of airplane crashing that distance into the water! The impact broke the outer struts on the left-hand side and snapped three vertical wires. At that, they were mighty lucky.

'With an exclamation of disgust, Harvey took the rabbit's foot which had been presented to him in Sacramento and tossed it into the sea. Instead of bringing good luck he said it had been a jinx. Well, the spirits of the Far North were against them, I guess.'

'Gentlemen,' said the Mayor of Prince Rupert, as he stood there in the snow looking like Santa Claus, 'you have arrived on the worst day in ten years!'

'We believed him,' says Arnold, 'and inwardly congratulated him on not trying to convince us that it was the worst day in forty years — a thing that an American would have been sure to do. These British are certainly a conservative race.

'Our flight of six hundred and fifty miles, through fog and sleet and against strong head winds, had taken us eight hours and ten minutes. Here at Prince Rupert we saw for the first time what splendid advance arrangements had been made for us by Lieutenant Clayton Bissell, who had preceded us by boat along this coast as far as the Aleutian Islands.

'As soon as we stepped ashore, the Canadians offered us hot tea, and other beverages for which Canada is famous.

Our first toast was to Bissell, who had paved the way for us.

'Our immediate problem was to see whether or not the *Seattle* could be repaired. Had the ship not been so wonderfully constructed by American workmen, it never would have withstood that thirty-foot plunge into the water without more damage than the snapping of a few struts and bracing wires. However, after a thorough examination, we discovered to our delight that the Major's ship had not been hopelessly strained and could be repaired. There are shipyards at Prince Rupert, and at one of them, with the aid of a crane, we hoisted the *Seattle* into a dock.

'Fortunately, British Columbia happens to be the home of the finest spruce in the world, and we had a local carpenter make new struts. Using these struts and extra wires we had carried along for spares, we worked all that day, all night, and part of the next day, before the repairs were completed, and the plane was then every bit as good as new.

'We oiled the wires on the other planes and looked the ships over with great care before risking them to the rigors of the next flight, which was to take us on into Alaska.

'The people of Prince Rupert gave us an official banquet, and many of those who attended were dressed as formally as though attending a ball in a Fifth Avenue or Piccadilly club. We, on the other hand, had shipped our dress uniforms direct to Japan from Seattle, and had nothing with us but the heavy woolen shirts and trousers, sweaters, chamois flying-jackets, fur-lined coats, and the Arctic pack shoes that we wore. A splash of color was added to the function by the presence of some officers of the famous Royal Canadian Mounted Police in their scarlet tunics, and we were greatly impressed by them.

'It was at this banquet that we passed through one of life's embarrassing moments, an episode that reminded us of how our educations had been neglected since the passage of the Eighteenth Amendment. When our hosts rose to drink to our success, we innocently made the mistake of standing with them and dumbly drinking a toast to ourselves!

'At the close of the banquet, we were presented with small Union Jacks as souvenirs, and, although we had never contemplated carrying the flags of any other countries, we were treated with such charming hospitality in Prince Rupert that some of us kept these Union Jacks in our planes in memory of the place whose citizens had welcomed us so warmly. As a matter of fact, everywhere we stopped on our way around the world people wanted to give us things to bring us good luck. But the good-luck charm that we were the most interested in was having plenty of gas and oil.'

All this North Pacific Coast is well known for its misty, rainy climate. Many years ago a Methodist preacher arrived in Prince Rupert, and in his opening sermon to the fishermen took his congregation back to the days of Noah, the first great navigator. When he had told the story of the Flood, a hefty trawler boy stood up at the back of the church and interrupted with 'Say, you can't put that over on us. Up here it has rained for forty years day and night and it hasn't even affected the tide!'

'We were wet through most of the time,' writes Arnold in his diary. 'Everything was so slushy and slippery that we were continually dropping wrenches and hammers overboard. Leigh Wade took off the front cowling [the hood covering the nose of the plane] and put it down for a moment on the wing while he turned to pick up a piece of rope. When he reached for the cowl again, it had slipped into the sea. Now the cowling of an airplane is not one of the things that you ever expect to lose. Although we had spare parts for almost every emergency, we hadn't any new noses for airplanes. The water where it slid off was fully sixty feet deep and, despite the fact that we fished for hours, we couldn't locate it. So Leigh got a coppersmith from the town to pound him out a substitute. From then on, for months, the *Boston* flew with a copper cowl instead of an aluminum one like the *Seattle*, *Chicago*, and *New*

Orleans. Poor old Leigh, in addition to being superstitious about such things as losing your plane's nose, is somewhat fastidious, a sort of Beau Brummel among birdmen, and the idea of the *Boston* flying around the world and appearing before royalty with a bulbous yellow proboscis was decidedly distasteful to the Sheik of Cassopolis.

'An old fisherman named John Toner used to row us back and forth from the shore to our planes out at Seal Cove. John's home was a floating shack — a sort of Arctic Noah's Ark, inhabited by dogs, fish, clams and crabs, and a rendezvous for all of John's fishermen cronies. Occasionally we would duck into John's shack to dry our clothing and get warm and we would sit around his sheet-iron stove listening to him spin yarns while we devoured the crabs and crackers and hot coffee that he prepared for us. The last day we were there, John had us sign our names in bold scrawl on his front door, then proudly had the door photographed, and varnished it in order to preserve our autographs as a souvenir.

'John's neighbors were envious, and when he went fishing one day he returned to find that some one had stolen his front door!

'We were mighty glad when it cleared up a bit and, even though it was raining, we left for Sitka. But in leaving, we felt that we had at least gained some valuable experience in buffeting storms, and in taking care of our planes.'

Major Martin decided that the boys should take turns leading, with Smith in the *Chicago* piloting the way on the next hop, then Wade on the long jump over the glacial fields to Resurrection Bay, then Erik on the flight past Mount Katmai and the Valley of Ten Thousand Smokes, then the Major again, and so on.

'We took off from Seal Cove, on the morning of April 10th,' says Wade, 'and followed Smith past the Indian town of Metlakahtla, made famous by Father Duncan, a missionary who devoted his entire life to educating and protecting the Indians. Without Father Duncan's help they would have been killed off by disease and the white man's liquor long, long ago. There are few white men in the Far North who have been more loved than this old priest, who for many years was almost an uncrowned king among the aborigines of these islands.

'Shortly after crossing into Alaskan waters, just off Cape Fox, we rounded the northern shore of Annette Island and passed the first important town in the "Frozen North," as Uncle Sam's empire in the land of the midnight sun was sarcastically called sixty years ago when Secretary of State Seward bought Alaska from Russia for a paltry $7,200,000. But we learned that enough fish are packed each year here at this southernmost Alaskan town of Ketchikan to pay the United States for what Alaska cost. Ketchikan, by the way, is referred to as the "place where they eat what they can and can what they can't."

'Word from Prince Rupert had been wired to Ketchikan that we were on our way, and as we came along under the clouds, flying low over the narrow channel between Gravina and Bevillagigedo Islands, we came within a hundred yards of the cannery piers that run out into the waters of Clarence Strait from this little Alaskan city.

'The wharves, all built on piling, were black with people, among them Americans, Indians, and Chinese salmon packers from the canneries, waving frantically. We were only fifty feet off the water, and so close to land that "Hank" and "Smiling Jack" could throw kisses for the belles of Ketchikan to catch. Although we could hear nothing over the roar of our motors, we could tell from the plumes of spurting steam that every cannery and steamer whistle was screeching a welcome.

'A moment later and the wooden streets and grinning totem poles of this town clinging to a mountain-side were a mere memory behind us in the mist. Once more we were flying in the great solitude of the North.

'The flight from Prince Rupert to Sitka, a distance of approximately three hundred miles, took us from 9.25 A.M. until 1.35 P.M. Next to the thrill of suddenly coming upon the Alaskan city of Ketchikan, with its picturesque location and crowds waving to us, our next excitement came about 11 A.M. when we were flying over the water to the right of Prince of Wales Island. By flying over a narrow neck of land only a mile wide on Kuiu Island, we knew we could jump direct from Sumner Strait to Chatham Strait and cut off about seventy-five miles of flight out of sight of land over Christiana Sound, past Cape Decision, and thence up the open Pacific along Baronofid Island to our destination. But when we tried to cut across this neck of land, the fog was so low that we were forced almost to the tree-tops and had to turn back and take the long way. We were flying along in single file up this narrow passage and it was a tricky maneuver for the leading planes to turn and fly back past the others. But by good judgment and careful piloting by all concerned, this was accomplished safely.

'It was while we were turning that "Hank" and I nearly floundered on the rocks. We happened to get into the "wash" of the *Chicago*. In a heavily loaded seaplane with large hanging pontoons a wash will make it gyrate wildly and in your wildest imagination you will be unable to conjure up a picture of what it is like and of what a shiver it sends down your spine, especially if one is only a few feet above the ground. The propeller wash from another machine is a veritable miniature cyclone. It shakes you and throws your ship about and puts you through a series of crazy maneuvers that will turn your hair gray if anything will. We were only twenty-five feet off the ground at the time, so we couldn't dive down out of it without smashing up on the rocky coast of Kuiu Island. We managed to get out of it by swinging to one side. But it was a close thing.

'At noon, just before arriving in Sitka the fog lifted and the air became perfectly clear and calm. As we flew over the harbor with its charming Old-World Russian church, we admired the view on this clear and bright afternoon. The city, as you know, was made the first capital of Alaska in 1804 by Alexander Baranof, head of the American-

Russian Trading Company. Certainly he chose a wonderful site: indeed, Sitka is perhaps the most picturesquely situated of the towns that we saw on our flight around the globe. A fringe of small islands covered with evergreen trees lies across the mouth of the harbor, and on the other three sides it is surrounded by precipitous snow-capped peaks. This harbor is named the "Three by Three" — three miles one way and three thousand the other.

'We were entranced by the sight. But on the following day we were to see it under circumstances that were to make us wish Baranof had picked a more sheltered spot for his capital. A storm came up that nearly wrecked our expedition just as a similar storm had brought to a tragic ending the expedition of Vitus Bering and Alexander Chirikov, who first explored this coast two hundred years ago.'

CHAPTER VIII

THROUGH ALASKAN BLIZZARDS

'WE seemed to have entered a new world — an Arctic fairyland,' continues Wade, 'when we left the open sea and flew past the islands at the entrance to Sitka Harbor. The water under us was so smooth it reflected our planes like a mirror. And there in front of us lay the tiny city clustered around its Russian church. Behind this fairy city, like the "backcloth" on a stage, ice-capped peaks rose sheer from the sea.

'Millions of seagulls flew toward us as though sent out as an escort. Then, hearing the roar of our engines, they flapped out to sea and only returned, by twos and threes, on the afternoon of the following day. As we drew near the shore and circled above the yellow buoys to which we were to moor, we noticed that the beach was white. We naturally assumed that it was snow. But later we discovered it to be herring spawn washed in with seaweed. It was on this spawn that the great flock of gulls had been feeding when we frightened them away.

'After we had moored to our yellow buoys, we went ashore and secured little rafts, manned them with Indians and put out from shore with cans of "gas" and oil. The rafts were made of trees cut just a few days before our arrival.

'After we had "serviced-up," boats took us ashore. As we grounded, an Indian band played martial airs. Officials of Sitka and representatives of the Governor of Alaska bade us welcome to the Far North and led us to a quaint little hotel. Imagine our surprise when we stepped into our rooms and found them full of huge bouquets of gladioli from the garden of an experimental station of the United States Department of Agriculture. More than ever, we seemed to have flown out of the fog into fairyland.

'But alas, Sitka turned out to be an Alaskan Circe and she nearly caught us in her toils. For the first twenty-four hours everything about the place fascinated us. We were entranced with the scenery. We visited the Alaskan village with its totem poles. We were overwhelmed with hospitality by the resident American ladies and their daughters, who acted as waitresses at a dinner given in our honor.

'Next day came disillusion.

'We had hoped to hop off for Seward at dawn. But when we awoke, a gale was blowing in from the sea, and with every hour it increased in violence until by noon it was blowing a hurricane. "Les," Jack, "Hank," and Erik and I were in a local photographer's shop looking at pictures when the door opened. An Indian entered, but none of us paid any attention to him. After five minutes or so the proprietor asked if there was anything that he wanted.

'"Yes," replied the Indian calmly and casually, "I just wanted to let these folks know that one of their planes is adrift."

'You should have seen us dive through the door and race to the beach! Sure enough, the *Boston* had been torn loose from her moorings, and the gale was blowing her toward the *New Orleans*. Some of us jumped into the nearest rowboats, while others rushed about town borrowing ropes and extra-heavy anchors from fishermen and hardware stores.

'But if it hadn't been for the *Ranger*, a fifty-foot Forestry Service motor-boat, and her plucky skipper, both the *Boston* and the *New Orleans* would have been wrecked. From three that afternoon until nine that night, we fought the storm. We got ropes and tied to the *Boston* and did everything we could to drag her out of danger. But the gale was so strong it was all we could do to keep the *Ranger* from going ashore, let alone execute any maneuvers with her.

'Although we battled all evening in the teeth of that gale, the most thrilling moment of all was when the

Boston came within a bare two feet of colliding with the *New Orleans*.

'Ogden and I were on board our plane by then. Erik was was in the bow of the *Ranger* giving orders to her captain; and Lowell and "Les" were in the stern of the *Ranger* hanging onto the rope we had attached to the *Boston*. The wind drove the *Ranger* around into a position that endangered her, and her skipper shouted to "Les" to cut the rope. But above the howl of the storm I could hear Erik shout for him to do nothing of the sort and for the *Ranger* to go hard astern. Erik had given the right command, and a few minutes later we had my plane away from the *New Orleans*, safely moored to a large fishing vessel.

'It was one of the critical moments of the Flight. But our adventures in Sitka were by no means over, and the next afternoon Erik and Jack had still another close call.

'The following day the storm abated. The wind was still high, however, and there was a big sea running. After lunch Jack and "Hank" and Harvey went out to look over the planes. Meanwhile Erik was sitting in the hotel addressing postcards. Just as he started for the post-office to mail them, he saw the *New Orleans* drifting toward the beach. Dropping his postcards right there on the sidewalk, he gave a whoop and set out at a run. Smith, who was upstairs, came down in three jumps. Both he and Erik rushed down to the beach and waded right out into the icy water up to their necks hoping to be able to keep her off the rocks.

'What had occurred was this: Jack Harding, who was on board the *New Orleans*, had thrown off the little snubber line that ran to the mooring buoy, not knowing that the gale had caused the shackle on the main mooring line to come unscrewed. So the snubber was all that was holding her, and when he threw it off she started at once toward the rocks. When Erik and Lowell reached the beach, Jack was already in the cockpit trying frantically to get the motor started, but they couldn't see him from the water. Just as Lowell and Erik had waded in up to their necks in the hopeless attempt to keep her off the rocks with their bare hands, they saw the old propeller start to spin. Ordinarily it takes a little time to get the motor started, but luck was with Jack. He jerked the canvas covers off the engine, untied the controls, primed the motor and ether, and got her running in less than a minute. Then he taxied her around and they soon got her moored again. But it surely was a miracle that she wasn't wrecked.

'To prevent the other planes from getting loose during the night, we reënforced the mooring shackles. It was long after dark again before we finished, and, as we were not yet hardened to this work and were worn out from the strain, we went straight to bed. Next morning to our delight the weather was clear and the gale had gone down. So we prepared to say farewell to this picturesque little place with its hospitable inhabitants and its inhospitable climate. At least we were in for a clear day, we thought.

'But once more we were deluding ourselves, for the hop from Sitka to Seward was to prove worse than anything we had so far experienced.'

Although every flight from the time they left America, flying into the West, until they returned to America, flying out of the East, was accompanied by its thrills, there are few stages more memorable than the flight from Sitka along the edge of the great Alaskan ice-fields.

'In accordance with Major Martin's orders that each pilot was to lead the flight in turn, on this hop we were to follow Leigh Wade,' says Lieutenant Erik Nelson. 'Our destination was to be Cordova, four hundred and eighty miles away, at the mouth of the Copper River. We had loaded each plane with three hundred and twenty-five gallons of gasoline, enough to carry all the way through to Seward, a distance of six hundred and ten miles, provided the weather was with us.

'By six o'clock the pontoons were checked for water leaks, the engine and cockpit covers were off, and we were ready to start. Final weather reports had not yet come through, however, so we waited until the radio station ad-

vised us that the skies were clear. At 8.45 we taxied off
down the bay between the ice-capped mountains. With
Wade in the lead, we were soon flying over the fjords and
glaciers and mountains of Alaska, with Sitka disappearing
behind us. It was a glorious, snappy morning, and the
liquid sapphire of the waters of Hayward Strait below us
was bordered with a diadem of silvery peaks whose summits glistened in the sunlight to our right.

'But this fair weather lasted less than an hour. After
passing Black Isle and Cape Edward, ninety miles out from
Sitka, we dived into fog. A few minutes later, as we flew
over the entrance to Cross Sound, a snow-squall caught us
and prevented our seeing Brady Glacier which was so
close to us on the right that we could feel the air grow
colder. The snow flew thick and fast, and it was all we
could do to keep in touch with the other planes. Below
were jagged rocks and to our right were ice-capped peaks.
We had to descend almost to the edge of the water and
crawl along the beach to keep from getting lost. Leigh
suddenly turned the *Boston* sharp to the left as though he
had seen a mountain looming up ahead. The rest of us
were so close to him that it was all we could do to bank
steeply enough to avoid crashing into each other. By the
time we had flattened out again, we were separated and
out of sight of each other in the snow. But luck was with
us, and we got together again in a few minutes as we passed
over Cape Fairweather.

'Just as we reached the entrance to Yakutat Bay, the
somewhat notorious sheet of water that leads into Disen-
chantment Sound at the foot of the glaciers that descend
from the slopes of Mount Seattle, we shot out into brilliant
sunlight again. There, looming in front of us was one of
the monarchs of the North, Mount Saint Elias, towering
up to over eighteen thousand feet. Between us and the
mountain lay the vast ice-field of the Malaspina, the largest glacier in Alaska. For nearly forty miles, from Yakutat
Bay to Icy Bay, we flew along the edge of it. Each day
millions upon millions of cubic feet of ice crack off from

this glacier and tumble into the sea with a thunder louder than the heaviest cannonading.

'The sight of this enormous ice-field, extending from the pellucid depths of the North Pacific to the distant summit of Mount Saint Elias, a glacial area larger than the whole of Switzerland, sent shivers up my spine despite the warmth of my fur-lined suit. We flew along the face of it, while Jack photographed the other planes between us and that prodigious wall of blue ice.

'There was something weird and terrifying about that apparently inert yet living creature of the Arctic, brooding there between the mountains and the sea. Moving on and on, crushing forests and even leveling mountains that lie in their paths, these glaciers of the North are as irresistible as the hand of Fate.

'Just off Icy Bay, and due south of Mount Saint Elias (where the Duke of Abruzzi first gained fame as a mountain-climber), we plunged into another snowstorm. This one turned out to be a real blizzard, and in comparison with it, the first one we had encountered off Brady Glacier was a mere teaser. Again we had to descend almost to the water, and with a sort of misery-loves-company idea we huddled together until the storm grew so thick we were in danger of running into each other and had to separate. The only way we could tell whether the others were ahead was when we would get into the wash from the propeller of another plane and wobble around and nearly upset on the beach before getting out of it.

'The beach was covered with snow, and the air around us was filled with it. Everything was one color and we might almost have been flying in total darkness. The only help was a strip along the beach where the waves kept washing and melting the snow, and this in contrast to the gray-white color of everything else appeared as a narrow black ribbon. We would drop down and cling to this line until we came to a bay, then we would shoot straight across until we picked up the beach again on the other side.

'Twice, when the density of the storm lessened for a

few moments, we passed over villages blanketed with snow, but with many of the roofs all caved in: they were abandoned mining towns, ghost cities of the gold-crazed adventurers of the past.

'Had there been a cliff or promontory jutting out, the chances are that all four planes would have crashed headlong into it. We couldn't see far enough ahead to have avoided it, and we were flying too low to have gone over it. But luckily the coast was straight and the beach clear.

'Sometimes we flew so low that our pontoons almost dragged on the water. Occasionally we passed over wrecked boats half buried in the sand, or over piles of logs washed up by the sea, and I kept wondering if we should hit them. Most of the time I flew standing up in the cockpit braced against the back of the seat with my feet on the rudder-bar so that I could look out over the front of the plane as well as over the side. Neither Jack nor I dared sit down because if we did we couldn't see the beach.

'Every few minutes I had to change goggles because the snow driving against my face melted, trickled down behind them, and blurred the lenses. Jack, of course, was as intently on the lookout from the rear cockpit as I was from the front. And we both kept wondering where the rest of the gang were until all of a sudden the plane would start to jerk and pitch, and we knew then that we were in the wash of some one's propeller.

'This second storm lasted nearly an hour. But even more suddenly than we had plunged into it, we came diving out into the sunshine again. Everybody looked wildly around for everybody else, hoping to see them and hoping that nothing had happened to any of the other planes in the blizzard. At first Jack and I couldn't see a sign of them. Then far ahead we spotted the *Seattle* and the *Boston*, and, looking behind us into the snow from whence we had just come, we saw the *Chicago* emerge.

'We passed more glaciers and ice-capped mountains, and below us on the beach we saw fishing boats and occasionally a wrecked steamer. Smith gave vent to his joy in getting out of the blizzard by diving around in the air and flying low over the boats simply out of curiosity to see what it was that kept them standing up so straight in the sand instead of lying over on one side. We all felt so relieved that we certainly would have "looped" if our Cruisers had been suitable for "stunting."

'After flying over Controller Bay and Katalla Post-Office, we headed out over Prince William Sound. The weather now was so gorgeous that we decided to push straight on to Seward instead of turning in to Cordova. Afterward we learned that the citizens of Cordova were very disappointed. They had arranged a reception, even sending all the way to the States for bunting with which to decorate their streets, and had arranged a banquet. We also were disappointed, but our one thought was to get on with our flight as rapidly as the weather would permit.

'Halfway to Seward, and not far from the little island town of Latouche, we passed over a tiny passenger vessel, the S.S. *Star*, that Lieutenant Bissell had used for getting our supplies out to the Aleutian Islands. She blew her whistle and Captain Johannsen and his crew waved to us. The *Star*, by the way, is known in the North as "the rubber-bottomed boat" because she is always getting on the rocks and then bouncing off again without damage.

'At 3.45 that afternoon we flew around Cape Junken, over a few miles of open sea, and then up Resurrection Bay, the most beautiful fjord in North America, at the head of which nestles the flourishing city of Seward.'

CHAPTER IX

FORCED LANDING OF THE *SEATTLE*

THE ruggedness of this Alaskan coast, the cold and the grandeur of the snowy peaks made a deep impression on Jack Harding, who had never encountered anything of this kind in sunny Tennessee.

'*April* 14: Snow, snow, snow. This is surely a good country for Eskimo,' he wrote in his log. 'We got up early this morning hoping to get away for Chignik; but the air is full of the biggest snowflakes I've ever seen, bigger and fluffier than we came through on our journey from Sitka. Having had quite enough excitement battling blizzards the previous day, we decided to sit tight and wait for more favorable weather.

'We had moored the planes several miles north of Seward in a sheltered arm of Resurrection Bay, near a cannery. We went out to the ships to get the batteries and have them re-charged at the local power plant. The wind was blowing hard and yanking at the planes in ominous fashion. So we decided to eliminate any risk of another experience such as we had encountered at Sitka, and borrowed heavy ropes and anchors from the cannery. Terrific blasts sweep off the mountains and are known as "Willie-was." Although only of short duration, they often reach a velocity of from fifty to a hundred miles an hour. At some places in the Aleutian Islands they are so frequent and so serious that cables have to be put over the houses to keep the "Willie-was" from ripping off the roofs.'

Seward is situated on the Kenai Peninsula at the head of Resurrection Bay, surrounded by towering mountains, and is the southern terminus of the new Government railway that is the key to the treasure lands in the heart of Alaska.

The Fliers arrived at Seward just ahead of the annual

ARRIVING AT SEWARD, ALASKA

WE ANCHORED IN FRONT OF AN ALASKAN SALMON CANNERY AT THE HEAD OF
RESURRECTION BAY

salmon run, but found the fishermen preparing for the coming of the 'silver horde.' When the salmon come, they come by countless millions! They sweep in from the open sea in vast schools and are in such a hurry to get upstream to the spawning grounds and so full of vitality, that they will jump six feet into the air, and leap cataracts and falls.

The females lay their eggs in the shallow water as far up-river as possible, and the males swim up to fertilize them. When the spawning season is past, the little fish go out to sea in schools and vanish into the depths of the Pacific. No one knows where they go. A year later they return to the stream where they were born, and like their parents, they, too, spawn and die.

'Seward is also the headquarters of the halibut fleet. In fact, the fishermen from a halibut schooner helped us to put extra heavy two hundred-and-fifty-pound anchors on our planes. Then we went on board their smack while she lay alongside the cannery dock.

'These Alaskan fishermen are the burliest, toughest, shaggiest-bearded *hombres* I have ever seen. We watched them unload their boat and then went down into their galley, had hot coffee, and fooled around listening to them spin yarns as they stomped about in their hip boots, slickers and rubber hats. Four of them tried to show "Les" how to tie a bowline knot, and then guyed him for his clumsiness. Most of the men who fish up here are of Finnish, Swedish, Danish, and Norwegian origin. They are big, two-fisted giants with picturesque names, like "Humpbacked Jake," and "Whiskey Nels."'

That night a brilliant moon came over the rim of mountains above the Fliers. Innumerable stars dimpled the surface of Resurrection Bay with their points of gold. It seemed to them as though, from the limits of sidereal space, the Lord of the Heavens looked down and promised them clear weather for the morrow.

'*April* 15: Up at 5. Out to the cannery, to get the planes ready, while the Major, Erik, Smith, and Leigh get the dope on the weather by radio. Sky clear as a bell.' Thus writes Jack Harding.

'At 9.45 we took off. Major Martin was the last to get under way, so the rest of us circled around for twenty minutes, flew alongside each other, took pictures, and fooled about in the air, amusing ourselves and the crowd below, until the *Seattle* finally joined us. It was 10.05 when we headed down the fjord between the two rows of extinct volcanoes whose snow-covered cones and glacier-filled valleys make Resurrection Bay one of the sights of the world.

'Our course on this hop from Seward to Chignik had been carefully worked out by Major Martin, Smith, Erik, and Wade. Our plane was to lead the flight, so Erik ascended to fifteen hundred feet, closely followed by the *Chicago* and the *Boston*. But for some reason, we don't know just why, and never did find out, the *Seattle* remained much lower, and when we headed off on the prescribed course over some low mountains near where Resurrection Bay joins the sea, Major Martin flew way out around Cape Aialik into the Gulf of Alaska. Just off the mainland we passed a freak rock, with a tunnel through it through which the sea rolled. Slowing up on the southern side of this rock, we jogged along until the Major caught us opposite McCarty Glacier and Nuka Bay.

'The *Seattle* did not signal to us, so we thought the Major had been flying low because he had suddenly decided to take the advice of some of the Seward people, who were of the opinion that the planes would be less likely to be wrecked by the "Willie-was" if they stayed five miles or so from shore. However, the "Willie-was" left us alone on this flight. We attribute this to the fact that they come down off the ice-capped mountains and spend their force near sea-level. We were high enough up merely to get a few bumps as they whistled under us.

'The *Seattle* kept up with us for a mile or so, but by the time we had reached Port Dick, she had dropped astern for the second time. Near Chugach Island, about a hundred miles out from Seward, we passed a lighthouse, and then an even more welcome light. It was the S.S. *Star*, and once again, just as when we passed her in Prince William Sound on the previous flight, she was headed in the same direction that we were. We could see her famous skipper and his crew waving as we sped by, and it sure seemed mighty good to pass friends away out there in that wilderness of water and ice. Later, the *Star* officially reported having seen three of the planes pass over her, with the fourth trailing ten miles behind.

'After passing over Barren Islands, we flew down Shelikof Strait, the treacherous stretch of water that separates Kodiak Island from the mainland of the Alaskan Peninsula. Here we encountered the first of another series of snow-squalls. The waters of Shelikof Strait, by the way, have the reputation of being the roughest in the world, with the exception of Bering Sea and the Straits of Magellan. Between squalls, the air was so clear that we could see the snowy mountains of the Aleutian Range from sixty to seventy miles to our right.

'Not far distant, we saw Mount Katmai, the gigantic active volcano which on June 6, 1912, had produced one of the most violent eruptions of modern times. The whole face of the mountain had been blown off and boulders as big as a house had been sent tumbling into the adjoining valleys. According to the explorers sent out by the National Geographic Society, who were among the first persons to reach the rim after the eruption, all of the buildings of New York City could be dropped into the crater without filling it, and there is no doubt they could be, for it is eight miles in circumference and thirty-five hundred feet deep.

'Although we were not flying close enough to see the wonderful land around the base of the volcano, called "The Valley of Ten Thousand Smokes," we could see clouds of steam rising from it. Had we not been engaged in pioneering an aerial route, we would have liked nothing better than to stop and visit this place, where scalding streams flow from under glaciers and where hot water and icebergs are found in the same lake. We were told that it ranks with the Yellowstone and the Grand Canyon as one of the awe-inspiring sights on the planet.

'Just as we were passing Cold Bay, shortly after we had seen Mount Katmai, we slowed down and Major Martin caught up with us. He did not signal that he had been having any trouble.

'At the southern end of Shelikof Strait we ran into several more snow-squalls, and although we lost sight of the *Seattle*, under the circumstances we all thought that the Major and Harvey would soon be up with us again. We kept looking back, and when fifteen or twenty minutes had elapsed, we began to fear that something had happened and that they had been forced to land. By then we were not over a hundred miles from Chignik, but we were flying against a stiff head wind that retarded us. In fact, we had been bucking a head wind most of the way and we had barely enough gas to carry us through. This meant that if we turned back to look for the Major and Harvey, the whole expedition would run the risk of being wrecked.

'The pilots speeded up the revolutions of their motors to over 1620 R.P.M. and sped past Cape Providence. Then a little later we ran into fog and more snow-squalls, but landed at Chignik at 4.25. A native boat came out to meet us. Smith, Nelson, and Wade immediately hurried ashore. A radio station had been established here by our advance officer, Lieutenant Bissell, and Smith at once ordered the operator, Sergeant Rogers, to communicate with the U.S. Destroyers *Hull* and *Cory*. He also radioed Captain Johannsen of the *Star*. We knew that they were all not far away, and within a few minutes replies came back that they were acting on Smith's suggestion and speeding toward Kanatak and Portage Bay. We knew that the *Seattle* must be somewhere along that part of the coast. Smith also sent a message to a Standard Oil radio station some miles inland from Kanatak where there was a crew prospecting for oil. The superintendent at once started overland on horseback through the snow on a long and hazardous ride to get every one at Kanatak to help in the search for the lost World Cruiser.

'The destroyers *Hull* and *Cory* radioed us that they were proceeding full speed ahead and expected to find the plane by daylight. Captain Johannsen, on his little "rubber-bottomed tub," the *Star*, overheard all of this radioing, and he also wirelessed us as follows:

'"Racing to the rescue full speed ahead."

'Then a little later he radioed again: "Hope to reach Martin ahead of the destroyers."

'But not long afterward another message arrived: "Destroyers have just passed us, making thirty-two knots. Best we can do is seven. By comparison looks as though we must be going backwards."

'We were all worried sick over the disappearance of Number 1. That day, as we flew above Shelikof Strait was to be the last time we were to see our plucky Commander and our old pal Harvey until our return to Seattle.'

Although a few brief dispatches were radioed out from the Far North, telling the world of the disappearance of Major Martin and Sergeant Harvey, the full story of their adventures has never been told. Since then, however, Major Martin has given an account of it which, of course, constitutes an important part of the chronicle of the Flight.

'At 2.40 P.M., after being in the air four hours and thirty minutes, Sergeant Harvey called my attention to the fact that our oil pressure was at zero. This forced us to land with the least possible delay. Fortunately, we were just off Cape Igvak, having passed through Shelikof Strait. The *New Orleans*, leading, was flying at a thousand feet.

'It was necessary to throttle the engine in order to glide within the shelter of Cape Igvak. The wind was from the northwest, blowing at forty miles an hour. The open sea was rough enough to make landing extremely hazardous, but, behind the shelter of Cape Igvak, the swells were not so high and it looked as though we could get down safely.'

The water was very deep in the harbor of Portage Bay and Major Martin reports that they were compelled to anchor a hundred yards offshore.

'Upon examination, we found a hole three inches in diameter in the crank-case on the left side, under Number 5 cylinder,' said the Major. 'The connecting rods seemed to be intact, and as no opportunity was ever available to determine the exact cause of this trouble, we assumed that it was caused by the loosening of a connecting-rod bolt, permitting all the oil to escape.

'Sergeant Harvey and I remained aboard the *Seattle* all that night. We had thought of trying to get ashore to build a fire on the beach, but we gave this up until morning, because we should have had to wade through icy waters for a hundred yards, and then dry our clothes before a bonfire.

'I tried the self-starter, and, to our surprise, it would not work. No doubt the spline was broken. This left us helpless in case we started to drift. After eating the few malted-milk tablets we had, we divided the night into watches of four hours each, in order to get a little rest. After two in the morning, however, neither of us could get to sleep owing to the cold. It was a calm, clear night with the moon shining on the precipitous mountains around us. The waters of the bay and the snow-capped peaks were a wonderful sight in the moonlight.

'At 4.55 I saw a thin wisp of smoke on the horizon to the southeast, near Kodiak Island. As the smoke drew near, we recognized through our field-glasses that it came from the funnels of two destroyers. They arrived off the entrance to Portage Bay at 5.30 A.M., traveling at full speed. At minute intervals we fired three rockets with our Véry pistol. When they were about a mile distant, we saw that they had a small launch swung out on its davits and that they had dropped anchor. When the launch approached, the officer in charge informed us that he was from the U.S.S. Destroyer *Hull*. We were towed over to the *Hull* and welcomed on board by Lieutenant-Commander J. C. Hilliard.

'After breakfast we were towed to the little village of Kanatak, where the entire population, about forty people, turned out to greet us. Upon going ashore we learned that this was their first calm day in eight months. From what we heard regarding the frequency and velocity of the winds, we decided to float the *Seattle* into a little creek at high tide, and then on into a small pond two hundred yards from the shore. This was accomplished on the high tide at eleven that night.'

Lieutenant Smith had radioed to Bissell at Dutch Harbor to rush a new engine, as well as a supply of gasoline and oil, out to Martin by the Coast Guard cutter *Algonquin*. While waiting for these, Major Martin radioed to the rest of the Flight to push on to Dutch Harbor, the main supply base, and check over their planes while waiting for his ship to catch up. When the engine and supplies finally arrived at Kanatak on the *Algonquin*, they were brought ashore in a whaleboat. Wading in the water around the plane and chopping away the ice from the pontoons, Major Martin caught a severe cold and was confined to his bed. But Sergeant Harvey, with one of the sailors from the *Algonquin*, worked all night by lantern-light in the snow installing the new engine.

'On the morning of the 25th, we arose at 3 A.M. and found the weather calm. But it was necessary again to break the ice around the pontoons and float the cakes down the creek before we dared move the plane.

'Then, by means of skids, and with the aid of a Holt tractor loaned by our Standard Oil friends, the *Seattle* was finally dragged to the edge of the bay. The wind had now increased to thirty miles an hour and the water had become very rough in Portage Bay. It was a critical moment, and it looked equally dangerous either to attempt to take her back up the creek or take-off through the high seas.'

A decision had to be made instantly, however, so Major Martin decided that the lesser of the two hazards would be to take off. Not many seaplanes have ever left the water under more critical circumstances.

At eleven o'clock they were in the air and circled over Kanatak three times — in doubt as to whether it would be safe to try to fly on to Chignik against the snowstorm and with a high sea running below them. But the favorable radio reports that had come through that morning decided the Major to attempt to rejoin the Flight rather than risk having the *Seattle* destroyed by a 'Willie-wa' on the bleak shores of Portage Bay.

CHAPTER X

FROM CHIGNIK TO DUTCH HARBOR

MEANWHILE the other members of the Flight were living in the cannery bunkhouse at Chignik. They spent their time between their planes, the emergency radio station, and a stove round which the fishermen spun yarns.

Chignik is in the heart of the region where the largest bears in the world are found, measuring from fourteen to eighteen feet from 'tip to tip.' The giant Kodiak brown bear weighs nearly a ton, and is one of the most powerful of all wild animals.

The town of Chignik consists of nothing but two canneries and a few dozen native huts. It is situated on the shore of a horseshoe bay, at the foot of mountains that are sheer walls of rock rising from four to five thousand feet right out of the sea. There is not a tree on any of these peaks and they are coated with ice and snow.

'While landing, we circled over the village,' says Lowell Smith. 'Afterward we learned that the natives had been nearly frightened out of their parkas and mukluks. As we flew up the harbor, the roar of our engines reverberated back and forth between the mountain walls, and the women and children ran indoors crying. They were sure that the Devil had suddenly taken wings.

'In addition to a hundred natives, the only inhabitants were some twenty whites, who spend each spring getting the canneries ready for the annual summer salmon "run." These are the men whom Rex Beach has told us about in "The Silver Horde." They are Americans, Russians, and Swedes. The leading citizens were the superintendent, Jim Osborne, and his wife.

'That first night, we sent Jack and "Hank" out to hang lanterns on the planes, so the watchman would be sure to see them from the shore in case a "Willie-wa" tore them adrift. But after they had reached the planes, they found the wind so high that it was impossible to light the lanterns, so they continued on to the native village and hammered at the door of a hut. When they got inside, out of the storm, they found a crowd of Aleuts dancing in celebration of the arrival of our "Thunder Birds." Jack and "Hank" stayed quite a while watching them, and even joined in the dancing. Of course we didn't know but what they were still out in the harbor, and after an hour had passed we began to fear they had capsized, because we knew that neither was an experienced boatman. In alarm, we ran up and down the beach blowing our police whistles, until we finally discovered them at the soirée. We carried our police whistles all the way round the world and used them in signaling between planes when not in the air.

'During our stay in Chignik we heard many bear stories from the "Sourdoughs." One fisherman, called "Dad," had passed "his threescore years and ten," and said, "I've the hang of it now and can do it again." His beard was so long that he tucked it inside his shirt to get it out of the way. He said that he was rowing up one of the fjords of Kodiak Island, when he heard some fierce growling and spluttering. Looking over his shoulder, he saw a huge brown bear swimming alongside. Reaching over, he said that he grabbed him by the ears, and that the bear towed him and his boat ashore!

'Not having his rifle along that morning, before reaching the beach he decided to turn Mr. Bear loose and row on home. But the bear followed close behind him until he reached camp. Dashing into his cabin, he grabbed his rifle, and, looking out the window, he saw a bear's head above a log a few yards away. Taking careful aim, he fired. But to his amazement, a moment later the bear's head appeared again. Taking even more careful aim, he pulled the trigger and, to his consternation, up came a bear's head once more. Ten times he fired, and nine times the head reappeared.

'"Next morning, when I went out to have a look,"

said Dad, "there were ten bears lying dead behind that log!!"

'Another "sourdough" then told a better one. Said he: "Last spring, when I was doin' a bit o' prospectin' up in the Kuskokwin, I went out to the diggings one mornin' without my rifle. Jest about halfway, while crossin' a stretch o' tundra, I noticed a grizzly follerin' me. You should 'a' seen me sprint across that tundra! But my mukluks war no seven-league boots, and the bear was a-gainin' on me. Thar wasn't a tree in sight fur me to climb. At last I seen a lone pine up ahead, and the old boy was so close behind me that I could feel his breath on my neck when I reached it. My heart sank into my boots when I saw that the lowest branch was twenty feet off the ground. But I made a great jump for it."

' "Did you make it?" we cheechakos asked.

' "Waal," replied the fisherman, "I didn't ketch it goin' up, but I caught it comin' down!!"

'One of these Alaskan hunters had a bear cub chained outside his cabin at Chignik. He offered to give it to Jack to take along in the *New Orleans* as a mascot, but he said, "Huh-uh, I'm afraid he'll outgrow me!"

' We rolled out of our bunks before dawn, on April 18th, hoping to start, but when the radio messages began to come in, it wasn't long until we discovered there would be no flying that day. I suppose some folks at home wondered why we were not getting along any faster. But you must remember that we were pioneering a route over a little-known section of the North Pacific, trying to carry the Stars and Stripes around the world, not to Davy Jones's locker.

'On the 19th, we were up before dawn again, and, after enjoying some of Mrs. Osborne's delicious mush, we started scurrying around in the frosty air, some of us heating cans of oil, and the others packing up. Harding, Ogden, and I had been aboard the plane for a half-hour when the pilots came out with the news that instructions had been received by radio from Martin for us to push on to Dutch Harbor and wait there for the *Seattle*. We were delighted to leave, both because we hoped to find better weather at Dutch Harbor and because we should have an opportunity to go over our planes, install a new motor in the *Boston*, and get ready for the flight to Japan. About that time a radio message came through from a thousand miles to the southwest with the news that all the harbors in the Kurile Islands were filled with ice and that it was doubtful if we could get through and on to Japan. But we didn't let that disturb us, and we decided that we were going to get to Japan, even if we had to put the planes on skis and slide across!

'There was a hellish wind blowing across the lagoon this morning when we left Chignik, and, as we crawled out on the pontoons and got down on our stomachs to release the planes from the buoys, the waves dashed over us and soaked us through. So you can imagine how we shivered and shook on that day's flight to Dutch Harbor.

'O boy, how the "Willie-was" whistled as we were getting under way! Being in between high mountains, we struck some awfully rough bumps in the air. The old wheel was fairly spinning in both directions and Wade and Erik and I had to keep kicking the rudder-bar to stay right-side up. This condition continued and the "Willies" threatened us until we reached Dutch Harbor.

'After leaving Chignik, we repeated most of the experiences of our previous flights, going around or under or over snow-squalls, looking down on rocky islands, and flying past ice-capped mountains. We knew that if we went down around Castle Rock and over Cape Ikti, it would take us some forty miles out of the way, while by going across Chignik Lagoon and over a ten-mile portage, into Kuiukta, the distance could be halved. I was leading on this hop, and chose the short cut.

'It was on this jump to Dutch Harbor that we bade farewell to the mainland of North America. The main difference in the scenery now was that we were passing many volcanoes and the islands were not covered with snow to the extent that the Alaskan Peninsula had been. But the region looked even more barren and desolate.

'Flying over Cold Bay, we passed a school of whales spouting and frolicking. They didn't even stop their game of water polo long enough to look up at us. After that we saw no living thing until we arrived at Dutch Harbor, but we hit a lot of squalls that tossed us around and gave us plenty to think about. Sometimes we would strike an air current that would throw us up for a thousand feet. Then again we would run into a downward current, and drop five or six hundred feet as though falling through a hole in the sky. All this in addition to bucking a head wind of from thirty to sixty-five miles an hour which greatly reduced our average speed. It was 6.05 P.M. when we reached Unalaska Bay. It had taken us all of seven hours and twenty-six minutes to fly a mere three hundred and ninety miles. Dog-tired, sopping wet from our ducking at Chignik, chattering with cold, disagreeable, and hungry, we tied our planes to the yellow buoys, and climbed aboard the *Haida*.

'The officers of the million-dollar Coast Guard cutter *Haida*, under command of Captain Hottel, welcomed us, turned over their own quarters, helped us get warm and clean up, and then ushered us into the wardroom where we sat down to a regular Thanksgiving dinner of roast turkey, cranberry sauce, sweet potatoes, fruit salad, and many other delicacies.

'Here, as the guests of the officers of the *Haida*, we were to wait for our Commander — our Commander who never came.'

For two weeks, while they waited at Dutch Harbor, hoping that Martin and Harvey would soon catch up, the boys had an opportunity of seeing life in one of the most remote places under the American flag. Between waiting for radio news from the ships searching for the lost aviators, and protecting their planes from the 'Willie-was,' they wrote their first long letters home.

'We are living in the home of Mr. Strauss, a white

trader, who buys fox skins from the Aleuts, and sells them
necessities like flour, tea, etc., in return,' wrote 'Hank'
Ogden. 'There are two villages. The one that is best
known is called Dutch Harbor where the wireless station
and oil tanks are. The other is the native settlement at
Illiiliyook, where the old Russian-Greek Orthodox Church
and Mr. Strauss's trading post are located. All whaling
ships on their way to the Arctic Ocean make this their
headquarters. Steamers going to and from Nome pass this
way. The Coast Guard cutters that protect the big seal
herds on the Pribilof Islands, just a little to the north of us,
make this place their headquarters and were under command of Captain Carmine.

'These islands are all volcanic in origin. One of the
volcanoes, Bogosolof, has erupted on several occasions,
vanished beneath the waves, and reappeared again as if by
magic. As Service said:

"There are Arctic trails that have secret tales
    That would make your blood run cold."

'But of all the stories we have heard here, the most
blood-curdling are of the early Russian fur-traders who
made slaves of the Aleuts, tortured and killed the men, and
carried the women off into the Arctic on their whaling
ships. It is one of the blackest pages in modern history and
makes me think that the twentieth century is not so far
removed from the age of the cave man after all.

'In flying down the Aleutian Islands, we were back-
tracking over the route by which the Russians came to
America in crude boats from Kamchatka. Other prehis-
toric migrations of man no doubt followed this route also.

'When we arrived here at Unalaska, we found Lieutenant Bissell, our energetic advance man, waiting for us, and
with him Hudson, a Pathé camera-man. Although we are
staying at the home of the trader, we are taking our meals
on board the Coast Guard cutter *Haida*. The food these
boys serve us is worth flying across the Pacific to enjoy.

'About five o'clock the first morning after we arrived,

Commander Jones from the *Haida* dashed in with the news that a "Willie-wa" had driven one of the planes from its original mooring-place and that it was adrift. Smith and Nelson raced out without stopping to awaken the rest of us, and found that the *New Orleans* had been carried across the bay. After towing it back to safety, the captain of a big freighter, called the *Brookdale*, unloading coal here, agreed to help us, and with the aid of their cargo booms hoisted her clear up over the *Brookdale* and onto the dock, where we could change motors.

'That afternoon we built temporary runways on the beach, so we could haul the other planes out of the water where we could work on them and the "Willie-wa" would have less chance to damage them. We also placed them where the *Haida* could swing her searchlight on them every five minutes during the night.

'They have turned their whole crew over to us and they do everything we suggest. Not only do we use their men, but we monopolize their machine shop and their other equipment. The spirit of the crew has impressed us greatly. They do things, not because they were given orders, but because they are keen to help us.

'Dutch Harbor, by the way, is our last big base until we reach Japan. Ahead of us lies nothing but barren islands and open ocean. So it is up to us to check the planes carefully, because if any little thing goes wrong on the next few jumps, our chances will be rather slim.

'*April 21:* A radio has just come through from Major Martin, saying that the sea is so rough at Portage Bay that it has been impossible for him even to get the motor ashore. So the Major and Harvey are having nothing but tough luck. The planes are right alongside of a big pile of coal and a "Willie-wa" came zipping down the mountain this morning and blew soft coal all over them. Although we attempted to wash the coal-dust off the wings with hot water, it froze as fast as we put it on, and then we couldn't even rinse the soap off, so we had to give it up. If we don't get out of this land of the "Willies" pretty soon, we'll have 'em ourselves. Yesterday the Storm King put on a special show for us. It had been perfectly calm for hours when, all of a sudden, a wild and woolly "Willie-wa" rushed down from the mountains at from fifty to seventy-five miles an hour. After it had blown for a few minutes, another came along from an entirely different direction. This one picked up big sheets of water and carried them right across the bay. A boat lying on shore went rolling end over end. Some iron barrels on the dock were scattered in every direction. Arnold and I happened to be walking down the street when we heard a clanking. A big iron drum came bounding along. We jumped out of the way and let it crash into a fence. Then the "Willie" hit a pile of lumber on the dock that had recently been unloaded and hadn't yet been lashed down. The boards went scaling off the top of the pile just like a deck of cards.'

'Les' Arnold tells of how on the night of April 24th the boys were sitting in the wardroom of the *Haida*, when a guard dashed in with the news that the planes were afloat.

'We thought they were surely safe, even at high tide. But a gale suddenly swept in from the Arctic Ocean and the waves dashed so high up on the beach that they tore the planes loose. It was a night that none of us will soon forget. Not only was it as dark as the nethermost pit, but it was snowing like the dickens, the wind was howling, and the waves were booming on the beach. Of course, every able-bodied man rushed out with us to the rescue, including sailors and officers on the *Haida*. We had no lights excepting our pocket flashes. But the searchlight from the cutter would reach its long finger of light into the gloom and help us. We were all rushing about wildly and wading around in the water trying to get hold of the planes before they were swept into the bay. Some of us floundered about in that icy water right up to our necks, and worked for two hours and a half. It was after midnight, with the weather near zero, before we managed to pull the planes higher on the beach, away from the threatening seas, and had them safely secured. One of the sailors from the

Haida proved himself a hero by diving into icy water, to prevent a large plank off of the broken runway from smashing one of the pontoons. When we got back to the trader's house that night, we were so cold that we couldn't even unbutton our coats.

'*April 25*: Smith has just received word from Martin that he is at last leaving Portage Bay on his way to Chignik. With a little good luck now, he and Harvey ought to be with us in a day or so, and then we'll be off for Japan.'

CHAPTER XI

MARTIN AND HARVEY LOST IN ALASKA

'No finer fellow than Major Frederick L. Martin ever climbed into a cockpit,' is the opinion of many who know him. But from that first day when he had a forced landing in the San Joaquin Valley, ill-luck dogged his trail on the World Flight.

We have seen how, after various misadventures, the *Seattle* left Portage Bay at eleven o'clock in the morning of the 25th of April, for Chignik.

'It was too dangerous to fly a compass course on account of the poor visibility,' says the Major. 'This made it imperative that we should follow the shore-line. According to our plan, Sergeant Harvey was to watch for obstructions such as projecting headlands, on the port side of the plane, while I was to keep a lookout on the starboard side. If the Sergeant saw anything that looked dangerous, he would kick the rudder, and several times we were forced to bank quickly to escape disaster.

'Two hours and fifteen minutes passed, during which we were far too busy keeping out of trouble to watch the map. But, instead of the storm being local, it seemed as though we were never going to get through into clear weather. The wind had been blowing from the southwest with a velocity of about twenty-five miles an hour, but finally we found ourselves over a quiet stretch of water. For fifteen minutes we continued over this, noticing as we passed that it contained considerable floating ice. Just as we reached the opposite side of this bay, we plunged into a still worse snowstorm. So we turned back, landed, and dropped anchor. The body of water we had been crossing turned out to be Kujulik Bay, just east of Chignik.

'After an hour and a half the storm went down a bit, so

we took off, and finally reached Chignik at 5.50 in the afternoon.

'Snowstorms and high winds prevailed on the 26th, 27th, and 28th. The spray from the whitecaps broke over the pontoons and froze on them, and even coated the fuselage and wings, making the *Seattle* look like an iceberg. This Arctic coat must have weighed at least four hundred pounds.

'The wind went down a little on the 29th, and for the first time since arriving at Chignik it was possible for us to get out to the plane. With a launch borrowed from the Columbia River Packers, we towed her to a more sheltered spot near the cannery, scraped off the coat of ice, knocked the icicles off the engine, and went over it thoroughly, serviced-up, and got all ready to fly on to Dutch Harbor.

'Next morning, the 30th of April, we were up at four o'clock. Although still snowing, it was perfectly calm, and the radio reports coming through from Dutch Harbor about ten o'clock led me to believe that we could make it; and not knowing how long we might have to wait for another halfway decent day, we shoved off. On the recommendation of Mr. Osborne, superintendent of the cannery, who said that the rest of the Flight had done likewise, we decided to take the same short cut over the portage to the west of Chignik.

'In trying to cross this portage, which was supposed to be low ground, we suddenly saw a mountain looming ahead. I knew this couldn't be right, and, thinking that we might have veered a bit too sharply in leaving Chignik Lagoon, I turned, flew back, took my bearings again, and flew over a level stretch for a short distance until we came to mountains with level ground extending to the northward. Feeling certain that only a slight change of direction could be necessary, I flew north for a short distance. As we were now flying over land, with pontoons instead of wheels, we were getting rather concerned. But blue water was visible to the westward, apparently only a short distance off, so we headed for it in an effort to reach the sea again with the least possible delay.

'Our ceiling now was about two hundred feet. But somehow that body of water never got any nearer. Instead we were approaching fog. I was now strongly inclined to turn back to Chignik and start all over again by way of the original course. But, as we had come this far and the water seemed near, we kept on. The fog grew so dense that it drove us down within a few feet of the ground. Still we found no water. But feeling certain that we had left the mountains behind us, I thought it would be safest to climb over the fog, which I felt sure would only extend for a short distance.

'In order to make sure of getting all the way to Dutch Harbor, we had taken on board two hundred gallons of gasoline and oil. With this heavy load she climbed slowly. We had been gaining altitude for several minutes when, suddenly, another mountain loomed up ahead. I caught a glimpse of several dark patches, bare spots where the snow had blown away. A moment later we crashed.

'The right pontoon hit first and struck an incline right on the top ledge of a thousand-foot precipice where the mountain tapered upward in a gentle slope. The plane came to a final stop about two hundred feet up this grade. The fuselage keeled over on a forty-five-degree angle. The force of the impact drove the right pontoon under the fuselage and jammed it up against the left pontoon. The pontoon struts were, of course, splintered and torn loose. The bottom right wing was demolished, and the one above it driven halfway back to the tail.

'Sergeant Harvey got out without a scratch and I escaped with a few minor injuries to my face.

'But the tragedy to us was that, so far as we two were concerned, the World Flight was at an end!

'We realized the seriousness of our situation because we knew that the Alaskan Peninsula was almost uninhabited. We packed up the emergency rations, as many other things as we could carry, and struck off to the south over the mountain into which we had crashed.

'We figured that we were not over ten miles from the Pacific Coast shore (on the east side) of the peninsula, but we knew we were cut off from it by a range of mountains.

'The fog was dense and white and seemed to blend into the snow. Everything around us was dead white. We were also troubled with not being able to walk in a straight line. Our sense of balance seemed to have deserted us. So we stopped frequently to check our course with the compass. Finally, after walking for two hours, we returned to the plane, because it appeared unlikely that we should be able to reach shelter before dark.

'Putting on our heavy, fur-lined suits, which we at first had abandoned on account of their weight, we built a fire out of broken parts of the plane, and, bundled up in our flying-suits, we huddled in the baggage compartment of the fuselage. We had to sleep on a slant, because the floor was tilted up at an angle of forty-five degrees. Although it was long enough, it was only two and a half feet wide, so first one would sleep with the other lying half on top of him, and then the other would take the lower berth. We were cramped and uncomfortable, and it was bitter cold, so we slept but little.

'Next morning, when we crawled out of the fuselage, we found the fog as thick as ever, so we decided to wait until it lifted rather than run the risk of walking blindly over a precipice.

'All that day and all the second night we remained there. Our fire finally melted the snow and ice until quite a pit was formed. Then we took a small spade from the plane and with it cut chunks of snow and ice about a foot square, stacked these up and made walls, used the wings for a roof, banked loose snow in the chinks to keep out the wind, got out our pipes and tobacco, and made ourselves as comfortable as possible.

'Next morning, May 2d, the fog was still with us, but we decided to make our way out to the coast. Our hydrographic charts were of no value because they failed to show enough of the interior. Leaving behind our fur-lined flying-suits, which were too clumsy to walk in, we set out in our ordinary clothes, which included light-weight woolen clothing, woolen breeches, flannel shirts, chamois vests, cotton overalls, heavy socks and shoes.

'In order to keep more nearly in a straight line, one of us would break trail for a time, while the other followed a little way behind, within shouting distance, in case the man in the lead started to zigzag. In this fashion we made our way over the mountain on which we had crashed, and to the top of another ridge. By that time the fog had lifted slightly. None too soon, either, because we were within a few paces of a fifteen-hundred-foot precipice.

'Realizing the hazard involved in trying to get over the mountains in the fog, we retraced our steps to a creek we had just crossed. We thought this creek would surely bring us out somewhere along the shore. It ran toward Bering Sea, and as long as we followed it we were not obliged to do any more climbing. Due partly to the smoke from our camp-fires of the previous day, and partly to snow-blindness, Harvey was having trouble with his eyes. But from 11 A.M. to 4.30 P.M. we kept on along the stream until we emerged from a small canyon into a level, marshy region. About four or five miles was as far as we could see, and we were still unable to tell how far we were from the ocean. Realizing that darkness would soon be upon us, we decided to camp for the night near a thicket where there were enough dead alder-bushes for fuel. Although our clothing was ample to keep us warm while walking, it was far from sufficient during the night. It was too cold to lie down, and of course it was essential that one of us should watch the fire and keep a lookout. Before morning we had made up our minds that it would be folly ever to attempt to reach the coast on the Bering Sea side of the peninsula, not only because there were sure to be fewer inhabitants there, but also because we had heard that there was no driftwood on those shores. So at daybreak, on the morning of the 3d, we retraced our steps to the airplane.

'Sergeant Harvey's eyes were now in a serious condition and he could hardly see despite the fact that he was wearing amber goggles. But by using boric acid from our first-aid kit the inflammation was reduced, and by the following morning his eyes were nearly back to normal. The fog had now lifted and we climbed the mountain to about twenty-five hundred feet. From its summit we looked off to the southward and could see nothing but a sheer wall of rock, and more mountains, the tops of which were hidden in the clouds. But off to the southwest, through our field-glasses, we saw a lake. Hoping that there might be a trapper somewhere on its shores, we set out about 11 A.M., but at 4.30 that afternoon we were still three or four miles from it. Once more we camped for the night in an alder thicket. But during the remaining daylight hours, we succeeded in killing two ptarmigan with an Army pistol. This bird is about twice the size of a quail and is indigenous to the Arctic. We cooked one in the meat can of my mess outfit and had it for supper. It was quite appetizing, too.

'Early next morning, after cooking the second ptarmigan for breakfast, we started out for the lake again, reached it about noon, and scanned it in vain with our field-glasses. But luck was against us, and so far as we could see there was not a sign of human habitation. By now my eyes were giving me trouble and I was suffering from snow-blindness, in spite of the fact that I, too, was wearing amber goggles.

'As our best chance now seemed to depend on finding a pass through the mountains to the southward, and as a lake and stream were indicated on our maps which conformed closely to those which we had crossed, we calculated that by following the stream at the southernmost point of the lake, we should come out at Ivanof Bay. But it turned out that, after a short distance, this stream flowed in the opposite direction. Nevertheless, hoping to find a pass through the mountains, we followed it. On account of my eyes, it was now necessary for Harvey to lead the way, and we kept on, notwithstanding the fact that we were weak and exhausted.

'At two o'clock that afternoon, we came to a desirable spot to camp, which we decided to do because I was snow-blind and helpless. Here we found plenty of deadwood for fuel, and with dry grass from a marsh we made a bed and managed to get about four hours' sleep, our first real rest since the crash. It never took us long to prepare a meal, for we usually had nothing but our emergency liquid ra-tion. According to the instructions we had been given, two teaspoonfuls per person were supposed to constitute a meal, but we increased this ration to three.

'On the morning of May 5th, we continued our march through the swamp, and finally reached a valley where this stream passed through the mountain range. The snow was deep and the crust was not strong enough to hold us, so struggling through it was tedious work. As we were both very weak, we halted at 3 P.M., and Sergeant Harvey, after investigating, reported that he had seen a body of water about three miles to the south. But we were too exhausted to go on that night, and again camped in an alder thicket.

'By seven-thirty the next morning, we arrived at the shore of the water, which Sergeant Harvey had seen on the previous afternoon, and there we saw a cabin only half a mile away. Here we found a small cache of food, including flour, salted salmon, bacon fat, baking powder, dried peaches, condensed milk, sirup, and coffee. There was also a quantity of wood cut for a small heating stove, and it looked as though the cabin might have been occupied the previous day, although the bedding had been removed.

'We made some hot cakes, but not having eaten any solid food for some time, about two of them was all we could stand. At any rate, we now had both shelter and food. Despite the wood fire we spent a cold night and awoke the next morning to find it snowing heavily. The storm lasted all day, that night, and through the next day.

'The morning of the 9th, we took a walk to try and

MAJOR MARTIN ENGAGED IN THE FRIGID OCCUPATION OF SMASHING PANCAKE ICE TO KEEP IT FROM
DAMAGING HIS PLANE

MAJOR MARTIN AND SERGEANT HARVEY AT THE END OF
THEIR ADVENTURE

locate our position, and finally decided that we were on
Moller Bay, an arm of Bering Sea. Later Sergeant Harvey
made a reconnaissance trip and verified this while I prepared
the wild ducks which we had killed near the cabin with
a rifle belonging to our absent host. The Sergeant also
brought back two snowshoe rabbits. Although our charts
did not indicate that there was a village or cannery anywhere on this bay, we noticed a "Port Moller Cannery"
label on a condensed-milk box. This was encouraging, but
as Moller Bay was still a mass of floating ice, we were afraid
the cannery might still be unoccupied.

'After a hearty breakfast of rabbit, pancakes, and
gravy, and after putting the cabin in order, we started out
on the morning of the 10th for Port Moller, which turned
out to be twenty-five miles distant. The weather was clear
and calm, so we made excellent progress along the beach,
except for three or four miles where cliffs jutted out into the
sea. At four that afternoon, we saw a wireless mast and
smokestack in the distance. Just as we were wondering
whether we should find anybody there, we saw smoke
coming from the stack, and, as we were crossing a sandy
stretch about a mile wide, a launch put out from the
cannery on its way to a native village, called "Hot Springs,"
on the western shore of Moller Bay. There were two men
and three women in the launch, all of them natives. The
man in charge, Jake Oroloff, ferried us across to the cannery,
where we were greeted by the superintendent and his men,
who seemed almost as overjoyed at seeing us as we were at
meeting them.'

Word was radioed to the rest of the world that the missing airmen had turned up at Port Moller and a few days
later they returned across the North Pacific to Puget
Sound on a cargo boat of the Alaskan fishing fleet. Thus
ended Major Martin's and Sergeant Harvey's adventures
on the Round-the-World Flight.

CHAPTER XII

FLYING DOWN THE ALEUTIAN ISLANDS

ALL this time, of course, the other six airmen were having adventures of a different sort in the Aleutian Islands, and we will now turn back the calendar in order to follow them until they heard that Martin and Harvey were out of the Flight for good.

'An interesting experience during that long stay at Dutch Harbor while waiting for Martin and Harvey,' says Henry Ogden, 'was the Easter service we attended in the little Russian church.

'During the early part of the evening of April 26th, Mr. A. C. Goss, the trader who owns fox farms on the adjoining islands, gave a party in our honor. Although the entire white population of Illiiliyook attended, there were only twenty-one men and six women.

'About midnight there was a wild pealing of church bells. We all went over to the church, where we found the population dressed in their Sunday best. The chief stood near the door selling candles to the worshipers.

'After buying their candles, the women took seats on the left while the men sat on the right side of the church. But once the ceremony started, no one was allowed to sit, from midnight to dawn. Long benches had been brought in for us, and simply because we were guests of honor who had arrived through the clouds, we were allowed to sit down, but not until the high priest had blessed the benches.

'Dutch Harbor is the official residence of one of the patriarchs of the Russian Church, and it was this Bishop of the Aleutian Islands, with long beard, flowing robes, and huge mitre, who led the service. The church was dimly illuminated by the flickering candles, and the chanting in Aleut was as weird as the winds and volcanoes of this remote island. As we sat there in our heavy flying-suits, it was so cold that we could see our breath congeal.

'In the center of the room before the altar was a draped casket, and at the height of the chanting, while the Aleuts continued their wailing, the Bishop, followed by priests and acolytes swinging their incense braziers, lifted the casket to their shoulders and marched out of the church followed by the entire congregation still chanting. Around and around the church they marched. When they returned, the casket was missing and the Bishop was carrying the shroud over his head to indicate that the Saviour had risen.

'As they reëntered the church, every one relighted his candle. The climax of the ceremony was when the Bishop returned to the altar. Suspended from the ceiling was an enormous chandelier. As the Bishop approached, an acolyte touched it with his candle and the flame sped from wick to wick so that in a moment the whole church was ablaze with light. Hanging from the ceiling were dozens of smaller candelabra and every few minutes to the rhythm of the chanting the priests raised and lowered these on chains.

'Shortly before two o'clock in the morning, the Aleuts lined up, men first, the women next, and the children last, still chanting, and marched single file past a cross and two sacred pictures which each person kissed in exactly the same spot. Tuberculosis is the curse of these islands, and in this kissing business they have certainly invented an ideal way of spreading it.

'The wailing of these primitive people in their strange tongue, the priest's strange vestments, the incense, the icons, the flickering candles, the howling of the storm outside, made me realize how far I was from my home in Mississippi.

'Every few minutes during the service, one of us would run out to see if the planes were still safe.'

'Sunday, the 27th, was the first day since leaving Santa Monica that we really had a chance to rest,' says Leigh

Wade. 'Monday found us still waiting for Martin. There was a concrete tennis court way up here, built by the Coast Guard, and although the weather was really better suited for skiing than for lawn tennis, we shoveled off the snow and played seven or eight sets.

'Next night the " Willie-was " went on another rampage. Several of them gave the Japanese freighter down the bay such a mauling that she wirelessed to the *Haida* for help. So our revenue cutter friends steamed to the rescue, and towed the Jap to a deeper mooring-place. It was a wild night and the " Willie-was " were blowing from every direction. For the first time we had an opportunity of observing their effect upon a boat at sea. They were coming at the *Haida* both from starboard and from port. Great sheets of water would smash first into one side and then against the other. Several times sheets were lifted right over the top of the ship. For a few minutes everything would be perfectly calm. Then, as suddenly as the wind had died down, it would come again and go whistling and screaming over us.

'Wednesday, the 30th, the weather seemed ideal for flying. The sun shone and it was our first day out from Seattle without a snowstorm. Major Blair, our meteorological expert, radioed Major Martin that the weather signs were favorable, and about noon a message came through from Chignik that the *Seattle* had at last set out to join us at Dutch Harbor.

'Naturally we spent the afternoon wondering how soon they would arrive. Hours passed, but no speck appeared on the horizon. Dusk came, but still no sound of a whirring Liberty. Between Chignik and Dutch Harbor there is a wireless station at King Cove. We were in touch with them, but they too had seen nothing of the plane. Then darkness came. We now knew that they had met with some mishap.

'The following message was sent by the wireless operator at False Point, Unimak Island, on the night of April 30th to the Associated Press:

Fears are expressed here for the safety of Major F. L. Martin, who left Chignik, at 11.10 A.M. for Dutch Harbor, and who was not reported passing any points up to six o'clock to-night. Residents at the small tannery station here have just passed through the worst five days known for this period of the year. The North Pacific Ocean has been lashed by terrific gales, the wind frequently reaching one hundred miles per hour. The air at the wireless station has been filled all day with snow blown from the mountain-sides and neighboring peaks. Even the seagulls making their home here did not fly to-day. The temperature has ranged from sixty to twenty-four degrees above zero during the storm. If Major Martin succeeded in reaching Dutch Harbor, he will be fully qualified for any bad weather that might arise later.

'All that night we tried to get Chignik by radio, and failed. As soon as it grew dark, Smith, with the rest of us constantly around him, remained at the radio station wirelessing every ship within reach, asking them to help in the search. We assigned each vessel to a separate section of the coast. The *Algonquin* started out from False Point; the *Pioneer* from Shumagan Island; the *Redwood, Modoc,* and *Redondo* set forth from King Cove, the *Unga* from Chignik, the *Warrior* from Squaw Harbor; the *Haida* also put to sea that night, and many fishing smacks and cannery boats put out from different points. For two days and two nights we remained at the radio station awaiting news. Search parties were organized by land, and both natives and white trappers took their dog teams and started for the interior. Later we learned that Washington had dispatched Lieutenant Earle H. Tonkin from Crissy Field, San Francisco, with a Curtiss JN airplane, which was boxed up for shipment to Alaska by boat.

'Then, on the 2d of May, the following message reached us from the Chief of the Air Service:

Lieut. Lowell Smith, command World Flight.

Don't delay longer waiting for Major Martin. See that everything possible done to find him. Planes two, three, and four to proceed to Japan at earliest possible moment.

'Major Blair, with the Bureau of Fisheries people on the *Eider*, had gone on ahead to the island of Atka where we were scheduled to make our next stop. He radioed that they were encountering severe storms which would make it hazardous for us to leave that day.

'Next morning, we were up before dawn, and with the help of a crowd of Aleuts we took advantage of high tide and launched the planes before breakfast. A few hours later, Major Blair radioed that the weather was fairly clear, and at eleven o'clock we taxied in single file out of Unalaska Bay into the Bering Sea.

'With a cloud ceiling at less than a thousand feet, we flew low enough to make out the reindeer herds grazing on the tundra. It seems that years ago, when the first white men, the Russians, came into the North in search of walrus, seal, and Arctic fox, the Eskimo and Aleuts began to starve, because they could not compete against the more efficient weapons of the white hunters. This caused them to die off rapidly. But when Uncle Sam bought Alaska and the Aleutian Islands, a doctor named Sheldon Jackson raised money by private subscription and introduced a small herd of reindeer from Lapland, in the hope that he might be able to build up a new industry and thus save the vanishing race of Aleuts. That was about 1892. Since then the Government has made further appropriations and introduced more herds of reindeer until now there are several hundred thousand in Alaska.

'One of these herds was assigned to the Aleutian Islands, but the half-breed Aleuts were too lazy to look after them. They turned them loose and to-day they are as wild as the caribou. So lazy are the Aleuts that they won't even go out to kill the reindeer for food!

'From our experience in Alaska, you might think it a desolate, wind-swept region. As a matter of fact we had to fly over the inhospitable parts: — ice-fields, mountain ranges, and volcanoes. But Erik and the boys who flew with Captain Streett, on the nine-thousand-mile flight from New York to Nome and return, passed through the interior of Alaska, and once they had crossed the mountain ranges they found themselves in a land of flowers and sunshine, an empire capable of supporting a vast population.

'Flying low over the Aleutian Islands, we passed schools of whales and frequently frightened flocks of Arctic birds called murres. Then, as we passed over the Islands of the Four Mountains, tens of thousands of sea-pigeons came whirring up to have a look at us. The air was thick with them. They were so excited that it looked as though it would be impossible for them to keep out of our way. We flew right through the midst of them, every moment fearing that we should hit one and break a propeller.

'Flying conditions were peculiar on this day. There was a dense layer of clouds at one thousand feet, and while the air was dark and gray, we could see for a long distance ahead, which was quite a relief from the fogs and snow-filled air we usually had to contend with.

'An hour before reaching Atka, we ran into the usual fog, and this soon turned to a heavy, driving rain mixed with snow and sleet, while visibility decreased to almost nothing. We followed our compass course, and when we did reach the island of Atka, it loomed up straight from the sea like a black wall, presenting no anchorage sites at all. For a few minutes we wondered if we had made an error. But on we went via the compass course; we skirted a cliff or two, passed over a protruding neck of land, and around another mountain-side, when suddenly we discovered a land-locked bay with a small village on the shore and the *Eider* awaiting our arrival.

'It was three in the afternoon when we flew over the island of Atka and saw the *Eider* riding at anchor in a little bay. Here we landed and were welcomed by another crowd of Aleuts and one lone white man, a school-teacher named William Nye — no relation to the humorist, by the way, for the original Bill Nye would have been hard put to it to make a joke out of life up here. The sole trading rights to this island of Atka are held by Mr. Goss, the trader who entertained us at Dutch Harbor. He comes here only once a year.

'As soon as Major Blair and the officers and crew of the *Eider* had helped us ashore, they hoisted anchor and sailed for Attu, the last island in the Aleutian chain. So we were left on this remnant of an ancient volcano without even a radio. Goss had told us to make ourselves at home in his trading store. Some of us bunked alongside stacks of flour and piles of condensed milk-tins, in the attic among the rats. However, I am not mentioning the rats out of disrespect for our big-hearted host, for he too gives Atka a wide berth and comes here only when obliged to do so.

'To Smith, our new leader, went the honor of occupying the bridal suite, to wit, the only bed on the premises. But Smith didn't have much the best of it after all, because it collapsed twice during the first night.'

'Living in the wilds was nothing new to him, and he volunteered to act as chief cook. Jack and Hank washed the dishes most of the time, relieved only by Arnold and Wade when the latter wanted to get their hands warm. As for me, I worked off my surplus energy by sweeping the floor every ten or fifteen minutes,' said Erik.

'Smith's repertoire, by the way, proved somewhat limited. He usually gave us eggs Vienna for breakfast, eggs Vienna for lunch, and eggs Vienna for dinner. This Viennese diet made some of us so desperate that we set out to forage for ourselves. In the store were some hundreds of cans of Eagle Brand condensed milk which Jack and Hank gulped down like Coca-Cola. Some of the rest of us, in prying about the island discovered that the local Aleut chief had a flock of chickens which he was apparently trying to keep hidden, and which he refused to sell to us. He also had a motor-boat. This gave us an idea, and one night we crossed the wires on the magneto so that the old motor wouldn't mote. Of course the chief knew nothing about engines and he came and begged us to fix it. We did. But not until he had given us two chickens! Smith cooked them.

'Sunday, May 4th, as usual it was raining, snowy, and windy, the water being so rough that it was impossible to board the planes. We kept careful watch of them all the time for fear they might get adrift. At night it was customary for us to hang lanterns on the planes so that we could watch them from a window. But the first night here the sea was extremely rough and Jack and Hank met with a wild adventure when they went out to fix the lanterns.

'The planes were lined up, with the *Chicago* nearest shore, then the *Boston*, and then the *New Orleans*. The wind was blowing from the land, and the boys thought their safest plan would be to row out to the *New Orleans*, turn round into the wind, and then visit each plane on the way ashore. But while they were rowing out, the wind increased in velocity from about twenty to fifty miles an hour. Not being expert oarsmen, they soon were in danger of being swamped. First she would dip away down on one side, and then she would tip to the other. They found the only way they could keep from capsizing was to put up their oars and huddle in the middle of the boat. In this way they were driven for a mile and a half right across the bay where the boat smashed onto the rocks in the dark. Jumping out, Jack and Hank waded in water up to their necks, pulled the battered boat high on the beach, turned her upside down, and then started hiking back to the shack through a driving rainstorm.

'Meanwhile, when we noticed that no lights were burning on the planes, in alarm we ran down the beach shouting for Jack and Hank. You can imagine how relieved we felt when we found them.

'At first we hired the village chief's son and his buddy to stand guard over the planes. First one would stay out in the rowboat for a few hours and then the other would take his place. That was the theory. But at night, when they thought we wouldn't know, they would come ashore and sleep on the beach. For doing next to nothing, we had to pay those two young loafers ten dollars a day. My bunk happened to be in the attic, and with a couple of pieces of wood I rigged up a triangular thingamajig similar to what surveyors use. The planes were arranged so that they were exactly in line, and by means of my triangle, I could wake up at any hour of the night and by merely rolling over could draw a bead on them and see just whether or not they were adrift. I didn't trust the chief's son, so I used to wake up about every hour. Next day he and his buddy decided that watching the "thunder-birds" was too arduous and they tendered their resignations in time to avoid getting the sack.

'To give you an idea of how energetic these Aleuts are, Mr. Nye, the school-teacher, had a cow that gave more milk than he could use. So he offered it to the natives, but they were too lazy to come for it. We had a like experience with them. At the bottom of our gasoline drums there was a little sediment, so we always let a gallon or two go to waste. What remained was purer than ordinary "gas" and would have been ideal for the chief's motor-boat. But do you think the old boy would come and carry it away? Not on your life! However, he did agree to accept it if we would drain it and bring it to him — He didn't get it! However, the Aleuts have their good qualities. For instance, Mr. Goss, the trader, leaves this fully stocked store wide open. The natives simply walk in and take what they want off the shelves. The commodities are staple articles and every one knows the price, so they either drop the cash in the open drawer or write on a slip of paper what they have taken. Apparently they are as honest as daylight.

'On May 5th, the Coast Guard cutter *Haida* steamed in and with the help of her men and boats we fueled the planes. The drums of gasoline here were stored on the beach. To transfer the "juice" from the beach to our planes, it was necessary for us to take a whaleboat as close in to shore as she would go, and then run planks from her to the beach, and wade into the water up to our waists in order to roll the drums up the planks. There was a stiff northeast wind blowing and a choppy sea which would frequently break over the whaleboat and drench us all. But being wet and cold had become a daily experience now.

'To our disappointment, the *Haida* had brought no news of Martin and Harvey. All they knew was that when last seen the *Seattle* was flying toward Black Lake and Bering Sea. But we had not given up hope, because we felt that

they had enough emergency rations to keep them alive
for about two weeks, and we were sure that the coast
of the Alaskan Peninsula had not yet been thoroughly
combed.'

'On Tuesday, May 6th,' says 'Les' Arnold, 'the planes
were all ready to fly on to Chicagoff on Attu Island, but
Major Blair on board the *Eider*, at the latter island, reported unfavorably on the weather. So we spent the afternoon hunting the bald eagles that perch high on the volcanic mountain crags of these islands. They wheel round
and round the steaming cones and are as difficult to shoot
as mountain goat. When we located one, everybody in
the party would blaze away at once. But invariably Mr.
Eagle would calmly flap his wings, "take off," glide gracefully about the sky, and then park on another crag.

'And, by the way, having these boys of the revenue cutter with us helped a lot in refueling the planes. They were
as fine a lot as we have ever met.

'*May* 9th. We were up at dawn this morning, hoping that
we might be lucky enough to get a favorable weather report
from Major Blair. Sure enough, at eight o'clock the good
news came through. In leaving Atka harbor, we had to
take off "cross wind." As Erik's ship left the water, a
"Willie-wa" came whirling toward him. Realizing that at
that altitude it might easily dash the plane back into the
water and wreck it, he attempted to turn in order to get
out of its path. He avoided it partly, but as he turned, the
ship settled in spite of all efforts to prevent it. By perfect
piloting he somehow managed to get her straightened out,
but when the *New Orleans* hit the waves, she must have
been going fully ninety miles an hour. This was another
close call for the *New Orleans*, because this is far too swift a
pace when your pontoons are on the water.

'It was 9.09 A.M. when we started on our five hundred
and fifty mile hop. On this trip we had to make two long
water jumps out of sight of land, of about seventy-five
miles each, excellent practice for the long flights that were
to take us to Japan. This gave the pilots an opportunity to

check their compasses and it was a real relief to find that they could hold their course over water without trouble.

'We saw nothing but sea and deserted islands to-day. Two oceans, the Arctic and the Pacific, converge here, and each has its own tide. When the two collide between the islands, they form whirlpools where nothing could long survive. At 5 P.M. we rounded the edge of a volcano and entered the sheltered harbor of Chicagoff, the most westerly abode of human beings under the American flag. Since leaving Seattle, each town had grown smaller and smaller. Chicagoff is tiny.

'Attu Island looks like the end of everything. And it is, in a sense. Beyond lies Asia.'

'During our first days away out here on the island of Attu, the most westerly bit of land connected with the American continent, we lived on board the little Bureau of Fisheries boat, the *Eider*,' said 'Smiling Jack.' 'Three of the officers, including Captain Paul Beck, turned their bunks over to Smith, Nelson, and Wade, while the other three of us slept in the fo'csle. Captain Beck proved to be one of our best friends. His long years of seafaring experience, combined with his enthusiasm for our adventure, helped us on several occasions.

'The other day at Dutch Harbor, I had said to Goss, the trader, "Say, when do your seasons change up here? When does winter end, and spring come?" "Don't be funny, young fellow," he drawled. "We only have two seasons. This winter and next winter!"

'Here in Chicagoff when the barometer starts to fall, it frequently slips down to 28.45, the lowest I have ever known. Our old friends the "Willie-was" have been performing for us again to-day and if anything, they have been the worst that we have ever seen them. And that's saying a lot. They made the sea so rough this morning that we couldn't even balance ourselves on our planes and we had to hustle aboard the *Eider*. Here on Captain Beck's steamer, we were only about a hundred yards from the planes. Each time a "Willie-wa" hit us, the little *Eider* leaned way over. When a "Willie-wa" hits our planes, instead of hopping up and down as you would expect them to do, they simply shove their noses into the wind and cling tight to the waves. We have spent the whole afternoon dashing back and forth to the portholes expecting to see them torn from their moorings. Thanks to Captain Beck of the *Eider*, our moorings were secure enough to ride out every gale.

'*May* 11. While dozing this morning, I heard some of the members of the crew of the *Eider* conversing in low tones about the Major and Harvey having been found. For a time I thought I was dreaming. But when it dawned on me that what I heard was real, I leaped out of my bunk with a bound. It seemed almost too good to be true. The boys told me that Port Moller had broadcast an announcement regarding the arrival of the lost crew of the *Seattle*. Well, it was great news and we were all much relieved. Although Washington ordered us to proceed with the flight, and although we had done everything possible by getting every boat in these waters to scour the coast, and every man with a dog team to search the interior, none of us had liked the idea of going on before the search was over. Now, at any rate, the mystery is solved and we are eager to proceed.

'This is still another day of rain and wind. The *Haida* has just arrived off the island, but the harbor entrance is too treacherous for a boat of her size, so she is remaining outside in the open sea. Immediately after anchoring, she sent one of her boats to confirm the glorious news that Martin and Harvey are safe at Port Moller Cannery. All along we have felt that they would surely get back alive. Even after a week had passed, we lost none of our confidence, but after ten days, and then eleven days, we began to grow uneasy. We have missed them a lot, and it's mighty tough that they are not here to push on with us. Although we have flown over a lot of wild country, on our way out here to Attu, still we are only a little more than a sixth of the way around the globe. So who knows what adventures may be in store for us from here on? Whatever they may be, we are looking forward to them and anxious to get on.

'Attu is the uttermost point of America, an island way out here on the edge of nothing. The population of the island is exactly fifty-nine, all Aleuts. The day we arrived, there was no one here in Chicagoff excepting twenty-four women and girls and one crotchety patriarch. Leigh Wade being the sheik of the party, we renamed the town "Wade's Paradise."

'The harbor of Chicagoff is well sheltered with mountains all around it — extinct volcanoes, of course. The village consists of three wooden shacks and a number of barraboras, native huts which the Aleuts burrow out of the ground. The roofs are made of sod and are dome-shaped. Each barrabora has one lone window, and from six to eight people live down there crowded into a small space. Here they cook, eat and sleep, in airtight safety — and stuffiness. We thought we should like to visit a barrabora. "Les," being a bold spirit, opened the door and we started to walk in, but after one whiff we ran out again.

'These huts look more like storm cellars than like places for people to live: they are divided into two tiny rooms. The first one is filled with clothes, harpoons, jerked meat, dried fish, and odds and ends. The partition between this and the "living-room" is a skin curtain. There squat the old Aleut women with their wrinkled, weather-beaten faces, weaving baskets or making garments out of hides.'

> ' " Behind the rest, on heaped-up skins,
> The oldest hag crouched on her shins.
> Her teeth were worn down to her gums,
> And rawhide thongs had scarred her thumbs.
> She split a sinew strip in two
> (Back sinew from the caribou);
> Between her sunken, oozing lips
> The stringy strip of sinew slips.
> She mumbles it twixt tongue and jaws,
> As through her mouth each strip she draws;
> She rubs it with her greasy claws

Until each soft and moistened shred
Becomes a long and pliant thread
Rubbed round upon her cheek."

'Colonel Broome, advance representative for the British Round-the-World Flight, recently passed here. Before he went on to the Kurile Islands, he left a cheery letter for us, telling us exactly where he had placed all his supplies, assuring us that we were welcome to use them if necessary, and wishing us the best of luck. We have found these letters from Colonel Broome all the way along the line. He is a real sportsman.

'There are only three wooden buildings on this island. One is the little Russian church which the Aleuts attend, and the other two belong to Mr. Shroeder, who controls the trading rights to Attu. He also has a number of fox farms on the smaller islands scattered between here and Atka.

'After the *Eider* had left Attu to take up a position midway between here and the nearest islands off the coast of Asia, in order to send us weather reports, we moved ashore to Shroeder's house and were delighted to find an excellent library. Our revenue cutter friends from the *Haida* have just come in and set up a portable radio outfit. Although with this outfit we can send messages for only about a hundred miles, we can receive from a much longer distance.

'Our chief of the Black Magic Department, Ensign Lee Baker, radio officer of the *Haida*, has opened up on his two-kilowatt arc and sent messages from behind the mountains of a land-locked harbor for a distance of sixteen hundred miles to a radio station on Vancouver Island, British Columbia. Even the alchemists of old and the voodoo men of Africa would blink their eyes at that, I guess! By the use of radio, we have been able to work in close coöperation with three or four vessels stationed hundred of miles apart. Of course during the days when Martin and Harvey were lost, the number of messages flashed back and forth across the North Pacific, the Gulf of Alaska, the Aleutian Islands, and the Alaskan Peninsula, must have been beyond all calculation. The importance of radio in connection with this flight through the Aleutians cannot be overestimated, and Ensign Lee Baker of the *Haida* deserves much credit for the way he handled our difficult requirements. One of these days, when an around-the-world aerial transportation system is established, radio is sure to be a vital factor in making it a success.

'After the *Eider* left, another gale swept down on us, a gale of such velocity that it blew the *Haida* way out to sea. We were in touch with her by radio all the time and Lee Baker radioed back that the wind was bowling along at a sixty-mile clip. The *Haida*, he said, had been having a bad time during the gale, so we could imagine what the little *Eider* had been going through on her way to the Siberian coast with our weather expert on board.'

'Incidentally,' added Smith, 'Major Blair certainly deserves his reputation as one of the foremost meteorologists in the world. So accurate were his forecasts that, had it not been for all the time lost in waiting for Martin and Harvey, we would have taken advantage of every flying day.'

On May 14th, the weather cleared long enough to enable the *Haida* to return to her anchorage outside the harbor. That day a correspondent on board the *Haida* radioed his office in Seattle the thrilling news that the Fliers had completed their final arrangements; that the weather looks clear to-night, and to-morrow the Fliers are to bid farewell to the Aleutian Islands and North America and attempt to fly all the rest of the way across Bering Sea and the Pacific to Japan, a feat never before attempted, and destined to be one of the most historic episodes of man's first flight around the world.

TO PROTECT THE PLANES FROM THE 'WILLIE-WAS' WE HAULED THEM UP ON RUNWAYS

TO KEEP FROM BEING BLOWN AWAY THE ALEUTS LIVE IN DUGOUTS

THE FLIERS' FIRST VIEW OF SIBERIA

CHAPTER XIII

THE FIRST AERIAL CROSSING OF THE PACIFIC

HISTORICALLY, the next flight is perhaps the most important single episode of our aerial journey, because for the first time airplanes were to cross the Pacific Ocean. To be the first to fly from America to Asia was an achievement comparable to the first aerial flights across the Atlantic made by the United States Naval seaplane NC-4, by Sir John Alcock and Sir Arthur Whitten Brown, and by the Portuguese from Lisbon to Brazil. It was as great an event in aviation history as Sir Ross Smith's feat in flying from England to Australia, and the first flight across Africa from Cairo to the Cape.

If we stop and think of what it meant to pioneer an aerial route from America to Asia, and then think of the small relative importance of this in relation to the whole journey, we then realize the really vast proportions of this World Flight.

'We rolled out of our bunks in the trader's house at Chicagoff about five o'clock on the morning of May 15th,' says Lowell Smith. 'Major Blair, our meteorologist, was on board the *Eider*, away out in Bering Sea near the Komandorski Islands, while the Coast Guard cutter *Haida* remained near us some twenty miles or so to the west of Attu. We depended much on our friends on the *Haida* and *Eider* to send us constant reports about the weather, for Bering Sea is an ugly place when blizzards rage.

'Several nights before, at a council with our Bureau of Fisheries and Coast Guard friends, we had decided to attempt to fly all the way to Paramushiru, Japan, a distance of about eight hundred and seventy miles, provided we got a clear day.

'The nearest land after leaving the Aleutian Islands is the Komandorski Islands. These barren masses of rock belong to Russia, and as Uncle Sam had not recognized the Soviet, no arrangements had been made with the Russians for us to land anywhere in their territory. To do so, we had been warned, might lead to serious complications, but the weather up here is so notoriously fickle that we all agreed that the *Eider* had better lie off about three miles from Bering Island in the Komandorskis; just so that in case of trouble we could at least come down in the lee of one of the Bolshevik islands, refuel from the *Eider*, wait for the weather to clear up, and then fly on to Japan. As things turned out, it was a mighty good thing we made this arrangement.

'At 11.35 on the morning of May 15th, we set forth across the Pacific, and at five minutes past midday we passed over the last bit of American soil that we were to see for a long time. At 12.20 we passed the *Haida*, and circled low to wave to our Coast Guard friends who had worked so enthusiastically for us. Bering Sea is one of the roughest bodies of water in the world, as we had long since discovered, and right here where it joins the North Pacific is the roughest part. So the *Haida* was rolling and tossing about like a cork, yet every man on board was hanging on with one hand and waving good-bye to us with the other.

'By now the sky in the southwest in the direction of Paramushiru had suddenly turned black, while due west it was still clear. So we headed toward the Komandorskis, deciding to take our chances with the Bolsheviks rather than face the wrath of the storm. For three hours we flew out of sight of land, wondering all the time what the Russians would think when they saw three giant planes swoop down out of the sky in this remote region where even ships only come about once a year.

' After we had changed our course to avoid the storm and headed for the Komandorskis, our nearest land was Copper Island, two hundred and seventy miles away. This island is nine miles long and one mile wide — not a very large object, and one that could be easily missed in an ocean, had our navigation been at fault. This was our first long water flight and consequently our first real test, so that, after straining our eyes for hours in an effort to sight Copper Island, it was rather a triumph to see it eventually "dead ahead," over our radiator caps.'

Nelson and Wade pay tribute to Smith for his skill as a navigator. Indeed, every one who has flown with him declares that his instinct for direction is like that of a homing pigeon.

'At 3.05 we arrived over Copper Island, the most easterly of the Komandorski group,' says Smith. 'That bleak bit of land out there in Bering Sea sure looked good to us. From a promontory, marked Polatka Point on my map, I headed northwest toward Bering Island, the largest of the group, and at five o'clock saw a dent in the coast and the wireless towers of the Soviet looming above the village of Nikolski. About the same moment I spotted the *Eider* five miles offshore. But it was too rough for us to come down away out there, and her officers, realizing this, steamed to three miles from Nikolski and dropped buoys while we circled above the island.

'Although it was early Wednesday morning of May 15th, when we left Attu, and we were only five hours in the air, it was Thursday afternoon, May 16th, when we landed at the Komandorskis, for we had crossed the one hundred and eightieth meridian, where time changes, and had dropped a day of our lives.

'As we taxied toward the buoys, a boat put out from shore, so after mooring we climbed back in our cockpits ready to take off again if necessary. The boat came alongside, with five men on board, two in uniform and three in civilian clothes. All had long beards, and looked just as Russians marooned away out here ought to look. None could speak English and of course we knew as little about their language as we knew about Chinese. Aside from their shaggy beards they didn't look specially savage, so we climbed down, got into the boats that had come over from the *Eider*, and motioned for them to follow us aboard her. Fortunately, there was a sailor on the *Eider* who was a

Lithuanian from Chicago and proved a capable interpreter.

'Afterwards we were told that newspapers back home described how these Komandorski Bolsheviki of Nikolski had told us to "get outski." But that was all bunk. They were exceedingly courteous, although they naturally did want to know who we were, where we had come from, why we were there, and whether we had permission to land.

'We explained that we had been forced to put in at their islands because of storms to the south. When we assured them that we were birds of passage winging our way round the world, and that we merely desired to remain overnight, they asked us to stay on board the *Eider* and not go ashore. That was exactly what we wanted to do, anyhow, and they knew it. In the meantime, they said they would send a wireless message to Moscow to see what Comrade Trotsky had to say.

'We heard nothing more that day officially. They sat around smoking cigarettes and chatting for a while. Upon returning to the village, they showed their good-will by sending out a flagon of vodka — which, however, we did not drink.

'Until ten o'clock that night we stayed with the planes, fueling up and getting ready to push off at dawn if possible. There isn't a harbor at Nikolski, merely an open roadstead, and if a southwester had blown up we might have ended our expedition just as did Vitus Bering. Fortunately, there was only a light north wind and it was twilight all night long. In fact, when we returned to the *Eider* at 10 P.M. it was still light enough to read on deck, and when we rolled out at 4.30, it was broad daylight again.

'Just as we were getting ready to take off, out came the bearded committee in their little boat with word from Moscow that we could not be allowed to stop there. We thanked them for their courtesy, and chuckled to ourselves a bit because we had already remained as long as we wanted. So I asked them if they would mind pulling their boats off to one side a little. Then signaling to Erik and

Leigh we all "gave her the gun" together, and I suppose the Russians are still stroking their beards and wondering what it was all about.

'The previous night, Captain Beck of the *Eider* had informed the *Haida* of where we were and what had happened and the latter had started full steam ahead toward the Komandorskis. That morning as we started from Bering Island for Paramushiru, far off on the horizon we saw our faithful friend, the good old *Haida*, speeding toward us. She was coming to our rescue and on her way to make quite sure we were not in trouble with the Bolsheviks. And that was the last time we saw our friends until we had completed our trip around the world.

'It was an ideal spring morning when we approached the Gulf of Kronotski, Cape Shipunski, Petropavlovski, and the mountains of Kamchatka. But as "Les" said, a few skis would come in handy if we had to land in that realm of ice and snow. We had covered the distance of one hundred and fifty miles over open water from the Komandorskis to the mainland at Cape Shipunski in just two hours' flying time. And at 9.30 A.M. on the 17th of May we were over a headland jutting out into the ocean beneath us and knew that we were at last above the continent of Asia and had completed the first aerial crossing of the Pacific.

'Long before we had even reached Attu, in the Aleutians, elaborate preparations were being made for our reception in Japanese waters, and ships of the American and Japanese navies were on their way north to meet us.'

No one had a better opportunity of really seeing the hard work of the American airmen than Linton Wells, Tokio representative for the Associated Press, for he transferred from destroyer to destroyer and followed the Fliers all the way from Bering Sea to India.

'I was in Tokio when the World Fliers left America,' says Wells, 'and was in daily contact with Lieutenant Cliff Nutt, in charge of the advance arrangements. This officer had

attempted to charter a boat to visit the Kurile Islands in
order to establish supply bases. But the lowest offer he
could get was six hundred and fifty dollars a day. Even at
that no one cared to take a ship there because of the notoriously nasty weather that usually prevails in the Kuriles.

'But the Navy stepped in and volunteered to send the
destroyers *John D. Ford*, commanded by Captain Hallo-
way H. Frost, and the *Pope* under command of Captain
John A. McClaren. Both belonged to the American
Asiatic Fleet, and on the 10th of April they arrived from
Manila and left Yokohama for the Kuriles.

'At first Nutt encountered obstacles with the Japanese
authorities, who feared the flight might be an excuse for
obtaining airplane views of their fortifications. But once
Lieutenant Nutt and Major Faymonville had succeeded in
convincing them that America contemplated nothing of
the sort, the Japanese joined heart and soul in making the
Flight a success and gave the boys a splendid reception
when they arrived in their territory. They laid out a special course for the Fliers to take, however, and instructed
them to follow this route in order not to fly over points
of strategical importance. It was also requested that the
boys should deposit their cameras with the commanding
officer of the *Ford* until after the departure from Japan.

'It was also arranged that each American destroyer
coöperating with the World Fliers should carry a Japanese
Naval officer and a representative of the Japanese Army.
Nor were any photographs to be taken by any one on
board these destroyers except with the consent and in the
presence of these Japanese officers. Even then, under no
circumstances were any pictures to be taken showing a
foot of coastline.

'It was on the U.S.S. *Ford* that I sailed north to see the
Fliers complete the Pacific flight. Two days out from
Yokohama we ran into an ice floe that stretched as far as
the eye could reach. For a night and a day we skirted this
ice, and upon arrival at Battobu Bay found it completely
blocked by the floe.

'We had gone up to the Kuriles to remain no longer than two weeks, and only had oil, food, and other supplies to last that long. But the two weeks passed and the Fliers were still away over in the Aleutians. Of course we knew little of the hardships they were going through except for an occasional word or two caught out of the air telling us that Martin and Harvey were lost.

'The temperature at Paramushiru hovered around zero all the time, we were running short of fuel and food, and gales of from fifty miles an hour upward were causing us to drag anchor all over the place. Meanwhile a Japanese destroyer arrived to act as our escort — the H.I.M.S. *Tokitsukaze*. They had plenty of food and often invited us aboard. Although Captain Frost would return their hospitality by inviting them to dine on the *Ford*, he could give them nothing but salmon and hard-tack. However, there was enough motion-picture film on board for eight evenings, and whatever the American dinners lacked in food they made up in entertainment. Each night there were speeches, and friendly relations between the two Navies were more firmly cemented. Few of the Japanese could understand English and only two Americans knew Japanese, but in spite of this handicap, they soon joined us in singing "Old Sailors Never Die."

'On May 3d the *Pope* arrived with fuel and provisions, and when the *Ford* steamed south I transferred to the *Pope*. I now had the questionable honor of being the oldest foreign resident of the Kurile Islands.

'When we had been three weeks at Paramushiru, a gale started that lasted for sixty hours, during all of which time Captain McClaren remained on the bridge.

'About seven o'clock of the second evening, Colonel Bratten, liaison officer for the Flight, and I were sitting in the ward-room playing "Acey Deucy" when McClaren came down for a moment to get warm.

'"Well, boys, better put on your life-preservers," he said. "The chances are a hundred to one we'll be on the rocks before morning."

'"All right," we replied, and went on playing Acey Deucy. We knew that the water was only eighteen degrees above freezing and that if the ship broke up we couldn't live in that. So it didn't really make any difference whether we put on life-belts or not.

'At that time the *Pope* had both anchors down, her stern to the beach, and was steaming straight ahead. The beach was only two hundred feet away.

'At ten o'clock Colonel Bratten turned in with the remark, "Well, if she's going to pile up, we might as well go to bed and not lose any sleep over it." But first he wrote a letter to his wife, and I wrote one. About three o'clock I woke up. It was perfectly calm — one of the most beautiful mornings I have ever seen. Arriving on deck I beheld a sight that I would not have believed if I hadn't seen it with my own eyes. It was the hot smokestack of the *Pope* coated with a layer of ice!

'That day we received a radio from the *Ford* saying that during the gale she too had had a close call and had rolled fifty-seven degrees from the vertical.

'A Japanese fishing boat, anchored not far from us in Murakami Bay, sank near the shore, and all thirty-eight of the people on board her were drowned or frozen to death.

'On the 11th the *Ford* came in with a fresh supply of fuel and provisions to relieve the *Pope*, and I transferred to her again. Meanwhile not a word had come through from the Fliers. The weather was now the most gorgeous imaginable, weather ideal for flying, and we kept hoping and hoping that the boys would hurry up and come through before another gale blew up. Captain Frost spent sleepless nights worrying about all this marvelous weather going to waste.

'One Wednesday morning, about two o'clock, when we were sitting in the radio-room trying to pick up any messages that might be floating about on the ether, this came from Smith:

> *Request you go to Kronotski and reconnoitre*
> *for possible landing places.*

JAPANESE AND AMERICAN NAVAL OFFICERS AWAITING THE
ARRIVAL OF THE FIRST AIRPLANES TO CROSS THE PACIFIC

The man in the black hat is Linton Wells, Associated Press representative,
who followed the flight all the way from Bering Sea to Baluchistan.

THE JAPANESE WELCOMED US BY WAVING AMERICAN FLAGS AND SINGING 'MY COUNTRY, 'TIS OF THEE' IN ENGLISH

'Out came the charts and we soon located the Gulf of Kronotski, away up on the east coast of Kamchatka.

Will not enter Russian waters under any circumstances except to rescue a plane

was Captain Frost's reply, at the same time adding a line to the effect that the weather was superb and that we were all "fed-up" waiting.

'Sixteen hours later, back came an ironical radio from Smith setting forth how overwhelmed they were with the realization of all the hardships that Captain Frost and his men were experiencing, and adding they had no intention of establishing a permanent residence in the Aleutian Islands.

'Thursday passed, but no further news came. Friday morning we intercepted a message that was evidently passing between the *Eider* and the *Haida*. Up to this time we had often been able to hear the *Haida*, but never before had we caught the response from the *Eider*. This meant that she must be quite near us and that the boys were getting ready to hop off from Attu. All day passed without news. Saturday morning the 17th, it was bitter cold and snowing and sleeting again. You can imagine how disgruntled we were to see storms setting in again.

'"Well, they won't come to-day," we said, and at 11.20 on the morning of May 17th I was up in the radio-room sending a message to my Tokio office urging them to try their best to keep the Flight story alive in the American newspapers, as the aviators were at Attu, and might possibly make the flight over the Pacific by Monday. Just as I was flashing this to Tokio, I heard some one shout:

'"There they come!"

'Jumping to the door and looking out, I saw three sailors leaning against the starboard rail looking east. The World Fliers had just appeared from behind a cloud. And believe me, that was the sight of my life. I have been in the newspaper game for twenty years, and as a result my friends say I am "hard-boiled." But after waiting up there on the edge of the Arctic for weeks just for this event, and then to unexpectedly see these cruisers coming out of a cloud — I'll say it gave me a thrill. And, judging by the way they whooped and yelled, it thrilled the honorable Japanese as well. No such uproar has been heard on the Kurile Islands since the last volcano broke loose.

'There they were, safe and sound, Smith in the lead, Wade on the right, and Nelson on the left, flying in perfect triangle formation.

'As soon as I had seen the planes coming in the distance, I jumped into the radio-room. I had made an agreement with the Japanese commander not to send any radio messages for thirty minutes from the moment the Fliers touched water, he figuring that this would enable him to announce the news of the completion of the first Pacific flight. But before the boys were out of the air, I shouted to the radio operator to kill my other message and take this:

> *Urgent. Associated Press, San Francisco. Fliers arrived Kashiwabara Bay, Paramushiru, 17th, at 11.35.*

'As a matter of fact they touched the water at exactly 11.37. In those two minutes I had scored a world news "beat." Then the radio operator on the *Ford* had to shut down for thirty minutes while the Japanese destroyers were notifying the War Office in Tokio. But before they could give the news to the other press organizations of Japan, my radio had reached San Francisco and had been flashed all over America.

'A few minutes later the boys came on board, half frozen, wet to the skin, and with icicles hanging from them.'

In the afternoon several radio messages came through to the Fliers from Washington, and among them the following:

Kashiwabara, Paramushiru, Kurile Islands, Japan: Congratulations. Yours is the honor of being the first to cross the Pacific by air. Through its Army and Navy, our country has the honor of having led in the crossing of both great oceans. The

Army has every faith in your ability to add the circumnavigation of the globe to its achievements.

(Signed)   JOHN W. WEEKS
Secretary of War

Then, as the boys sat around the ward-room, they told of their flight down the peninsula of Kamchatka, how they had crossed the Gulf of Kronotski and had suddenly encountered a layer of fog that completely obliterated the earth, but extended up to an altitude of only five hundred feet. Above the fog the weather was perfectly clear. So all the way down Kamchatka they flew above it and saw nothing but a range of volcanoes rearing their ice-capped summits above a billowy cloud continent.

Although they could neither see the ocean nor the terrain beneath, the summits of Koryatskay, Vilyuchinskaya, and Povorotnaya loomed up like Arctic sign-posts to tell them where they were. As they flew close to one towering peak, there was nothing to break the smooth surface of the snow excepting a lone track down the mountain which they imagined must have been made by one of the giant bears for which Kamchatka is famous.

A hundred miles south of Cape Shipunski the fog suddenly stopped abruptly, as though sliced off with a knife. But in front of them at an altitude of two thousand feet was another bank of it, and from there on to the Japanese island of Shimushu, their flying ceiling grew lower and lower until finally they plunged into snow and rain and were just skimming the water.

CHAPTER XIV

IN THE LAND OF VOLCANOES AND HAIRY MEN

'WHEN we arrived at Paramushiru, it seemed as though we had descended from the clouds into a new world. To be sure, there isn't much difference between the islands off the Alaskan coast and these near Siberia,' says Wade; 'for both are away up on the edge of Bering Sea, the birthplace of blizzards, and as barren as islands can be. Just the same, we were mighty tickled to have the Pacific behind us. The presence of the Japanese destroyers with their snappy-looking little sailors contributed chiefly, I think, to the illusion of a new world. And when we looked at the un-pronounceable names on our maps, that helped too.

'A gale blew that first night at Paramushiru, and it was a stem-winder. The officers insisted on giving us their bunks, and the one I occupied must have been a little wider than usual. At any rate, there was nothing I could brace myself against, and when the ship rolled, I rolled, and my recollection is that the ship never stopped rolling. The cabin was full of trunks, shoes, and all sorts of things that kept slamming back and forth. On one side was a book-case, and once when the destroyer gave a lurch the books all tumbled out on top of me. I got up and put them back carefully. But a moment later she gave another lurch with the result that Webster's Abridged Dictionary hit me on the jaw and nearly broke it; Mark Twain's "Innocents Abroad" plumped on my stomach; while a little volume of "Much Ado About Nothing" nearly put out one eye. Just as I reached up to switch on the light, Irwin Cobb's "Roughing It De Luxe" caught me in the ear. Never had I been so intimately in touch with literature!

'The sea stayed rough all Sunday. It was not until later in the afternoon that Jack and Hank could get out to the planes to look them over. But it was most fortunate that they reached them when they did, because, as far as the *Boston* and *New Orleans* were concerned, the World Flight nearly ended right there. The gale had blown them back and forth until two of the mooring bridles were almost cut through. The *Boston* was held by one strand, and in a few minutes that would have been chafed through.

'This evening we all went over to one of the Japanese destroyers to a party given in our honor, but at 2 A.M. Monday morning we took lanterns and rowed out to the planes. Until then the sea had been too rough for us to service-up. At 7.10 A.M. we took off for Hitokappu Bay on Yetorofu Island and made the coldest flight of the entire trip since leaving Seattle — colder than anywhere along the Alaskan coast. Now and then we would stamp our feet just to see if they were still with us. We kept plunging in and out of snow-squalls and hopping over one Japanese island after another. We were later amazed to discover that there are more than four thousand islands belonging to the Empire of Japan, extending all the way from the latitude of Alaska to the latitude of Madeira and Cuba. They are inhabited by more than 66,000,000 people, but, as we flew above the islands and looked down on mountain ranges, active volcanoes, and primeval forests, we realized that only a small portion of them were or could be populated.

'After the desolate stretches of country we had been flying over up to this time, it seemed good to look down sometimes and see villages and human beings. We also passed herds of sea lions sunning themselves on the rocks, or swimming about. Halfway to Yetorofu we passed over Shimushiru, Uruppu, and innumerable smaller volcanic islands. Until we started on this trip we never realized that there were so many valves of hell in the whole world as there are over here in Japan, where there are not only over a hundred extinct cones, but also a score or more that are still on fire. And as we felt their hot breath we had visions of terror-stricken mobs fleeing through ashen darkness.

'At that time, I was laboring under the delusion that the great earthquake which had nearly wiped out Tokio was a rare occurrence. But to my astonishment I learned that there had been 13,750 earthquakes recorded during the past thirteen years, or approximately three and a half shocks daily! During our short stay Mr. Vulcan's batting average was fully one thousand per cent, and we were shocked more than three times per day — nor am I referring to the Japanese bathing customs.

' We flew over another active fire mountain, on Ushishiru Island. Then, after diving down for a close view of the perpendicular cliffs of the mountainous island of Ketoi, we peered into a smoking crater on Shimushiru, and a half-hour later saw clouds of steam coming from two cones on the little island of Rebuntsiriboi. Only one large island, Uruppu, now remained between us and Yetorofu where we were to land. Uruppu, incidentally, possesses two more chimneys of Vulcan's forge. The island is utterly deserted excepting during the fishing season when the primitive folk from near-by islands come here to fish in the bays facing the Sea of Okhotsk.

'When we got to Tokio, I learned a few things about volcanoes that I didn't know before. Among the professors at the Imperial University with whom we came in contact, there was one who had devoted his life to seismographs and the study of geophysical phenomena. He amazed me by saying that scientists no longer believe the earth to be molten in the center with volcanoes for vent-holes. He said they were merely local boils on the face of Mother Earth. That was news to me.

'Yetorofu, one of the largest islands of the Kurile group, is one hundred and ten miles long, from two to twenty miles wide, and has five steaming volcanoes with their bellies full of fire. Indeed, one was in violent eruption quite recently and belched forth storms of pumice, ash, and flames.

'Arrangements had been made for us to come down and refuel on the shore of a lake just a mile inland from Hito-kappu Bay, on the Pacific Ocean side of Yetorofu. As we passed over the bay, which is just a little over halfway down the island, we saw the American and Japanese destroyers waiting for us. On the shore of the lake were several hundred school children who had walked fifty-four miles to see us arrive: that is, they had walked nine miles to the lake and back on three successive days, expecting each day to see us fly down from Paramushiru. They were from the town of Furebetsu, the capital of Yetorofu. And it was easy enough for us to tell that they were school kiddies because the Government requires them to wear uniforms. The little boys have black caps and kimonos, while the little girls wear trousers and carry parasols. As we walked past them they sucked in their breath with a whistling sound as a mark of respect, and put out their hands to touch our flying-suits.

'One of the teachers, bespectacled and wearing a dark gray gown, clattered up to us on his wooden sandals, and in response to our questions told us many interesting things about the schools of Japan. He said that, just as in America, all children are obliged to attend school until they are fourteen. He also said they had more than thirty thousand schools, attended by nearly ten million children.

'One thing that impressed us was the sturdiness of those two hundred youngsters who had trudged so far on their wooden shoes to see us land on their island. The only thing they couldn't quite understand was why we didn't flap our wings when we flew! The teacher told us that all of them go through rigorous exercises every day, and that the boys are not only taught to fence with swords, to swim like seals, and to master jujutsu, but that they are put through courses in military drill before they even enter high school. When we asked him what subjects the children studied, he named over the usual things taught in America, and then added that English is the most puzzling of all to them because we of America have such a quaint custom of writing backwards from left to right while they do it the way it should be done and both write and read from right to left! They also think we are a bit dumb because we take our hats off and keep our shoes on when we enter a house. "It isn't your hat that's dirty, it's your shoes," say these spotlessly clean little people.

'We were completely worn out as a result of having slept only an hour or so the previous night. The five hundred and ninety-five mile flight we had made through the cold upper air had kept us awake and alert, but now we were utterly exhausted, and several of us fell asleep at dinner.

'One interesting thing about the flight is that most of the time we were away off the beaten track. For instance, on our trip down the Kurile Islands, we were seeing a region that few tourists even know exists, let alone ever see.

'Among other things we discovered that up here in the northernmost part of the Japanese Empire lives a race of people, a mere remnant now, that once ruled over all Japan. These aborigines are utterly different from the ruling race to-day. Their eyes don't slant. They are of the brown race instead of the yellow.

'Like Esau, these Hairy Ainos are great hunters, and even crawl into the dens of bears and kill them in hand-to-hand combat with knives. According to their own folk-tales they are descended from the mating of a beautiful princess with a grizzly bear. Some say they are a mixture of Mongol and Caucasian stocks. They live in primitive huts, wearing clothes made out of the bark of trees, and are as uncivilized as their ancestors of ten thousand years ago.

'Only about eighteen thousand Hairy Ainos survive, and the most of these live along Volcano Bay on the island of Yezo, while a few are to be found here and there in the Kuriles. The men have long hair which they cut off at the shoulders. Their beards and mustaches are of astonishing length and give them a patriarchal appearance. When one Aino meets another, they say "how do you do" by stroking their beards.

'Curiously enough, the women of this hairy race are unable to raise even a trace of down on their faces, a fact that is a source of grief to them, so they do the next best thing and tattoo imitation mustaches on their upper lips.

'The religion of the Hairy Ainos is a worship of the sun and moon. They also attribute divine power to grizzly bears, but that doesn't stop them from killing and eating them. One of their chief religious ceremonies consists of getting absolutely "blotto," as our British friends say. And the more hilariously "biffed" they become the holier they are. They believe that strong drink purges both sexes of sin, and would look upon our Eighteenth Amendment as the work of the Devil himself.

'Next morning, May 20th, we rolled out of our bunks at Hitokappu, before dawn, and at 3.30 A.M. sat down to breakfast in the ward-room. We then walked inland to the lake where the Cruisers were moored and got ready, hoping to fly south before sunrise, to the exotic lands of the lotus-eaters, of which Erik, our much-traveled sea-rover, had told us during those long nights in the cannery bunk-house at Chignik, where each evening, before turning in, we circumnavigated the world over our charts.

'We waited for hours there on the shore of Lake Toshi-moye for the fog to lift, but were disappointed. However, as the day progressed, we were not sorry. Indeed, had it not been for the fog we should have missed our most intimate glimpse of Japanese village life.

'About twelve o'clock on the morning of May 20th, we left the planes and started out to explore Yanketo, the village near which the American and Japanese destroyers were riding at anchor in Hitokappu Bay. What a pleasant contrast this village was to those clusters of baraboras in the Aleutian Islands! Everything here seemed so diminutive that we felt like six Gullivers among the Lilliputians.

'Of course we had heard that the Japanese were discarding their picturesque customs for those of Europe and America. But in the Kuriles, we saw Japan just as it was three quarters of a century ago when our own Commodore Perry landed at a little fishing village called Yokohama, and astounded the semi-barbarous inhabitants by showing them telegraph instruments, a toy train, and other inventions of the West.

'The people and country here are much the same as when Marco Polo, the Venetian, returned to Europe from the court of the Great Khan of China with tales of a mysterious island called "Cipango," where even the dogs wore golden collars, and where the "roofs and floors of the Emperor's palace were entirely of gold, the latter being made in plates like slabs of stone, a good two fingers thick."

'We were fascinated with the village with its tiny houses that looked like eggshells. Here for the first time since leaving Sitka, Alaska, we saw trees. But they were squatty, stunted ones, flat on top as you see in old Japanese prints and fans. Here, too, for the first time since Seattle, we saw horses, shaggy-haired little animals no bigger than a Shetland pony. Dogs with golden collars we failed to find, but Marco Polo had better opportunity than we of studying the fads of the smart set.

'We were strolling down the street when a Japanese gentleman, with much smiling and bowing, indicated that he wanted us to follow him. He led us across a little garden and at the door of a house which proved to be the home of our new acquaintance, we were met by a little maiden who knelt down and bumped her carefully coiffed head several times before us. This was the first time that any of us had ever had a girl at our feet. It had always been the other way. Rather embarrassed, we took off our shoes. About all we knew of the customs of Japan was that footgear must always be left outside.

'We went shuffling along in our woolly flying-socks. And, by the way, if you can take off your shoes and still retain your dignity, "you're a better man than I be, Gunga Din!" The room we entered was as innocent of furniture as Erik's head of hair. The matting on the floor looked so spotless that we hesitated to tread upon it, even in our stocking-feet. The walls were of paper through which came a mellow, restful light. The maid brought in a small iron stove that stood on three legs. We all sat around on cushions while the lady of the house, who had also come in with more bumping-of-the-head-on-the-floor, deftly arranged the tiny pile of charcoal in the hibachi so that it would burn better. The amount of heat given off by that little stove was surprising. As we smiled one to another and attempted in vain to carry on a conversation by means of gestures, our hostess brewed tea in a brass kettle. Then the maid insinuated herself softly through one of the panels with a tray of wee cups.

'Thus far the only thing regarding our World Flight that General Patrick and Lieutenants Streett and Brown had overlooked was to give us a course in Japanese etiquette. So how should we know that we were being rude when we failed to show our appreciation of the tea by sipping it noisily?

'Much as we enjoyed this little surprise party and much as we appreciated this really rare privilege of entering a Japanese home, the affair had its painful moments because our host spoke no English and the only word of Japanese that we knew was that for "thank you." Moreover, we were more or less conscious now of having made a *faux pas* in failing to whistle our tea as we sipped it. As a matter of fact Jack did turn away for a moment and try it. But instead he laughed and blew the wrong way, with the result that he sprayed it over me like a Chinese laundryman sprinkling clothes. Worst of all, however, was our embarrassment in not being able to make our feet inconspicuous by sitting on them after the fashion of our honorable host.

'At last we were obliged to leave, and with much bowing on both sides we betook ourselves to the wrestling matches that had been specially arranged for us by the crews of the two Japanese destroyers. We were much impressed by the superb physical condition of these men. Although a cold afternoon, and although we wore our heavy flying-clothes, they were stripped and seemed to need no protection. There were two teams, each made up of five wrestlers. The idea seemed to be to push each other out of a circle. Two adversaries take the ring. When one gets thrown out, another from his side jumps in, and before he can be declared winner, he has to throw out all five opponents. Then the

referee steps up and presents the victor with — a lead
pencil! The wrestlers sprinkle salt in front of each other
and mutter a few magic words of gibberish. This drives off
the devils. Then they slap their knees, grunt a bit, and
hop at each other like game-cocks.

'After the match was over, the Japanese officers served
all the spectators and wrestlers with food — much of it in
bottles. That night Commander McClaren regaled us with
blood-curdling tales of how the Chinese do away with
prisoners and criminals by burying them up to their chins
and then leaving them. So when I turned into my bunk
it was to dream of wrestlers, volcanoes, executions, and
maidens in beautiful kimonos making obeisance before me.

'The next two days we arose at midnight and by 2 A.M.
were at the lake waiting for the fog to lift, and on May 22d
we hopped off for Minato, at 5.30. On this trip we flew over
more islands, smoking volcanoes, and above a cloud-bank
that completely cut us off from the world for a stretch of
eighty miles. Perhaps the most interesting feature of this
flight was seeing the villagers rushing out of their huts and
running down to the shore to watch us. Occasionally we
passed a village near the base of a mountain, and there the
inhabitants would be right up on the tip-top of the peak
where they could see us from the best point of vantage.
Every one along the route seemed to know we were coming.

'In spite of the fact that we had sent wires requesting
that no reception be arranged for us at Minato, an elaborate ceremony had been prepared. There must have been
twenty or thirty thousand people on the beach, huge "welcome" signs, reception tents, and a luncheon all set. Giant
fire-crackers and sky-rockets were touched off as we taxied
to our moorings, and the governor of the island unrolled his
manuscript and prepared to make a speech.

'It was here that we were met for the first time by
Lieutenant Cliff Nutt, advance officer for the second
division. Cliff knew just what we wanted, and the moment
we settled down on the water he put out from the shore
with sampans loaded with gasoline, oil, and water, and

on each sampan an American interpreter. Minato has no harbor, but is located on an open roadstead. Large rollers made it very difficult to refuel and as the wind was increasing, it was imperative for us to get away from there at once. Since we were trying to reach Tokio that day, we decided not to go ashore despite the fact that it was sure to appear discourteous. So we gave poor Cliff the thankless job of expressing our regrets to the governor and committee. Without even stopping for lunch, we taxied away from the hospitable shores of Minato, and sped on toward Tokio. Just after "taking off," the *Chicago* developed a bad miss and it was a "nip-and-tuck" affair to get in closer to shore for a landing where the water was smoother. Smith hastily climbed onto the motor, located and corrected the trouble, and ten minutes later the *Chicago* was bouncing across the waves, took to the air, and rejoined the other two planes that had been circling around waiting. At last we were flying over Hondo, the main island of the Japanese Empire. The air was balmy, and we were thrilled with the thought that this flight would bring us to the heart of the Cherry Blossom Kingdom of the Mikado.'

CHAPTER XV

ADVENTURES IN TOKIO

'THERE is something Alice-in-Wonderland-like about the appearance of Japan, even from an airplane,' says 'Les' Arnold. 'The main island, along the eastern edge of which we flew from Minato to Tokio, is far from monotonous. The coast-line under us was dotted with dozens of little fishing villages, and on our right we saw rice-fields, mountains, forests, and towns slip by. Whenever we passed over a village, as we did at the rate of about two a minute, we could see people scurrying out of their thatched houses to see us. Off to our left were thousands of sampans, fishing smacks, and junks bobbing up and down on the Pacific.

'One of the Americans who had come out on a sampan load of "gas" for us at Minato told us to be on the lookout, on our way south, for Matsushima, one of the "Three Principal Sights" of Japan. Matsushima turned out to be an archipelago of forest-covered islands about halfway down the coast of Hondo from Minato to Tokio. There are nearly a thousand islands, all of soft, porous volcanic rock. The waves of the Pacific have worn them into fantastic shapes, and to each one of them the Japs have given a picturesque name, such as "Never-Growing-Old-Island."

'It was an ideal afternoon in May. The shadows of our Cruisers blended in the water with the shadows of the white-and yellow-sailed junks. The waters of the shining sea under us were so smooth that the freakish islets with their dwarf pines looked as though painted on a mirror. Here and there we saw tiny tea-houses and rustic bridges. These Japanese are so quaint about the things they do that they remind one of elves.

'A few minutes after five we saw Lake Kasumigaura ahead of us to the right. It is only about forty-five miles north of Tokio, and we had come all the way south from

Hitokappu Bay, a distance as great as that from Chicago to New York, in ten hours. There must have been twenty or thirty thousand people waiting for us, generals, admirals, representatives from our own embassy, and dignitaries from many other countries, and of course many representatives of the Imperial Government.

'In flying from Seattle to Tokio, we had covered a distance of 5657 miles and our time in the air had been 75 hours and 55 minutes.

'Long concrete runways extended out into the lake and led up to a stone pier where the throng waited to give us the first big reception that we had encountered since leaving Seattle. There were three of these runways, and motorboats came out to tow a plane alongside each. As we approached the pier at the Japanese Naval Air Base, the people waved thousands of American and Japanese flags and shouted "Banzai." They shouted as though they really meant it. There were photographers to the front of us, photographers to the left of us, photographers to the right of us, behind us, on platforms, on poles, and even on the roofs. There also were newspaper correspondents from all parts of the world — French scribes with beards, Englishmen with monocles, and Americans with straw hats and horn-rimmed glasses. As the reception committee led us through the throng, the Japanese patted us on the backs and kept on shouting "Banzai."

'There were thousands of frail-looking little Japanese women in their fancy kimonos and sashes, with their hair piled up on their heads so neatly. For variety and color we had never seen anything like it. And their smiles — ah, we knew we were going to like Japan!

'After a formal reception at which we were cordially welcomed by Japanese officialdom, and after we had made our planes fast for the night, we were taken to the Naval Air Service Club near by and each assigned a separate room and an orderly. Our quarters were just as modern as they would have been in a New York hotel. Special cooks prepared American dishes for us and the service was splendid. Some English aviators came out here after the war to teach the Japanese how to fly, and they built the club.

'We had been up since midnight and had flown nine hundred miles in ten hours. So we were dog-tired. But after dining with the Japanese officers, when we retired to our rooms we were handed the first mail from home that we had received. So it was just like heaven to us. I can't exactly explain it, but coming down from the Arctic to Japan was like I imagine a cat feels coming out of the snow of a winter's day into a warm room, finding a dish of cream by the fireplace and then stretching out and going to sleep.'

'Much as we all wanted to see Tokio,' says 'Hank,' 'we spent all next day getting the planes ready for overhauling, and we checked over the supplies, and made ready to take the ships out of the water in order to change pontoons. It was lucky, too, that we were going to change them because when Smith and Arnold were on the *Chicago* that morning a boatman came rowing alongside, and when they asked him to move on, he put his oar against a pontoon to push himself away, and of course he shoved a hole right through it.

'Later, when "Les" was on the *Chicago* alone, being towed into the dock, the motor in the boat stopped, and while he drifted helplessly he nearly crashed into a steamer. Never have I heard quite such frantic yelling! "Les" couldn't speak Japanese and no one around him could speak English, although they were trying to help. First "Les" hopped over to the power boat, but, unable to get it started, he took a flying leap back to the pontoon, and in doing so collided with a Jap who fell overboard, kimono, American straw hat, and all. Then "Les" crawled out to the edge of one wing, the wing that was about to hit the steamer, and he held them apart by sheer strength until another motor-boat was sent out to rescue him.

'A few minutes later, a Jap who had been helping him dropped a screw-driver overboard. It was one that "Les"

THE ARRIVAL AT LAKE KASUMIGAURA, JUST A FEW MILES
FROM TOKIO

THE FINISH OF THE FLIGHT FROM THE UNITED STATES TO CHINA

used all the time, and when he looked rather fed-up about it, the Jap dived right off the pontoon, swam around at the bottom of the bay like a pearl-diver, and two or three minutes later came up with it in his mouth.

'That evening we had our first introduction to the tea-houses and geisha girls of Japan when one of the admirals took us to dinner in the town of Tsuchimira. Having often heard of the geishas and wondering just who they really were, although tired, we all looked forward to this party. Nor were we one whit disappointed. When we stepped from our limousines to the veranda of the tea-house, checked our shoes, and were welcomed by a crowd of Japanese maids in flowered kimonos, it seemed as though we had stepped into the pages of a story-book.

'We entered a room with a floor covered with straw mats and with walls that were mere screens made of wood and paper. The admiral invited us to kneel on silk cushions. Then a tiny table of lacquer was placed in front of each of us by the pretty geisha girls who were there to serve and entertain us — demure, delightful, laughing-eyed, sixteen-year-olds. Each time one of them brought in another course she would kneel and touch her forehead to the matting. Each geisha devotes herself exclusively to the man she is waiting on, removes the various courses, brings others, lights his cigarettes as he reclines on his cushion, fills his little cup with warm *saké*, and initiates him into the mystery of using chop-sticks.

'The Admiral had ordered nothing but Japanese food, but we were too busy attending to our instructors to care much about what we were eating. Just try eating rice with two knitting-needles and you will know what it's like. You should have seen me! I had it in my eyes, my ears, and even in my hair! The rest didn't do much better either. Smith appeared to be the most adept with the knitting-needles, and after a little training his geisha had him swinging a wicked chop-stick.

'*Saké* was another thing we knew nothing about until we got to Japan, but it is served everywhere and flows like water. It is a funny sort of light wine made from rice, and instead of serving it in a pail of ice they put it on the stove and heat it! Japan surely is a topsy-turvy land. Or is it that we ourselves are queer?

'After we had dined, the geishas danced and sang to weird music. But the dancing was most artistic and the polar opposite of our American jazz. In bright silks, with dainty fans, the geishas simply postured before gold and silver screens. It all seemed in exquisite taste.

'It was an evening of a lifetime; indeed, just like a dream, as I said before.'

The rather long stay of eight days that they made at Kasumigaura was necessary, not only to overhaul the planes and change pontoons and motors, but courtesy demanded that they at least attend a few of the many official receptions and banquets that had been arranged in their honor.

'Our uniforms arrived from Tokio, Saturday morning, May 24th,' says Erik, 'so we blossomed forth in regulation Army Air Service dress for the first time since leaving Seattle. That day we caught our first glimpse of Tokio.

'The Japanese naval officers took us to the station in automobiles accompanied by a naval escort. A special train had been arranged for us, with separate coaches for our naval and military escorts, and for our crowd of newspaper correspondents and photographers. The Japanese reporters not only plied us with questions all the way in to Tokio, but they even handed us pencils and pads and asked us each to compose a poem appropriate to the occasion! We apologized and put them off with the explanation that we had lost our poetical touch while flying through the "Willie-was" of the Alaskan coast. But Smith made them glow with pride when he assured them that if we remained in flowery Japan very long we should soon be composing lyrics.

'When we alighted from the train, it looked as though there were a hundred thousand people to meet us, including all of the movie and "still" photographers who had bombarded us at Kasumigaura. A reception committee, made up of high Japanese officials and nearly all of the members of the Imperial Aviation Association, greeted us on the station platform. Lieutenant-General Gaishi Negoaka delivered an address of welcome and his tiny granddaughter addressed us in English and gave Smith a bouquet. It was a dull day, so the photographers had to use their "flash-guns," and with a hundred or more of them going off like bombs it not only was a picturesque Oriental welcome, but a noisy one, like an old-fashioned Fourth of July.'

'Thoughts of the recent earthquake were uppermost in our minds as we drove to our hotel in Tokio,' says Commander Lowell Smith. 'Knowing that it ranked as one of the most terrible disasters of modern times, we expected to see a city in ruins. As we passed the Prince Regent's palace, we saw great cracks in the walls and places where even the massive stones had been blistered by the fire that had swept the city following the earthquake. But there really was surprisingly little evidence of the disaster. Already the débris had been cleaned away, and fragile, temporary structures erected over the ruins. There is a wonderful spirit of optimism in the air and the people of Tokio say that within a few years they will have remade their lost fortunes and will build a new earthquake-proof capital. Their dream is that the most beautiful city in the world may arise out of the ashes of old Tokio. The Imperial Hotel, to which they drove us, was the only building in the heart of the city not affected by the earthquake. An American designed it and now, of course, he is the most sought-after architect in Japan.'

After paying their respects to Ambassador Woods, the American airmen were officially welcomed by an impressive gathering of statesmen, educators, and military and naval leaders, at a great banquet which included members of the Imperial Cabinet and the President of Tokio University, and arranged by Field Marshal Kawamura and his aide, Major Watari.

In the afternoon they made an official call on Lieutenant-General Ugaki, the Minister of War, who presented them with beautiful silver *saké* bowls. This is one of the highest honors that any one can receive in Japan, because these bowls are only awarded for great feats of courage and endurance. On the bottom of each bowl was engraved an exact replica of a Douglas Cruiser and an inscription stating that it was presented in honor of the completion of the first trans-Pacific flight.

After more official calls and a reception by the American residents of Tokio, Major Faymonville, of the Embassy, took them to the grand ballroom at the 'Imperial' where they met the entire diplomatic corps. This was the first time within the memory of those present that every member of the Tokio diplomatic corps had attended a function, and this despite the fact that it had been arranged on two days' notice.

The next day, the Fliers were received by Prince Kuni, brother of the Prince Regent, and head of the Imperial Aeronautical Society, who presented each of them with the medal of that society. From there they went to tea at one of the show places of Tokio, the home of Soichiro Ansano, owner of shipping lines and one of Japan's empire-builders. Like the Imperial Hotel, this is one of the few landmarks around Tokio that escaped the earthquake. Here they met the flower of modern Japan — men, of course, because Japanese gentlemen are rarely accompanied by their wives and daughters.

'Even our hostess, Madame Ansano, and her petite daughters, merely came in long enough to be presented,' says Lieutenant Wade. 'They went through the usual Japanese formality of kneeling and touching the forehead to the floor, stood silently to one side for a moment, then a panel opened and they were gone. According to custom, the entertaining of guests must be done by the male members of the family assisted by the human dolls of Japan, the

geisha girls. Each geisha on this occasion had a tiny
American flag fluttering from the back of her flowered
kimono.

'On each of the six tea-tables placed before us there was
a silver pepper-shaker in the form of the Oriental God of
Laughter, weighted at the bottom so that if you pushed it
over it would bob up again. "I have made and lost several
fortunes," said our host, "but like this image I have always
managed to come up smiling. On this first flight around
the world you are sure to encounter many obstacles, some
no doubt seemingly insuperable ones. This image with its
habit of never staying down is emblematic of the spirit that
is going to enable you to reach your goal. Take these
images as a souvenir from Old Japan — and remember
that you can't keep a good man down!"

'While we were having tea, we suddenly felt an uncanny
rumble, like a heavy truck going by. Immediately, our
host stopped conversing in English and said something
quickly in Japanese. After a moment, things quieted down
again and Mr. Ansano explained that we had just experienced an earthquake. In fact, we had three distinct shocks
served with our tea — perhaps arranged by Fujiyama to
add a touch of local color.

'No event during our hurried visit to the capital of Japan
impressed us so deeply as the luncheon given in our honor
by the Faculty of the University of Tokio, at which the
President, Dr. Yoshinao Kozai, addressed us in English as
follows:

Officers of the Army Air Service of the United States,

It is an honor and great delight to us to welcome you to our
University — you, who have come to our shores over the seas,
through the air. All here assembled, both the Faculty and the
members of the Aeronautical Research Institute of Japan, cannot
but admire your dauntless spirit and congratulate you on the
success you have achieved. At the same time we envy you, for
your daring is backed by science. Indeed it is the happy union of
courage and knowledge that has gained you your success and this
honor of being the first of men to connect the two shores of the
Pacific Ocean through the sky. This same spirit and skill, I am

sure, will soon make you the pioneers of aerial flight around the globe.

Looking a little into the past, it is to your nation that the honor is due for having produced the pioneers of aviation, Langley and the Wright brothers, and during the two decades that have followed their first successes in the air, the progress of aviation accelerated by your fellow citizens has been simply marvelous. Your pioneership is a manifestation of your valor which implies daring and indefatigable spirit in conjunction with deliberation and endurance. Your success is not merely a result of adventure, but it is the fruit of study and research in the wide and complicated domains of physics, chemistry, mechanics, and meteorology.

Gentlemen! Your honor is, of course, the pride of your nation; but the honor and pride are to be shared by all mankind, because they are a manifest expression of moral and intellectual powers in the human race — the will, ability, research, means and methods, all illustrate through your success man's control over nature.

More than four hundred years ago slow sailing vessels carried Christopher Columbus across the Atlantic. Two centuries later, your pioneers crossed the Rockies with weary horses and carts. Nearly a half-century elapsed before the two oceans, the Pacific and Atlantic, were connected by rail. And now you are encircling the earth by machines flying through the sky.

Again I say, we admire and envy you. Again I say that your honor is to be shared by all mankind.

Wing westward, farther and farther to your home! Then start anew toward the west and come again to our shores, then on to our neighbors and to yours, and through all the continents of the world! Thus through your efforts and successes will the nations of the earth be made closer friends and neighbors.

To the west, east, north, and south, we shall everywhere follow your journeys with admiration and congratulation! We bid you God-speed!

'All the time that we were in Tokio great crowds milled back and forth in front of our hotel. Of course, the people kept changing all the time, but no matter whether we came out at seven o'clock in the morning or went in at midnight, the mob was always there,' says Wade. '"Les" and I dropped into the leading department store to do a bit of shopping. While wandering about, suddenly there was a commotion. Up bristled a little Japanese all out of breath. And with much bowing he told us that he was the proprietor, and that he was overwhelmed both with joy and grief; with joy because we had deigned to honor his miserable store (the finest in all Japan) by entering it, and with grief because he had not known that he was to be accorded this unprecedented honor, and had therefore not been able to put up special decorations! He begged us to stay until he could assemble his board of directors from various parts of the city to wait upon us. He fairly overwhelmed us with courtesy and hospitality, and when we apologetically explained that we must hurry off to keep an appointment with the Minister of the Navy, he accompanied us to the street, and when we disappeared into the crowd, he was still there in the doorway bowing to us.'

The Japanese Government had arranged official receptions, banquets, and other functions in honor of the American World Fliers that would have kept the boys in Tokio for two weeks. But they begged the Japanese to telescope all the important events into forty-eight hours and cancel the rest, because they still had six full days of work to put in at Kasumigaura, installing new engines, changing pontoons, and going over every inch of the planes.

'Our final adventure in Tokio,' says 'Les' Arnold, 'was a dinner at the famous Maple Club where we were the guests of Lieutenant-General Irasumitsu. Geisha girls, and chop-sticks were, of course, the order of the evening. And it sure gave us a kick to see our illustrious host and our dignified American Ambassador, Mr. Cyrus Woods, padding around in their stocking-feet.

'The walls of the tea-house were the usual movable panels, and about twenty minutes after we arrived these panels began to do some mysterious sliding. Through a narrow slit came an arm and a yellow hand clutching a metal object much like a German hand grenade. The thought flashed through my mind that we were surrounded by nihilists of some Japanese Yellow Hand Society. As I saw the index finger on that hand pulling down on a trigger, I was uncertain whether to swoon into the arms of my geisha girl or take another sip of *saké*. Just as I was about to do the latter, there was a loud explosion, the walls shook, the room filled with smoke, my *saké* cup jumped from my hand, and the panels sprang back into place.

'Peering through the smoke to see how many casualties there were, and finding none of my gallant comrades nor their geishas stricken, I realized that we had been shot again, for the thousandth time, by Japanese photographers!'

CHAPTER XVI

ACROSS THE CHINA SEA

COLONEL L. E. BROOME, the advance officer for the British flight, tells the following characteristic story of meeting with our boys in Tokio and of MacLaren's disaster:

'The American Round-the-World Fliers had arrived in Japan, and on a Sunday morning, May 25th, I had arranged to breakfast with them in the bedroom of their leader, Lieutenant Smith, at the Imperial Hotel, Tokio, where we should be free from interruption and could talk flying shop and swap experiences to our hearts' content.

'I found a merry tousle-headed party in various stages of déshabille, rushing in and out of their bathrooms and getting into their neat uniforms in readiness for the day's programme of receptions that all Japan was showering on them during the few days of their stay in Tokio.

'These cheery boys would be the last to think or to realize that they had only a few short hours previously written their names to the same tablets of fame as Vitus Bering, and had plucked a laurel of fame to wear forevermore on those rumpled heads of theirs! Yet so it was, for they had just succeeded in crossing the Pacific by way of the air for the first time in history — through gales of wind, snow flurries, rain squalls, and bitter weather, as I can vouch, having wallowed over six thousand miles of this route, laying the British dumps a week or two ahead of them.

'Well, we laughed and chatted and the time flew and the hour for the first of their engagements for the day drew near, when there came a knock at the door, and the Japanese "boy" handed me a telegram:

MacLaren crashed at Akyab. Plane completely wrecked.
Continuance of flight doubtful.

'Without a word, I handed it to Lieutenant Smith, and he read it and passed it on to the others, and I think I then remarked: "Two years' work gone west!" I thought of Major MacLaren and his companions at Akyab, their beautiful machine a wreck, and that he must be thinking of how he could get the spare one that I was that very day loading on the trawler's deck in Hakodate Harbor, five hundred miles to the north of Tokio, as a spare machine for our Pacific flight.

'A thousand thoughts were tumbling over each other in my mind, when Lieutenant Smith said, "We'll get the machine to MacLaren somehow. Let's come upstairs to Commander Abbot's bedroom and have a talk with him."

'Within five minutes, these great-hearted sportsmen had roughed-out practical plans — how Captain Abbot, on his own responsibility, would rush a destroyer to Hakodate and then load and carry the huge cases to Nagasaki, where his beat, so to speak, ended, meanwhile cabling Admiral Washington, commanding the American Asiatic Fleet, for permission to take them farther — all the way to Akyab if necessary.

'I left them then, so that I could get a radio off to the British Commander-in-Chief of the China Station, asking if it were possible to trans-ship the plane to a British man-of-war at Hongkong.

'Meanwhile, hurried measurements were taken of the available deck space on the American destroyer *John Paul Jones*, then in Yokohama Harbor, and it was ascertained that it was just possible to get the biggest case on board — no small feat on the crowded deck of a destroyer, where every inch of space carries some engine of war.

'An answer came from Admiral Washington within a few hours, offering to rush the plane to Major MacLaren at Akyab, by trans-shipping it to another American destroyer at Hongkong.

'The same evening I received an answer from our own Commander-in-Chief:

Greatly regret I have no vessel available for this purpose.

'The first message — that the Americans would get our machine to Akyab — I had already cabled to MacLaren, who answered next day in just two words: "Well done." It was sent to me, whereas it should have been addressed to our great-hearted fellow airmen, not our rivals or opponents, but our very gallant friends and competitors.

'I called on the American Ambassador, Mr. Cyrus E. Woods, and wired to Admiral Washington, but the spoken or written word cannot convey the gratitude due for what will always remain a wonderful memory — help and sympathy in our ill-fortune — the first prompt and practical, and the second as tender as it was welcome.

> "Life is mostly froth and bubble,
> Two things stand like stone:
> Kindness in another's trouble,
> Courage in one's own." '
>
> (*Adam Lindsay Gordon*)

To get the cases containing the giant British amphibian aboard the U.S.S. *John Paul Jones*, it was necessary for Commander Hall to dismantle the wireless apparatus carried by his ship, and even cut away pipes and other gear that are a part of a destroyer's deck equipment. But he finally squeezed her in, between the after engine-room hatch and the main mast. Putting out to sea again at full speed, with the turbines parting the foam at twenty-five knots all the way, the *John Paul Jones* arrived at Hongkong on June 3d.

At Hongkong, the three huge boxes — one containing the motor, one the fuselage and wings, and the other filled with spare parts — were transferred to the U.S.S. *William B. Preston*, commanded by Lieutenant-Commander Willis A. Lee, Jr. Lee wirelessed MacLaren that he would have his plane at Akyab for him not later than the 13th of June, and the *Preston*, after battling a typhoon and encountering rough seas and storms most of the way, arrived at Akyab on the 11th.

Whatever were the reasons for the refusal of the British Admiralty to help MacLaren — probably economy, even Drake and Raleigh's ships, we recall, were starved of supplies, England's adventurers having always relied on their own daring rather than the help of Whitehall — the incident had a pleasant sequel in London, for when the American airmen landed, the First Lord of the Admiralty told Lowell Smith that he would gladly place the British Navy at the disposal of the World Flight for patrolling the North Atlantic, if Smith wished. However, it was not necessary for him to avail himself of this sweeping offer because the American Navy was already detailed for the task.

But to return to the scene at Tokio. After two days crammed with receptions, the six airmen returned to Kasumigaura. Although delighted with the hospitality of the Japanese, and anxious to see all they could of life in Japan, they had gone to Tokio solely for diplomatic reasons. After all, they were out to fly around the world and bring the honor to America before the airmen of some other nation got ahead of them. With MacLaren and his British crew back in the running, with Captain Pelletier D'Oisy breaking records for France, and with both Portugal and the Argentine after the prize, it still was anybody's race.

So Smith and his companions went back to tuning up their mounts, realizing that on the next few flights south through Japan and down the China coast, they would be flying through a region famous for its typhoons.

'But we could not work at night, and one evening, before we had completed the work on the planes,' wrote Arnold, 'we were again honored in a way that seldom falls to the lot of a mere visitor to Japan. Commander Yaragushi, the naval officer in charge of the base at Kasumigaura, invited us to dine at his home. The only persons present were the Commander and his cousin, and the six of us. We sat in groups of four at two small tables, with a three-legged bronze charcoal-stove between. Our two hosts prepared our food over the glowing coals. The meal consisted of thin, "tender slices of beef, and a delicious but somewhat mysterious gravy mixed with bamboo shoots and young rice stalks, all cooked together. This was our fourth real Japanese meal, and by now we were getting so that we could wield a chop-stick.

'During the evening, as is the custom in Japan, our two hosts kept exchanging places so that we might have ample opportunity to talk to both. After dinner they entertained us with ancient Japanese war songs. Before the evening was over, the Commander called in his wife and presented her, but of course she was not allowed to dine with us because of the peculiar status of women in Japan.

'The earthquake had destroyed all the water mains in this part of the island, as well as most of the sources of supply. The only water available was said to be full of diphtheria germs. So practically the only beverages one could obtain were tea, light wines, and beer. Coming from a water-drinking country like America, you can imagine what a hardship this was.

'On our way back to the club that night, while walking along a dark road, we suddenly came to a sharp turn. On either side were paddy fields flooded with water, and without fences around them. There was no moon, nor were any stars visible. Erik happened to be striding on ahead, and, not being able to see the road distinctly, when he came to the turn he went straight on and suddenly found himself floundering up to his waist in a paddy field.

'Saturday night, May 31st, we finished overhauling the planes, and at 3 A.M. next day were on the lake ready to start for China. The Chief of the Japanese Air Service and a special train packed with officials arrived from Tokio at dawn to see us off. We were much surprised to see them, but they replied that they looked upon the circumnavigation of the world by air as an event sure to usher in a new age, and an age in which they intended Japan to play a leading part.

'As we all shook hands, their last words were: "Keep a lookout for Fujiyama off to the right."

'All our lives we had heard of the sacred mountain of Japan and seen thousands of pictures of its symmetrical, snow-capped cone. Indeed, there were few sights we were looking forward to more than the opportunity of catching a glimpse of old Fuji.

'The weather was ideal for flying and the sun was just appearing as we left Kasumigaura and set our course south toward the southern end of the main island of Hondo. Just ahead to the left was O-Shima, an island volcano belching forth clouds of smoke and steam. We knew that Fuji was somewhere off to our right, but a cloud-bank obscured the view. Suddenly as we flew across the entrance to Yokohama Harbor, the clouds to the west rolled apart, and there, with his snowy summit standing out against the cobalt sky, was one of the loveliest sights I have ever beheld.

'As the clouds parted, it was just as though old Fuji had rolled aside two cosmic curtains and revealed himself to encourage and inspire us.

'No wonder this is a sacred mountain! No wonder that from the earliest times Japanese poets have sung of Fujiyama's beauty and charm! No wonder the people of these islands are Nature worshipers, with this dazzling, snow-capped volcano ever before them!

'The Japanese officers had told us that it was twelve thousand four hundred feet high, eighty miles in circumference at the base, and two miles and a half around the rim of the crater. For two hundred years Fujiyama has been asleep. But situated as it is here in the midst of an active volcanic region, amid geysers and hot springs, and in a belt where earth tremors destroy great cities like Yokohama and Tokio, it is not unlikely that old Fuji merely slumbers, just as Vesuvius slept for centuries. For what are a hundred years or so in the life of a mountain like this?

'No words could convey the thrill we got. To see the sacred mountain of Japan from an airplane is surely one of the great moments of life.

'A few minutes later, we plunged into a bank of rain and

fog, and from then on for two hours we saw no land and flew a compass course. The last hour of the flight was in a gale, and by the time we arrived over Kushimoto, where we were to refuel, the wind was fairly screaming. The sea was kicking up such choppy waves that we flew around half a dozen times before landing, and when we did come down, we bobbed about so that for an hour we were vainly attempting to moor the planes. Lowell ran the motor while I parked myself face down on the left pontoon. One moment we would be near the buoy, and the next moment we would be way off from it. When we got up to it again, first it would drop way down, and then the next wave would switch us around and it would be way up above me and I'd be down in the trough of the sea. Time and again the waves broke right over the pontoon, nearly washing me off.

'Finally we had to give it up. We taxied before the wind to the lee of a small island about half a mile away, where we used our emergency anchors. While waiting here for the destroyer to pick up the buoys, bring them over, and drop them again, we watched the *Pope* maneuvering about. Turning round, our hearts jumped into our throats, for we had blown within a few feet of the rocks. The *New Orleans* was in the same predicament, and the *Boston* was being carried in rapidly. Of course, Lowell and Erik and Leigh at once switched on the engines and taxied farther out, but it was a close call, for if the engines had failed we'd have been done.

'We finally got the buoys planted and the bridles fastened, and went aboard the *Pope* for the night. The leading officials of Kushimoto had arranged to come out and welcome us, but the sea was so rough they couldn't even get a boat alongside the *Pope!* So we spent the night in slumber — that is, all of us but Smith and Captain McClaren, who discovered the *Chicago* was drifting. Knowing how exhausted we were, they let us sleep, took some sailors, launched a small boat with difficulty, and went out to fasten an extra anchor to the Cruiser. It was raining and the storm was still raging.

'Next morning, June 2d, after the storm had subsided, we went ashore, listened to another flock of speeches, received medals, an enormous artificial flower trophy which is now in General Patrick's office, and six fascinating little Japanese dolls. By this time we had accumulated enough souvenirs to start an Oriental museum. Nearly every city in Japan had shipped something to Tokio for us. Among these were six exquisite panels with scenes painted on them by one of the foremost artists of the country. They are said to be very valuable and we treasure them highly.

'Among the decorations we received were three presented the day we landed at Kasumigaura near Tokio. Smith begged the Japanese to make up three more for Jack, Hank, and myself, and to present all six at once, since they were so kind as to honor us. He explained that we were simply six American airmen flying around the world together, and that we were all on an equal footing. This was mighty decent of Lowell and we all appreciated it, but none more so than Ogden, who had been a sergeant up to now. Lowell cabled Washington from Tokio, asking General Patrick to make Hank a lieutenant like the rest of us. So from here on we were all lieutenants.

'About one o'clock, the weather cleared enough to enable us to hop on south to the city of Kagoshima, where we were to take off on our important flight all the way across the Yellow Sea to Shanghai. We had to buck a stiff head wind the first part of the way, which cut our speed down to forty miles an hour. We flew from island to island, and had three open-water jumps of about sixty miles each. As we crossed different islands, the flooded paddy fields glistened in the sunshine and the shadows of our planes pursued us in the water.

'In the midst of the long water jumps we frequently passed steamers, junks, and fishing craft of all kinds. We also spotted two of our destroyers, the *Perry* and *Stewart*, out patrolling for us. Wade had trouble with his motor overheating and had to come down in a little bay and fill up

WHEN THE BOSTON AND THE NEW ORLEANS REACHED
SHANGHAI, THE YANGTZE-KIANG WAS SWARMING WITH
JUNKS AND SAMPANS

SPECTATORS IN SHANGHAI BROUGHT THEIR LUNCH

AND SHOPKEEPERS LEFT THEIR SHOPS

the radiator with salt water, while we circled above until he rejoined us.

'It was getting late now, and the sun, sliding out of sight into the Yellow Sea, tinted the landscape with a harmony of colors. Ahead of us loomed a range of mountains, and we knew that, if we flew round them just to keep over water with our pontoons, it would be dark before we could get to Kagoshima. So we flew right over them and came down in Kagoshima Bay.

'The shore was black with people. There must have been fifty thousand or more. Fully twenty thousand were school children who had marched in from all the surrounding country, and every child was waving a flag. It was an inspiring scene. When we got ashore, the band from the U.S.S. *Black Hawk* and this vast throng of Japanese kiddies burst forth into "My country, 'tis of thee," which they sang in English as they waved their American and Japanese flags. It was almost as thrilling as seeing old Fujiyama, and was one of the most impressive receptions we had anywhere in the world.

'Although our visit to Japan followed right on the heels of the passing of the Japanese Exclusion Bill by Congress, at a time when feeling was running high against Americans, we saw not the slightest evidence of it. In fact, we were amazed at the genuine enthusiasm shown by the Japanese educational authorities over our American attempt to fly around the globe. Throngs of children met us everywhere, and the day we went by train from the naval air base to Tokio, school children were drawn up in military formation to see us and give us their Japanese yell at every station where the train slowed down even for a moment. Although we hadn't yet flown a fifth the way round the world, they seemed to feel that ours was the type of undertaking that might inspire the younger generation.

'Kagoshima is the southernmost city of Japan proper, situated on a bay which forms one of the finest harbors in the Orient. In the midst of the bay is the impressive volcano of Sakurajima.

'After the reception we dined with the officers of the U.S.S. *Black Hawk*, mother ship of the Asiatic destroyer squadron, and one of them told us that Japan had not actually shut out foreigners right up to the time when Commodore Perry pushed his way into Yokohama Harbor. In fact, long before that the missionary priests from Spain and Portugal were welcomed, and after them the Protestant Dutch, led by a vigorous English evangelist. But once more, history repeated itself, and the foreigners, the representatives of the various Christian sects, started quarreling, and the Japanese became so bewildered that they sent their learned men to Europe to find out just what this contradictory Western religion of "brotherly love" was like at its source. After seven years, they came back with the verdict that Western nations were so corrupt and vicious that they should be avoided. So the Shogun of those days issued an edict warning every European to get out, bag and baggage, and to get out before he was thrown out. Those who made trouble were beheaded. Only a few Dutch traders were allowed to remain, and they were held virtually as prisoners and merely allowed to act as intermediaries between Japan and the outside world

'Two hundred years went by. Then came Commodore Perry with smiles and guile and his American fleet. The Commodore won the good-will of the shy Japanese and reopened the island empire.

'We stopped only one day here, just long enough to enable the destroyers to string out across the sea from Japan and China. The following day, June 4th, we planned to get away at daybreak. The water was calm and glassy, and there was not a breath of wind. Disturbed water, with fair-sized ripples, is almost essential in order to enable a seaplane to get into the air when heavily loaded. In smooth, mirror-like water, when there is no wind, the attraction of the water for the pontoons makes it almost impossible to break the suction. To overcome this, one plane used to taxi across the water to disturb it, so that the other two could get off on the waves left in the wake of the trail-breaker. Then the leading plane would rise in the rough water kicked up by the two others as they passed. But this day the *Chicago* missed the waves made by the *New Orleans* and *Boston*. Seeing us still on the water, Erik and Leigh circled around, but Lowell waved to them to fly on toward China.

'Suspecting that there was something wrong with our pontoons, we taxied back to our moorings, donned the bathing-suits that had been presented to us by the people of Portland, Oregon, and spent the rest of the day swimming about under the pontoons. We discovered that a metal strip had been torn away by the force of the water, so that there had been just enough resistance to prevent us from getting off as we should.

'Swimming around under the pontoons was a job for a mermaid, not for an airman, and we swallowed quarts of water. But we finally got it fixed, and the following morning the *Black Hawk* sent two fast motor-boats in front of us to kick up the surface of Kagoshima Bay, enabling us to follow the others toward China.'

Meanwhile the *New Orleans* and *Boston* had headed out across the open sea, and for six long hours had flown out of sight of land, making the longest sea journey up until this time.

'With the shores of Japan melting into the sky behind us,' says Nelson, ' the thoughts of all of us were of the interesting time we had had in the land of the Mikado, of the honors that had been showered upon us, and of the brilliant people we had met. It was so wonderful that we were still in a bit of a daze.

'But my thoughts, as we clipped off mile after mile and hour after hour of open sea between Japan and China, were of the days when I was a sailor on a tramp wind-jammer. What a difference there is between a ship that takes from one or two years to sail round the world, and a Cruiser like the *New Orleans* capable of making the circuit of the globe in less than two weeks' flying time! In a little more than ten years I not only had seen this miracle, but had taken part in it. And as we flew on and on toward China, my engine was running so smoothly that the ship seemed to be flying herself. I dropped into a reverie, and seemed to see dozens of giant planes passing me in the sky with passengers making week-end trips between Shanghai and San Francisco, just as they now do between Paris and London. It seemed to me that the airplane was destined to be the agency that would bring the races of the world into such intimate contact with each other that they would no more feel inclined to wage wars than the people of Oregon feel like fighting the inhabitants of Florida.

'If our Flight helps in any way to hasten this era, we shall be repaid a million times over for our efforts. Just what significance it will have to our fellow countrymen, we do not know. But there is one thing we do know, that it has done much to stimulate enthusiasm for aviation in Japan!

'Part of the time, while speeding across the Yellow Sea, I just let my mind browse, while Jack took the wheel. We often relieved each other like that. Nor is there a more ideal place in the world for meditation than the cockpit of a plane as you race across the sky at seventy or a hundred miles an hour. If the air is clear, and you are high enough from the earth not to be interested in its affairs and if your motor is singing a melody of power that is one long rhythmical harmony, you and your plane seem to merge into one. The swiftness of your flight seems to blow the cobwebs from your brain, and you can do more clear thinking in two hours there than you can do in two days in a crowded city.'

CHAPTER XVII

FLYING DOWN THE CHINA COAST

'WE left Kagoshima Bay at 8.25 on the morning of June 4th,' continues Erik, 'and flew across the junction of the Yellow and China Seas. An hour off the coast we had passed the *Ford*, first of the destroyers detailed to keep an eye on us. Forty miles off the China coast we could tell we were approaching the mouth of a great river because the sea changed color from deep blue to green, and then, as we drew nearer the mainland, it turned to liquid gold in the sunlight.

'We knew we were approaching the delta of one of the largest rivers of the world, the Yangtze-Kiang, which traverses a stretch of country from source to sea greater than the distance between New York and San Francisco. The Yangtze-Kiang is the Mississippi of the Far East, dividing North and South China. Tens of millions of people live on its shores, or on its turbid stream. Indeed, it is the most densely populated body of water on earth. Among the cities on its banks are Shanghai, about the size of Philadelphia; Nanking, nearly as large as Boston; Hankow, which is equal to St. Louis and New Orleans combined; Soochow, in the delta, about the size of Detroit; and a score of other cities with a population of one hundred thousand.

'As we flew across the mouth of the river and drew near Shanghai, we were amazed at the number of craft below us. The river teemed with tens of thousands of junks, sampans, and steamers. But we found when we came down that the harbor-master had held up all traffic in the river for hours. Just in one bunch there were over two hundred and fifty boats loaded with fish, and these hardly represented a hundredth part of all that Bedlam of boats. Not knowing just how much space we should require, the harbor-master had cleared several miles of water-front in order to save us from the fate of D'Oisy, the French world flier, who had crashed on the outskirts of Shanghai a few days before.

'This lower part of the Yangtze-Kiang is so broad, and the fall is so slight, that the tide runs all the way to the city of Wuhu, two hundred miles upstream. Owing to the speed of the tide, we found it difficult to moor, but it was finally accomplished, and we boarded an excursion boat where we were met by several hundred Chinese officials and representatives from the American and European quarter.

'Some thirty or forty thousand Americans and Europeans were living at the time in this treaty port, which is the commercial metropolis of the China coast. Although there are several million Chinese inhabitants, the city is one of the most cosmopolitan in the world. In addition to Chinese from every province, there is a colony of Japanese, many Malays, Hindu money-lenders, long-haired Sikhs from the Punjab, Parsees from Bombay, Koreans in their tall hats, Annamites, Siamese, Singalese with hair knotted around tortoiseshell combs, Javanese in gay sarongs, Turks, Russians, and in fact people from the four corners of the earth. And they all appeared to be on the river in boats waiting to see us complete the first flight from America to China. Incidentally, this was the first flight we had made with perfect weather conditions, since leaving Seattle.

'Clustered around the excursion boat, where the reception was held, were a number of sampans, each flying a flag with the letter "S." When we asked about them, Captain Eisler, the Shanghai representative of the United States Shipping Board, explained that they were for us, and were supplied by the Standard Oil people. All we had to do when we wanted to go back and forth to our planes was to call one and jump in.

'On our way across the junction of the Yellow and China Seas the exhaust pipe on the right-hand side of my engine had become so overheated and cracked that the rubber had burned off the ignition wires. If we had been obliged to fly an hour or two longer, Jack and I might have had a ducking. On reaching Shanghai, we had short exhaust stacks put on all the planes, because we had been having trouble with the longer ones, which burned out the exhaust gaskets. A machine shop in a Chinese shipyard worked night and day to turn them out and from then on we had no more trouble from this cause.

'After the reception on the excursion steamer, we rowed back to our planes and went to work. But in so doing we disappointed people ashore who had drawn up the reserve militia, mounted and in full regalia, to receive us. We were sorry to miss meeting these folk, but I am afraid we were the cause of similar disappointments all along the line. Our work was first, for we were not on a joy ride. Often we finished our work by lantern light and then were up again before dawn.

'It was dark when we left the ships and were taken to the Hotel Astor. Upon entering the lobby, had it not been for the Chinese attendants, we should have thought ourselves in a hotel in New York, Paris, or London. Later in the evening, cars whisked us through the streets to the home of a merchant prince. Upon entering, we were told to stand in front of two massive double doors. They swung open and we nearly dropped through the floor with surprise. There we were, facing a great throng in evening dress. Some one gave us a shove, and as we ran the gauntlet, an orchestra struck up and little girls in sweet little dresses led the way strewing roses before us and singing.

'It was a brilliant affair. The women wore Paris evening gowns, with pearls, tiaras, and ostrich-feather fans, and their escorts were arrayed in the uniforms of a dozen different nations. The movie-stars of Los Angeles could do no better than this.

'Next day Smith and Arnold arrived, and again the reception committee, the foreign colony, and vast throngs of Chinese were out on the Yangtze-Kiang to meet them. Again we worked on the planes until dark. When "Les"

and Leigh returned to the hotel, they had on their greasy
union-alls and the native footman at the door of the Astor
ordered them around to the tradesmen's entrance! Such
is life.

'Shortly after reaching the hotel, we were waited upon
by the strangest committee that we encountered in any
country. Apparently both in China and in India stealing
is a recognized profession. At any rate these worthies were
none other than the heads of the Thieves' Union of Shanghai and they had called on us to present us each with a life
membership in their society!'

That night, some of the boys jumped into 'rickshaws,
rode along the Bund and dipped deep into the tortuous
alleyways of the native city, past temples and tea-houses
and over zigzag bridges, to the accompaniment of gongs,
bells, and cries. They were going to a Chinese dinner given
by General Li, one of the heads of aviation in China. The
menu included sharks' fins and bird's-nest soup and
century-old eggs. The meal started at eight and would
have continued on through the night, but the boys were
very tired and took leave of their courtly host as soon as
they politely could.

In the meantime Smith was busy with the naval officers,
planning the best way to 'take-off' from Shanghai, and
arranging for several destroyers to drop down the coast and
prepare a special landing-place where they could refuel.
To have attempted to refuel in the Yangtze-Kiang would
have been extremely unwise, for they foresaw that even
with a light load of gasoline and oil, it would be difficult to
avoid hitting the swarming sampans.

In spite of precautions, Erik and Jack had a narrow
escape on the morning of June 7th, when attempting to
'take-off.' The traffic on the river was so great that the
harbor-master had not been able to clear a very wide
stretch. The first time the three planes attempted to fly,
they couldn't rise in the space available, nearly collided
with the river craft, and had to turn and make a second
attempt. This time the *Chicago* and *Boston* succeeded in

GRANDMA JONGG COULDN'T SEE HOW WE COULD FLY WITHOUT
FLAPPING OUR WINGS

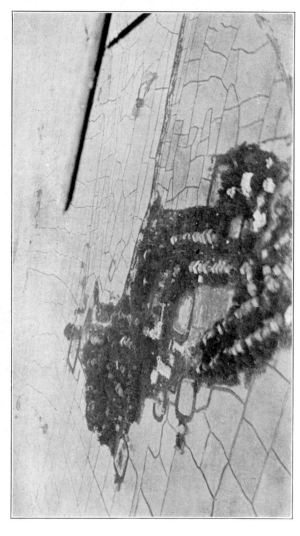

ON OUR WAY DOWN THE CHINA COAST WE PASSED VILLAGES AT THE RATE OF TWO OR
THREE A MINUTE WITH A CHECKERBOARD OF FLOODED RICE-FIELDS IN BETWEEN

getting off all right, but the *New Orleans* turned to avoid a sampan and Erik and Jack went sailing up the Yangtze-Kiang at sixty miles an hour, dodging the traffic with giddy skill. The other boys watched them with their hearts in their mouths fully expecting to see a head-on crash, but Erik's hand on the control wheel had never been more cunning and the *New Orleans* at last zoomed into the blue a few inches over the mast of a junk.

With only enough gasoline for five hours, they flew from 7.50 A.M. until 12.20 and descended near a destroyer in Tchinkoen Bay, a body of water that turned out to be far more boisterous than Smith had supposed. But they had to descend because they were nearly out of fuel. They got down all right, but their 'take-off' through the rollers was another of the many anxious moments of their adventure.

'In cruising on down the China coast to Amoy, we flew so low,' says Jack Harding, 'that we could smell China, an aroma that was still a novelty to us. Nor at that moment did we doubt but that there were four hundred millions of people living in the country. We had no sooner passed one village than we were above another. The streets seethed with people and the country roads were also dense with spectators, while chickens and pigs filled the yards. Far out into Formosa Strait the water was dotted with sampans with strangely painted eyes, each boat holding several families gazing upwards at the white devils.

'Whenever we got tired of villages and rice-fields, we would take a swing out to sea and play leap-frog with the junks for a while. Smith and Les would pick out a junk. Leigh and Hank would take another. Erik and I would spot a third. Then all three planes would dive toward them, full tilt. But just as the Chinks thought that plenty bad joss was coming all one piecey top-side and had doomed them to a watery grave, we would shoot over the tops of their masts, and in two minutes be miles away. It was fun for us, and I dare say it helped to break the monotony of life on board the junks.

'In northern China wheat, barley, and millet are the

principal crops, but from Shanghai to southward, rice, tea, and cotton are more in evidence. In many provinces the soil is so rich that the farmers raise three crops a year. But I should think it would need all that and more to keep all of these swarming slant-eyed folk alive in their countless, clustered villages and jammed-tight junks.

'At 5.30 in the afternoon, after having flown six hundred miles, we came down in front of the Standard Oil pier in the harbor at Amoy, with pagodas and temples all around. While we were mooring, a sampan came alongside and I heard a voice shout: "Hello, Tennessee." The visitor turned out to be a fellow Southerner who used to live within a few miles of Nashville. We worked on the planes until long after dark and then spent the night on board the destroyer *Preble* as the guests of Commander Glassford.

'Although we didn't go into the city, the city came to us. Next morning, Sunday, June 8th, when we were called at daybreak, we saw hundreds and hundreds of little Chinese boats crowded around the planes. More kept coming from shore until we could scarcely see the water. We hurried out, got up on the pontoons, and for an hour struggled to keep them from drifting into us and damaging the planes. Some of the sampans had sails and the wind kept blowing them toward us. Others were so full that their occupants could not control them. The launch from the *Preble* tried to protect us, but the officer in charge got disgusted and decided the only way to drive them off would be to sink a few. Something had to be done to prevent the planes from being crushed by those thousands of boats. So he backed off a few feet, and then shot his boat full speed ahead. Some of the sampans capsized, throwing the occupants over into other craft or into the water. It wasn't long until he had cleared a space. From then on the boatmen kept at a respectful distance.

'The city of Amoy is on an island of the same name. Its population is about equal to that of Seattle and Spokane combined. All through history it has been the abode of buccaneers who swooped down in their fast war junks and plundered villages and passing ships. Possibly that accounts for the way the people of Amoy treated us. At any rate, if it hadn't been for the *Preble* launch, they probably would have smashed us up.

'Not far from where we were moored, an antiquated Chinese destroyer, bristling with guns, swung at anchor. Her story was quite in keeping with the lurid history of Amoy. The captain, it seems, had deserted from the rest of the Chinese fleet and anchored here two years ago. Training his quick-firers on the city and sending word to the inhabitants that henceforth they were to pay tribute to him, he and his men then went ashore and drove off the local military detachment. Since that day he has never lifted his anchor and to-day he is the ruler of all the territory within range of his guns.

'We had only three hundred and ten miles to make on our way down the China coast to Hongkong, so it was not until ten o'clock that we got under way. But we would gladly have said farewell to Amoy at sunrise had it not been for the congested "aerodrome."

'As we flew down the coast we ran into the edge of a typhoon. This coast is the home of typhoons, springing from vortices of climatic disturbance as yet little understood, and causing terrible havoc among villages and shipping.

'The typhoon signals were out when we left Amoy. At any moment, out of a clear sky, one of these furies of the deep might sweep landwards with a velocity of one hundred miles an hour, carrying a sheet of hissing water as its vanguard and a tidal wave in its wake.

'The barometer dropped with startling suddenness. The horizon was a solid mass of soot-black cloud, through which lightning flickered like a snake's tongue. A wind, such as sweeps round the Poles, struck us abaft, increasing our ground speed to one hundred and fifty miles an hour.

'But we were only on the edge of the typhoon's path. It swept by, as suddenly as it came, leaving a strip of eerily calm sea. Then we met fog and driving rain, which seemed normal and soothing after the cataclysmic forces we had just escaped.

'For ten miles we skimmed over a narrow inlet between high hills. We kept just over the tops of the hundreds of boats passing in and out. All this traffic assured us that we were nearing the far-famed British city of Hongkong, one of the greatest ports in the world in tonnage cleared. We arrived at 1.32, and the weather cleared enough for us to see something of this harbor which is rivaled in beauty only by Rio and Naples. It was, indeed, a wonderful sight. Covering over fifteen square miles and almost surrounded by high hills, it was filled with warships, liners, and tramps from every corner of the globe, as well as native craft of every description. Stiff-sailed sampans cast curved and typically Chinese reflections on the land-locked waters of the lagoons. Hulking prosperously against the sky, stood the Peak, where the white men live and where land values are mounting as vertiginously as the funicular railroad. The British have owned the island since the Treaty of Nanking in 1841. When they took it over, it was deserted. Now a million souls and a million tons of shipping make it about the busiest place in Asia.

'As ill-luck would have it, the letter explaining where we were to moor in Hongkong Harbor had got lost in the mails. So we flew around for some time looking for our yellow buoys. Not finding them, we flew down close to an American destroyer and they waved us over to the opposite side of the bay, where we finally moored in a little cove near the Standard Oil dock. All that afternoon and the following day was spent refueling the planes, repairing all three propellers, and helping Smith and Arnold doctor up the pontoon that had troubled them in Japan. It was now leaking badly and it was necessary to hoist the plane onto a wharf where a new pontoon was installed.

'The Standard Oil people gave us invaluable help and sent lunch out to us, as well as some Chinese merchants with beads, pearls, and silks for us to look over in case we wanted to reduce the weight of our bank-note rolls.

'Next morning the sun was blazing hot. We were drawing nearer and nearer to the Equator. There was no mistaking that. Early in the morning on June 10th, we launched the *Chicago*, taxied across the harbor, and then left for Haiphong in French Indo-China. It was a clear day and we flew up to two thousand feet because we had been told that from there we might be able to catch a glimpse of the largest city in all China. Sure enough, away to the northwest in the delta of the Pearl River, we could see the gray splotch that was old Canton, city of silks and sedan chairs, and birthplace of revolutions.

'Thirty miles south of Hongkong, we passed Macao, the oldest outpost of Europe on the China coast. By defeating the pirates, the early Portuguese navigators and traders had won the good-will of the Chinese officials in this vicinity and had established a colony which is still under the control of Portugal. But Hongkong long ago lured away its trade and now Macao is merely the "fan-tan" Monte Carlo of the Far East.'

'On our way from Hongkong to Haiphong,' adds Smith, 'we made a forty-mile hop over a peninsula between the South China Sea and the Gulf of Tongking. Of course, crossing such a strip of land with pontoons is a rather risky business, because if obliged to make a forced landing you are sure to crack up. We had three different maps showing this peninsula, and each called it by a different name. On one it was marked "Leih-Chew," on another "Quan-Chaw-Wan," and on a third "Luichow." It is a part of China proper, and is the southernmost extremity of the province of Ewangtung of which Canton is the capital. This is the most tropical part of China, a land of banyan and camphor trees, cocoanut palms, temples and pagodas. Although densely populated, there are more tigers and leopards here than anywhere else in China. The majority of the Chinese who have settled in the Malay Peninsula, or who have migrated to Australia, South Africa, and America, have come from this province.

'Evidently the natives of Luichow Peninsula had never

seen airplanes before. We flew only about five hundred feet off the ground, and as we came roaring into view we could see Chinese running in every direction. When we caught up with them, they would swing off either to the left or to the right to avoid the dragons that seemed about to gobble them up.

'The scenery of Haiphong Harbor was most impressive. First we passed scores of little islands, some of them mere needles of rock. Then we sailed over high cliffs, and small lagoons with attractive-looking bungalows dotted here and there. Any one of the lagoons would have made an excellent place to moor.

'At 6.40, just as the sun went down behind the palms, we reached the mouth of the Red River which flows into French Indo-China from the mountains of Yunnan.

'Here we moored near another Standard Oil pier. The French officials wanted us to come at once aboard a destroyer and attend a reception. They couldn't understand why we should have to remain and work on our Cruisers, when they had a tea-party all arranged for us. Becoming impatient, most of the ladies and gentlemen who had gathered to greet us embarked on launches and came over and watched us. One boatload pulled right alongside the *Chicago* and a Frenchman with a luxurious beard made several attempts to clamber upon the pontoons. "Les" kept pushing him off, and each time the bearded visitor tried it again, sputtering volubly the while. Later, we discovered that he was one of the French officials delivering an address of welcome, and were very sorry at our unintentional discourtesy.

'It was dark before we had finished "servicing-up" the ships, and when we climbed aboard the destroyer nearly all of the guests had given us up as hopeless and gone home. But the French Governor-General was still there, patiently waiting with his speech of welcome, and invited us to attend a formal reception and ball to be held ashore in our honor that night.

'When we had so much trouble getting off the water the

day we left Japan for our hop across the Yellow Sea, we
had lightened our loads by throwing overboard every unnecessary thing, including all our clothes excepting those
in which we flew. This meant that we couldn't attend
functions unless we could borrow suitable apparel. But by
now we had reduced the borrowing business down to a fine
art. As soon as we boarded a destroyer at the end of a
day's flight, we would size up the officers. Then, without
their being aware of our evil designs, each of us would pick
out an officer about our own size whom we would later
relieve of a pair of white trousers, socks, shoes, white shirt,
tie, and sun-helmet. This would enable us to board the
waiting 'rickshaws and sally forth to the evening's festivities
as snappily groomed as any cake-eater of the China coast.

'At the reception in Haiphong that night, our French
hosts told us that they had just received a radio with the
news that two of our competitors, the Portuguese world
fliers, had arrived in Rangoon, Burma. The last we had
heard of them they had crashed in India. But the British
Royal Air Force had supplied them with a new plane in
which they had been fortunate enough at least to get past
Akyab, the "hoodoo" town on the Bay of Bengal where so
many airmen had crashed. MacLaren, the British flier,
was still at Akyab, awaiting the arrival of the American
destroyer bringing his Vickers-Amphibian from Japan.

'This news of the progress of the Portuguese was like a
tonic to us. Excusing ourselves from the reception, we
hurried back to the destroyer, got a good night's sleep and
were up at dawn the next morning, June 11th, hoping to
reach Saigon, or at least to get halfway down the coast of
French Indo-China that day.

'Our Libertys seemed to be humming a song of joy and
contentment as we warmed them up to the accompaniment
of the temple bells of Haiphong, and little did we dream
that before night we should be stranded on a lagoon in the
heart of the Tongking jungle.'

CHAPTER XVIII

A FORCED LANDING IN
THE JUNGLE OF FRENCH INDO–CHINA

Owing to the dead calm on the river at Haiphong, it took the Fliers three hours to get off the water, and even then they couldn't 'get on their pontoon step' until they had taxied for ten miles to the ripples at the mouth of the Gulf of Tongking. Wade, at fifty-five miles an hour, sped down the river, missing tanks and sampans by only a few feet. Dodging and swerving to prevent a crash, he taxied twelve miles before he succeeded in breaking the vacuum underneath his pontoons, and bounced into the air. Once under way, they crossed a narrow peninsula and headed for Tourane, a seaport of French Indo-China midway between Haiphong and Saigon. Some ten miles of flooded rice-fields passed beneath them. As the World Cruisers roared low over the Annamite farmers in their curious conical hats the water buffalo yoked to their ploughs would gallop madly across the paddy, scattering men and women right and left. The farther south they flew, the denser became the jungle. After a time they rarely even passed a village, although they sometimes saw a few huts near cocoanut groves, belonging to fishermen. One hundred and fifty miles of this flight were made over open sea.

'Thirty miles off the coast, our motor started to overheat,' says Lowell Smith, 'so I turned west toward the shore — for we were out over the Gulf of Tongking. At 2.28 P.M., according to the log, we landed in a lagoon called "Kuavictorpalms" and filled the radiator with salt water. Meanwhile the *Boston* and *New Orleans* circled overhead until they saw us take-off again. But we kept on losing water and couldn't make out just where the leak was. In fact, the water kept streaming back into our faces.

'For another twenty minutes we passed over wild

ON OUR WAY TO HONGKONG WE FLEW OVER THE LADRONES, OR THIEVES ISLANDS

ALONG THE CHINA COAST THEY FLEW PAST MANY WEIRD JUNKS

ENTERING THE LANDLOCKED HARBOR AT HONGKONG

FLYING OVER 'ISLANDS OF OPAL THAT FLOAT ON SILVER SEAS,' WITH HERE AND
THERE 'PALE PORTS OF AMBER AND GOLDEN ARGOSIES'

jungle and rough, unprotected arms of the sea, where there wasn't a hope of getting down without crashing. By now the motor was red-hot again and pounding badly, so we were obliged to turn out to sea, all the while scanning the country for some sheltered lagoon where we might come down. I spotted one at last, some three miles inland, so we hopped across the jungle and dived toward it. Nor were we a minute too soon. As we started to glide toward the lagoon, everything in the motor seemed to be going to pieces, for a connecting rod had broken and poked a hole through the crank-case. I couldn't tell at what moment the ship might catch fire.'

Immediately they landed, Arnold jerked loose his safety belt, grabbed the fire-extinguisher, and bounded over the side.

Fortunately they were not on fire. But they were stranded on a lagoon in a remote corner of Indo-China, with a wrecked motor and without food or drinking-water — none too pleasant a situation.

The *Boston* and *New Orleans* flew down past them several times. Smith and Arnold signaled that their motor had failed, whereupon the other two cruisers landed alongside, gave them what drinking-water they were carrying, and promised to get a new motor for them as quickly as possible, returning overland with it from Tourane.

Subsequent inspection proved that the loss of water had been due to a cracked water jacket on one of the cylinders. But this defect was hidden under the cowling and the metal nose of the plane had to be taken off before the discovery was made.

The lagoon in which they had come down was full of native fishing-traps made of bamboo poles driven into the muddy bottom. The landing was made alongside one of these. 'We always carried a rope,' says 'Les' Arnold, 'so we hitched our aerial mustang to a bamboo pole and then took a look around the lagoon. For the first half-hour, we saw no sign of any living thing excepting an occasional bird, or a crocodile slithering into the water with a plunk that brought the gooseflesh out on me in spite of the tropical heat. Evidently the natives, seeing three huge birds drop down out of the skies, had fled to the remoter parts of the forest.

'At last a dugout shoved off from the shore. One man's curiosity had overcome his fright. Although he had black, kinky hair, his lips were not thick like a negro's. As he looked us over and rested on his paddle alongside the *Chicago*, he spat a stream of crimson juice into the lagoon and we saw that his teeth were all black and worn off almost down to the gums. Whether they get that way from chewing betel nut, or whether their ivories are filed off, we didn't discover. He seemed worried about our being tied to one of the bamboo stakes that was holding his fish-trap, and tried to take off the rope, gibbering like a cageful of anthropoid apes in a zoo.

'While he entertained us with his simian small-talk, Lowell and I had got out the anchor and ropes, so that we could moor properly. To keep our caller from untying us, we coaxed him up on the pontoons and I gave him the sixty-pound anchor to hold — just to keep his claws out of mischief. When we were ready, we cast off, allowed ourselves to drift a little farther out into the lagoon, and then threw the anchor overboard.

'Meanwhile the rest of the lake-dwellers, reassured by the fact that this one man had not been chopped-up and cooked, paddled up to us in dugouts. Where they all came from was a mystery, because we could see no huts. But from our new location nearer the middle of the lagoon we noticed a small building back in the palms, that looked half Oriental temple and half church. Later, we discovered that it was in fact a mission house. The natives became friendly when they found no harm was likely to befall them; in fact they were just a bit too chummy.

'They wore no clothing beyond the usual breech-cloth, so we were not afraid of letting them stand on the pontoons and inspect the monster that had ruffled their quiet waters. But presently they began to swarm onto the plane in such numbers that the pontoons were rapidly becoming submerged. So we shooed them off, Lowell policing one side of the ship while I guarded the other.

'We hadn't had a thing to eat since daybreak, and it was then past three o'clock. There was no shade and, as the hours slipped by, our thirst increased, for we soon consumed our meager store of water. While debating whether it would be safe for one of us to get in a dugout and explore ashore, a boat came alongside, paddled by a hollow-cheeked, melancholy soul who looked neither native nor European. He had on a white robe and a soiled sun-helmet and addressed us in French, turning out to be a missionary who lived all alone out there in the jungle. All he seemed interested in was whether we would sell him some cigarettes. He wanted them, but stipulated that he would not pay more than two cents a carton for them. Evidently he thought we were aerial tobacco agents. Or perhaps he was a little cracked. Who wouldn't be, living out his life by this hot lagoon?

'When we explained in "doughboy French" that we had no cigarettes for sale, he lost all interest in us and refused to get food and water. Mumbling to himself, he paddled back to the shore in his dugout. I followed him in another, and behind the little mission church I found a spring. In spite of the loud protests of the cigarette-hound, I filled a bottle. Our native friend who had held the anchor for us also brought out a bunch of bananas and some cocoanuts which he split so that we could drink the milk. In return we gave him some cigarettes.

'About sundown a sampan arrived with three more priests who came from a neighboring village three and a half miles away. They were more friendly than the first, and when I explained, as best I could, that we were hungry and again out of water, they said that if I would go with them, they would provide us with such supper as they had. Smith, whose outward display of mirth rarely goes beyond a whimsical smile, roared with laughter at my pidgin French and pantomime. However, I got my ideas across to the holy fathers, and with a final plea to Lowell not to drink any of the dirty water that the natives had brought for us in the bottom of their dugouts, I paddled off to the village.

'It was dark when we arrived. The priests took me to a spring. But I didn't like the look of it. Before leaving America we had all been warned about drinking water in the tropics or eating green foods. My hosts then produced a glass of sacramental wine. O boy! I'll tell the world it braced me up. I asked them to let me have a supply to take back to Lowell. We debated about the price for some time, without my being able to convince them that it was their Christian duty to give us food and drink. But glancing around the little chapel I noticed there wasn't a window in it, and this gave me an idea. Now the smallest "greenback" I happened to have with me was for fifty dollars. No doubt ten iron men would have accomplished the same purpose, but it wasn't a time to haggle, so I put down the fifty and told them to buy windows for their church. That settled the argument about the communion wine. Labor is so cheap here that with the fifty they could almost build another church.

'Happy over my success and carrying a small bottle of Lachrima Christi away with me, as well as some boiled rice wrapped in leaves, and several baked yams that turned out afterward to be inedible, they paddled me back to the plane. I had been gone three hours and a half! Meanwhile Lowell had been having a troublesome time keeping the aborigines from damaging the pontoons of the *Chicago.* In desperation he had unhooked the Véry pistol which each Cruiser carried for signal purposes, and fired over the heads of the natives. After doing this a few times, he got them trained so that whenever he turned his pocket flash on them they thought he was going to open fire again.

'The evening had been sultry and nearly as hot as the afternoon. So thirsty had Lowell become that he had taken a few swallows of the water from one of the native dugouts. And that no doubt was what brought him down with dysentery a few days later when we got to Rangoon.'

While Lowell Smith and Arnold are waiting for help, we must follow the adventures of the *New Orleans* and *Boston*.

Less than an hour after leaving the lagoon, the other four reached Tourane. Mooring the planes and leaving 'Jack' and 'Hank' to 'service-up,' Erik and Leigh hurried aboard the American destroyer that was already in the harbor awaiting them. They decided that while Erik should go back and find Smith and Arnold, Leigh should get a new engine up from Saigon by destroyer.

The advance officer for this division was Lieutenant Lawton, the same officer who had arranged supply bases and mooring places all down the China coast. Here at Tourane he had appointed the Standard Oil agent, M. Chevalier, a Frenchman, to look after the boys upon their arrival. Erik found him aboard the destroyer. They hurried ashore to M. Chevalier's house, hunted up a map of Indo-China and tried to reckon the exact location of the lagoon and how best to reach it.

French Indo-China is larger than France itself and is populated by seventeen million people of Mongolian origin. From Nelson's description, M. Chevalier knew that Smith and Arnold were not many miles from the old city of Hué, capital of the Province of Annam. He suggested that they motor there before venturing into the jungle. So leaving Wade, Ogden, and Harding to look after the *New Orleans* and *Boston*, and to get the new engine up from Saigon, Nelson and M. Chevalier started for Hué to consult the French officials there.

'The highway we drove over was an excellently constructed gravel road,' says Erik. 'We wound through the jungle, past native bullock carts and mountain ranges and teak and tamarind forests. It was wild jungle country. Occasionally we would zipp through a village, or stop to be ferried across a stretch of water by a native barge.

'It took us three hours to get to Hué, and none of the

officials had even heard that any airplanes were in that part of Asia. But when I pointed out on the map where I thought the lagoon was located, they told us it was impossible to reach it by car and that we would have to go part way by sampan or dugout.

'At the little hotel in Hué we bought sandwiches, milk, soda water, and other things to take along for the boys, engaged a native who spoke a little French to guide us, and at 11 P.M. that night we were off in the automobile again. There are many waterways through this part of Annam, so we decided to make first for a place owned by a friend of Chevalier's, who owned a rice plantation on the river which ran into the lagoon we were looking for. We got within two miles of the plantation in the motor: then we had to load our food and other supplies into a sampan and continue by river.

'It was pitch dark, not even a star. How the natives could find their way around the bends in that stream on such an inky night was beyond me, but evidently their eyes are better trained for penetrating darkness than ours. This is a great tiger country, and the Annamites live in mortal terror of "Master Stripes." They also have a wholesome respect for crocodiles. Before we got into their sampan they threw a little cooked rice into the river and offered up a prayer to the spirits of the night, imploring them to protect us.

'In another half-hour we arrived in front of the plantation, and were greeted by a pack of dogs that yelped as if they had seen the Forty Thieves. Chevalier shouted to his friend, who had been aroused by the barking. He came out and told us he had seen nothing of the planes. But after we had all studied the map again in his bungalow, he advised us to journey overland for a few miles to a place where he said a native priest lived. This priest would be able to locate the lagoon, if any one could. He rounded up some of the natives for us, and after considerable bickering and bargaining we found five who agreed to carry the food and guide us through the forest.

'Just how far we hiked I do not know. We proceeded single file, and what impressed me the most was the multitude of little shrines all along the way where the natives said their prayers and left offerings for the tigers and their other forest friends. Every traveler who goes this way leaves a banana or a bit of rice on these altars. There were shrines every five minutes, and occasionally we passed a good-sized temple. On both sides of the trail there was dense jungle, that could only be penetrated by cutting your way through with an axe.

'At last we arrived at the thatched house of the priest. While the natives remained outside, he invited us in, told us he had neither seen nor heard any airplanes, but would send for some of the natives who had been out fishing that day. At the same time he ordered one of his servants to notify the mandarin who lived a mile or so away. The fishermen were unable to help us, but they did say they had seen two monsters flying through the air that afternoon.

'The mandarin came to the priest's bungalow dolled up in a gorgeous silk costume and followed by quite a retinue. He was most polite and offered to place sampans and men at our disposal. So we set off down the river again. Exhausted, I stretched out in the bottom of the sampan while Chevalier inspected the banks with the two flashlights we had brought along. Occasionally we passed a native village, and then the night would be rent by the cries of the natives on shore and those paddling us who answered shout for shout.

'An hour or more went by before we encountered any one who could give us encouraging news. At last a native told us that there was an airplane in a lagoon not far away. Eureka! We knew we were on the right track. From then on, we kept the flashlights going continuously, and called out every few minutes. At last we heard an answering shout.'

Meanwhile Smith and Arnold had managed to get a little sleep, although the mosquitoes nearly devoured them alive. After drinking their wine and eating their rice and bananas, Smith curled up in the tool compartment with his head out of the doorway, and 'Les' stretched out on the bottom wing. They were awake when the rescue party approached.

Not only had Nelson and Chevalier brought food and drinks, but they had had the forethought to pack the latter in ice. So a feast was obviously 'indicated.' It was a memorable night for the Frenchman and the three fliers, supping on that still lagoon at three o'clock in the morning. Erik remembered that it was the 12th of June, his birthday, so they pledged his health in Lachrima Christi and drank success to the Flight.

After they had finished this birthday party, they went ashore, aroused the natives in the nearest village and arranged with them to have a fleet of sampans tow the *Chicago* out of the lagoon and for twenty-five miles along the Hué River to the capital of Annam, there to await the arrival of a new engine.

At dawn, three war sampans were ready, with ten naked paddlers in each. These craft were hitched like tugs onto the *Chicago* and with a whoop and an Annamese 'Ho heave-ho' they started to haul the plane to Hué.

The wives of the paddlers followed alongside in other sampans, passing water, food, and cigarettes to the oarsmen during the journey. For ten hours they paddled without ever letting up for a moment, except when one of them would snatch a bite of food or take a puff at his wife's cigarette.

In the bow of the leading boat sat a patriarch with a tom-tom, the paddlers dipping to the rhythm of the drum. The chief of the tribe accompanied the party in his royal sampan, his junior wives paddling, while he reclined under a sun-shade. His favorite concubine sat beside him, not only rolling his cigarettes and lighting them for him, but also supporting him with draughts of toddy and comforting him with bananas throughout the twenty-five-mile trip to Hué.

AT SEA

THE ANNAMITE WHO GAVE LIEUTENANT OGDEN
HIS WILD RIDE THROUGH THE JUNGLE

A FORCED LANDING IN
FRENCH INDO-CHINA

AN ANNAMITE DOWAGER TAKES A CHEW AND GIVES US THE ONCE-OVER

'SMITTY' AND 'LES'

'"Les" and I took the cushions out of the cockpit of our plane,' says Smith, 'and rigged up comfortable seats under the wing where it was shady and fairly cool. Our greatest regret was that we hadn't a camera. Every bend in the river revealed a view that would have been worth photographing. And to see the *Chicago* come towing through that jungle behind the war sampans was a sight in itself.

'Erik and Chevalier accompanied us for twelve miles until we came to the place where they had left their automobile the previous night. Chevalier said the jungle through here was the favorite haunt of tiger, and he begged us to stay long enough to spend one day hunting with him, but of course we couldn't. Occasionally we saw elephants plodding along under the cocoanut and banyan trees with enormous loads of sugar-cane, and we passed herds of them bathing and throwing water over each other in shady pools near the villages.

'Our French friend had sent a courier ahead to warn the inhabitants of Hué that we were coming. So when we arrived the whole population was out to meet us. Erik and Chevalier who had arrived ahead of us by motor, had rounded up a company of Annamite soldiers to guard the plane, which we beached close to a bridge that looked as if it would be a good place for changing engines. And so it was: for it was much simpler to use the bridge for raising the engines than to attempt to rig up a derrick.

'By that time we were pretty well tired out, but stuck to it and worked until dark. Next day at dawn Nelson and Chevalier left for Tourane and we resumed the work of getting the motor disconnected, but by eleven o'clock the heat was so terrific that we grew dizzy and faint and were forced to stop. M. Bruel, a professor in the local Annamite college, insisted on taking us to his home for lunch in spite of our protests that we were too dirty, and were dressed in overalls. When we arrived at his home, the professor had his servants give us cold baths by throwing buckets of water over us and he then dressed us in his own white suits. As, however, our host was a six-foot giant weighing two hundred and twelve pounds, we looked like small boys dressed in father's clothes. But while we were at lunch, M. Bruel's servants attended to our laundry with such speed that our things were ready to put on before we returned to the hotel about 3 P.M. From then until dusk we worked in order to have everything ready upon arrival of the new motor.'

It was at this French professor's home that the boys had their first introduction to the *punka*. A little native girl sat outside the door pulling a cord which agitated a heavy cloth suspended over the table. This stirred up enough breeze to make the Fliers feel that life in the tropics had some attractions after all. That night they were entertained by the staff of the local college, but turned in early, expecting that the other boys would arrive the next morning with a new engine.

The spare 'Liberty–12,' meanwhile, had been rushed by destroyer from Saigon to Tourane under arrangements made by Leigh Wade, who, however, had himself to remain at Tourane to see that no mishap occurred to the *Boston* and *New Orleans*. As soon as the engine arrived, Nelson, Harding, and Chevalier started for Hué by automobile, while Ogden and four American sailors accompanied the precious mechanism in a motor truck.

'The driver of that lorry,' Ogden said later, 'cared little for his own life and less for mine. We left Tourane after sunset and it was so dark I couldn't tell what sort of country we were going through or what pace we were making, but it must have been fully thirty miles an hour. Traveling at that rate in a truck over a jungle road is enough to shake your toe-nails to your throat.

'Up and up and up, we went. It seemed as though we must be ascending Pike's Peak or Mount Everest. Occasionally I saw two balls of fire gleaming through the trees, and knew that it must be some wild animal. Finally we came to the top of the mountain range and started to coast down the other side. And didn't we coast! I'll say we did!

If we were making a mile an hour, we were doing between forty and fifty. Sometimes we'd skid around a corner on one and a half wheels — if I had had a stick of dynamite, I certainly would have put it under that — Annamite is a good name for him! — and then driven the rest of the way myself.

'Suddenly the bumping ceased and I felt as though I were riding in an airplane again. Sure enough, we were flying, and a moment later we flew into some trees. Mr. Annamite had buzzed right off the road into the jungle. It took us thirty minutes to disentangle the truck from the underbrush and get it back on the road. But even this experience taught him nothing. On we went, as if kicked by an army mule. Fifteen minutes later, we jumped off the highway again and crashed into a pile of rocks. Next day, on the return journey, I had a look at this place and noticed that on the far side of those rocks there was a thousand-foot of precipice, so the good Lord was watching over us on this trip.

'When we got to the bottom of the mountain, there was a place where the road went diagonally across a railroad track. Instead of continuing on the road, the fool Annamite swerved off and went bumping over the ties. It took us another half-hour to drag the truck back to the road.

'We crossed a second range of mountains, and on our way down grade this time the brake-band broke. I had climbed into the seat next my neck-or-nothing chauffeur, hoping my presence might tend to sober him somewhat. It was lucky I had, for he had just brain enough to do what I signaled, to throw the engine in low speed. In doing so, however, he let go the steering-wheel, so we left the road again. If it hadn't been for some trees, I am sure we should be going yet, because there was a deep valley right under us. My heart stopped beating at least ten separate times that night.

'When we reached the next valley, we came to a lagoon over which the truck had to be transported on a barge. Seven natives poled it, and it took them more than half an

hour to make the trip when all went well. This time things
didn't go well, for when we reached the middle I noticed
that the barge had sprung a leak and was sinking lower and
lower. When I called the attention of the Annamites to
this, they became pop-eyed with fright and immediately
started to pole her back to where we had started from. We
got there just in time. In another five minutes barge,
truck, and the new motor for the *Chicago* would have been
hors d'œuvres for the saurians.

'By this time, the first streaks of dawn were showing
through the cocoanut palms, and the crew on the barge
halloed across the lagoon to their friends on the other side
who came over with a less leaky barge.

'When we got to Hué, we located Smith and Arnold at
the little French hotel and in a short time we all were at
work changing motors. Under the bridge near where they
had beached the plane, there was a track and a car on
wheels. We lifted the "dud" motor up out of the *Chicago*,
rode it along on the track, dropped it on the beach, and
then hoisted up the new "Liberty–12" and dropped it into
place. The whole job took us less than four hours. Although I have changed motors hundreds of times, I have
never seen the job done with such speed, and I believe we
broke all records out there in this lonely corner of French
Indo-China.

'Only seventy-one hours had elapsed between the time
when Smith and Arnold had had their forced landing on
the lagoon, until a new motor was installed and running.
During that time we had had a conference with Smith,
flown on to Tourane, Erik and M. Chevalier had returned
by night and located them. They were towed twenty-five
miles up river by sampans, a new motor had been brought
five hundred miles by destroyer from Saigon to Tourane,
had been transported sixty miles by night to Hué, and had
been fixed and tested on the *Chicago's* engine bed.'

It is in crises such as these that the boys showed the stuff
they were made of. When the *Chicago* was in flying trim,
Nelson, Harding, and Ogden drove back to Tourane, and

Smith and Arnold flew to the same place in about forty minutes, arriving before nightfall on June 15th.

Next morning, the boys were out on their planes before dawn and shortly after 5 A.M. 'hopped off' for Saigon. On the way down the coast of Indo-China they passed a lighthouse on a rocky promontory. There was a French flag flying and as they drew near, the lighthouse keepers dipped the flag three times as a salute to the World Fliers, and the boys 'zoomed' three times in response. Three hundred and twenty-five miles south of Tourane they passed over Kamrauh Bay which leapt into fame during the Russo-Japanese War when the fleet under Admiral Rozhestvenski, which had reached the Far East from the Baltic by way of Cape Horn, united with Admiral Negogatov's fleet which had come via the Suez Canal.

After flying over more jungle, lagoons, paddy-fields, and indentations that were once the roost of Malay pirates, they arrived at the mouth of the Mekong River at 1.30 P.M. and moored in front of the city of Saigon, known as 'the Paris of the Orient.' They were now farther south than they were to be at any other point, and only a few degrees from the Equator.

CHAPTER XIX

FROM INDO–CHINA TO THE LAND OF THE WHITE ELEPHANT

'WE spent our first night in Saigon as guests of the manager of the Standard Oil Company,' says Wade. 'We had been having all kinds of trouble taking-off from inland rivers and we saw that here at Saigon we were likely to have the same grief we had at Haiphong. The best way to remedy this is to fly light. So we only "serviced-up" with a small amount of "gas" and oil and arranged for one of the destroyers to go on ahead and establish a halfway fueling station. So we had to wait over for twenty-four hours to allow her time to get into position

'This day we worked on the planes until late afternoon and then borrowed some respectable clothes from our naval friends on the *Noah* and sallied forth to see the sights of Saigon. Arrayed in the immaculate white shirts and trousers that had been loaned to us, we jumped into automobiles and started to "do" the so-called "Paris of the East."

'First we turned into a sidewalk café, which brought back to some of us happy memories of Paris days and nights. After sitting for a while at the jolly little tables, we became conscious of the fact that the waiters were taking care of everybody but us. Moreover, they scowled at us in an unfriendly way.

'Calling the head waiter, we started to give him our orders, when he interrupted and said that he could not serve us and that we would have to leave. When we asked the reason, he said that no one without a coat could be served at that café! We fully appreciated that it was somewhat uncommon for Europeans to be without coats, and we tried to explain who we were and how, as Air Service officers, we could put on our naval friends' trousers and shirts in order to come ashore, but that it was impossible for us to wear their tunics and masquerade as members of another branch of the United States Government service.

'All he said to this was that he knew who we were, but that it made no difference, and we would have to go away at once.

'This frosty reception didn't increase our enthusiasm for Saigon and we voted the city a "washout." To make the affair all the more unpleasant, the Frenchmen sitting at adjoining tables apparently relished our embarrassment and sided with the café management.'

This affair had its sequel, however. Later, when the boys finally arrived at the real Paris, the President of France welcomed them and the heads of the Republic did everything possible to make their visit memorable. One night at a banquet the Minister of Foreign Affairs, who was sitting next to Arnold, asked him how he had liked the capital of French Indo-China. 'Les,' of course, preferred to say nothing about it. But the Minister noticed his hesitation and begged him to be frank. So he learned the whole tale. He was furious at the treatment accorded them, apologized profusely, made a number of notes, and it is likely there was some sighing in Saigon soon after.

'On the morning of the 18th of June, we were up at three o'clock,' continues Wade, 'and as we climbed into the cockpits, shortly after four, we saw the loveliest tropical sunrise we had ever beheld. The colors in the sky, combined with the luxuriant foliage, the leaning palms, the thatched native huts, and the picturesque fishing craft, made it a scene too gorgeous for words.

'Immediately after the cathedral spire and pagodas of Saigon had dropped out of sight, we reached the delta of the great Mekong River which rises far up on the plateaus of Central Asia. Some stretches of it are famous for the number of crocodiles that lie in wait to devour the plump natives, while others are renowned as haunts of the rhinoceros. But from where we looked down upon it, the

Mekong was merely a muddy streak, like the Mississippi in lower Louisiana seen from the air. From then on, we flew over another densely populated equatorial region of canals, paddy-fields, cocoanut plantations, pagodas, herds of water-buffalo, and several fairly large towns with paved streets.

'The major part of this flight from Cochin-China to Siam was over the ancient Kingdom of Cambodia, which is known to archæologists because of Angkor, the ruins of which lie in the heart of Cambodian jungle just a few miles to the right of our course. Marco Polo wrote of this ancient city when he returned from his travels. Before that, the Romans had sent ambassadors to the court of the Khmers of Angkor. We would have liked to have seen the ruins, but we had to hold our course straight over the old Venetian's "Land of the Golden Chersonese," heading our magic carpets for Bangkok at eighty miles an hour.'

'The Gulf of Siam was a glassy sheet of sapphire blue,' says Commander Lowell Smith, 'but, as though to prevent monotony, the Creator of this fascinating world round which we were flying, has dotted the Gulf with a hundred magic isles, fringed with tall cocoanut palms and beaches. Some of these islets are covered with elephant grass that makes them look as smooth as lawns at home. So enticing were they, that we flew lower, to explore them with a view to coming here on our honeymoons — that is, if any of us really do get married! Erik's sweetheart flew right along with him on the instrument board. Printed on celluloid, to protect her from spray and storms, this picture was his inspiration all the way around the world.

'Our second landing of this flight was on the Menam River at Bangkok, and dodging about between junks, and houseboats, and nearly colliding with carcasses floating out to sea, we spent the rest of the afternoon working on the planes. A few minor repairs were necessary so that we remained for a day in the capital of Siam before flying on across the Malay Peninsula to the Bay of Bengal. Some of us spent the night on the destroyer, while the others,

ON OUR WAY UP THE MEKONG AND ACROSS THE JUNGLES FROM COCHIN-CHINA
TO SIAM

LEAVING THE REALM OF THE KING OF SIAM AND HEADING
TOWARD BURMA 'ON THE ROAD TO MANDALAY'

THROUGH STORMY SKIES, OVER RICE-FIELDS AND JUNGLE

THE DARK PENINSULA OF MALAYA, WHERE STRANGE AIR-
CURRENTS SUCKED THEM DOWN

IN THE JUNGLES OVER WHICH THEY FLEW WERE ELEPHANT HERDS, TIGER, AND FEROCIOUS SLADANG

tempted by thoughts of nice beds, insect-proof nets, and electric fans, went up to the Royal Hotel of Bangkok hoping to escape the mosquitoes and other sleep-destroyers that take the joy out of life on every river in the tropics.

'Next morning, while making our repairs, "Les" saw the body of a baby bobbing past the *Chicago* with the current. Much agitated, he called the attention of some English people who had come out in a launch to look over the planes. They smiled and said they were really surprised that we had been in Bangkok so many hours and had seen only one corpse floating by. They said this was just a little touch of local color to which nobody paid any attention.

'We were delighted with the Siamese, and particularly impressed by the intelligence, courtesy, and charm of the upper classes. We liked them the instant we met them. In fact the welcome of Bangkok was so warm that once again our planes were in danger of being crushed by hundreds of sampans. But the Siamese officers strung circles of police boats around each Cruiser for protection.

'Just before we started ashore with Mr. Dickinson, the American Chargé d'Affaires, a squadron of planes appeared over the cocoanut palms and banyans. Right down the Menam River they flew in formation. When directly above us, they dipped and gave us the salute of the Siamese Royal Air Force. Siam is indeed a land of contrasts. Around us were sampans filled with naked people, while overhead flew the airplanes introduced by King Rama VI, an Oxford man.

'I imagine we saw nearly as much during our half-day ashore in Siam as many visitors see in a week. The representatives of King Rama, the officers of the Siamese Royal Air Force, and our own countrymen escorted us about the city. First they took us to the internationally famous palace of the monarch of this tropic realm. The King himself was unfortunately detained in the country, so we did not have the privilege of meeting him.

'As we passed the gold elephants at the outer portal of

the palace, the Royal Bodyguard presented arms. Up the marble staircase, and through great doors of carved teak, we entered a vestibule whose walls were hung with the coats of mail of ancient Siam. From there we were ushered into the Council Room where the King reclines on a gold couch to receive ministers and envoys. Behind this combination throne and divan hangs a portrait of a bald Buddhist pontiff who looks down upon the assemblage with half-closed eyes.

'Although we passed Javanese, Burmese, Cambodians, Malays, Chinese, Shans, Was, Karens, and Japanese, on the tamarisk-lined streets of Bangkok, the state religion of the Siamese is Buddhism. Every Siamese youth is obliged to become a monk for a time just as the boys on the Continent of Europe are compelled to serve in the army. Of the eight million people in the country more than eighty thousand are Buddhist monks.

'From the Council Room, the generals, admirals, ex-prime ministers, and other dignitaries who were showing us the sights of Siam, took us into another chamber where we saw two huge and exquisitely carved elephant tusks. Then they marched us into the throne room with its lofty ceiling of inlaid glass, its frescoed walls and glittering gold leaf, its dazzling crystal candelabra, its mosaic floor, and the King of Siam's chief throne underneath a nine-story pagoda. The magnificence of this palace, and the fact that we, like characters of the Arabian Nights, had flown here through the sky, made us pinch each other to make sure we were awake.

'Although the king business is getting to be even more dangerous than the flying game, being King of Siam would certainly have its compensations.

'From the palace we were taken to the stables of the royal white elephants. As a matter of fact they were not white at all — but pink. These albino pachyderms are still the royal animals of the country, although since the present Oxonian monarch ascended the throne, taken unto himself just one wife instead of eighty, and introduced typewriters, phonographs, American automobiles and airplanes, the white elephants have been rather under a cloud.

'A few years ago, whenever one of these royal beasts was caught in the jungle, he was tied with silken ropes, given a group of Siamese nobles to serve as his valets, bathed with perfumed water, fed on tender shoots of bamboo and griddle cakes and fruit syrup, elevated to a peerage at court, and baptized by the Buddhist priests. Those were palmy days for the white elephants of Siam. But times are not what they used to be. In fact the people as well as the Court are acquiring many ideas from the west.

'For instance, we visited one Buddhist temple where we saw a statue of Saint Peter at one of the gates, and a statue of a Dutchman smoking a pipe at another. One quaint old world custom, however, remains as popular as it ever was — decapitation. As a special honor, it was suggested that a beheading bee should be arranged for us. This gay event was to have taken place a fortnight later, but we were told it could easily be hastened for our benefit: no doubt it would have been had we not sent our regrets at being unable to attend the frolic owing to our desire to get on with the Flight.

'Before concluding this half-day jaunt around Bangkok, which, by the way, was the longest honest-to-goodness sight-seeing tour that we had had time to make from the time we left America, we visited also the temple of the Sleeping Buddha, whose big toe is as big as a bed and who measures one hundred and fifty feet from the gold top-knot he wears to the mother-of-pearl soles of his feet.

'Finally we stopped to pay our respects to the ranking Siamese prince, who happened to be in the city. When we were ushered into his drawing-room, imagine our surprise when we saw a picture of our own General Mitchell, occupying the place of honor on the Prince's table. General Mitchell had been there on a tiger hunt only a few weeks before and every one in Siam was loud in praise of the man who has fought so hard to make the people of America ap-

preciate the fact that the world has at last reached the era
of travel by air.

'We were in a daze by the time we had finished with
Bangkok. That night we slept on the destroyer, in order to
be ready early next morning for the "road to Mandalay."'

CHAPTER XX

FROM SIAM TO BURMA IN A DAY

To fly from Siam to Burma, Commander Smith had to decide whether to go around the Malay Peninsula, or fly over it. If the former, they were faced with a flight of nearly a thousand miles across the Gulf of Siam and the South China Sea, to Singapore near the Equator and thence up to Rangoon. Their planes were still equipped with pontoons, so it was advisable to keep over water as far as possible until the arrival in Calcutta, where they were scheduled to change to wheels for the flight across India. If, on the other hand, they flew over the northern end of the Malay Peninsula, and ran the risk of engine failure over a jungle where a forced landing meant disaster, then a flight of only one hundred and thirty miles would take them overland from one sea to another and shorten their journey to Rangoon, by over eight hundred miles. Smith decided on the short cut.

Friday morning, June 20th, they went through their usual couple of hours of aquatic sports taxiing up and down the glassy river in attempts to rise. The Menam, like many other inland waterways, is so smooth that it is difficult to ruffle up the surface sufficiently to take-off with a heavy cruiser. But they succeeded at last and the pagodas of Bangkok melted into a background of forest verdure.

On nearly every leg of their journey round the world, the Fliers encountered some new phenomenon. This 'jump' across Malaya was no exception. Just as the giant jungle creepers twine themselves around trees and strangle them, so the strange air-currents from the forest reached up and gripped them with unseen but ferocious power.

By the time they had flown to the beginning of the peninsula, such invigorating quality as there is in the air at dawn even in the tropics had gone: instead, a dank mist arose from the vast, dripping forest below them. Clouds of steam rose from the damp roots of the jungle veiling mountain-tops as well as valleys.

'At times our pontoons barely skimmed the jungle-covered summits of these untrodden mountains,' says Jack Harding. 'We would shoot out over a valley and suddenly a downward current of air would catch us with such a bump that I thought we'd be impaled on the horn of one of those rhinos that live down there.

'While crossing a fissure in the middle of the peninsula, we were suddenly drawn down toward the jungle just like a gnat inhaled by a green monster. The *Chicago* and *Boston* were to our right at the time and were not affected by this particular "pocket," although they too were having the bumpiest trip they had ever experienced. It just seemed as though we couldn't get over that ridge, so Erik banked to the left and we flew right back the way we came in order to get out of the depression and into a "raising" air current. But again when we started over the ridge we were drawn into that valley of vapors.

'Meanwhile, the other boys were wondering what had happened. So they flew back and circled around waiting for us. At last we made the ridge, and I'll say we were the happiest airmen east of Suez when we finally succeeded in climbing out of the pocket and winding through the mountains until we reached the sea. A few minutes later we sighted the destroyer *Sicard* that was waiting for us at Tavoy to give us a fresh supply of fuel. While "servicing-up" the tide changed, the monsoon wind swept in from the Andamans, and the sea became almost too rough to get off. But we were forced to attempt it, because there was no sheltered cove to which we could run until the storm passed.

'Smith managed to get off, but Wade on his final bounce before leaving the water hit a big wave and one of his wires gave way. When we followed along behind the *Boston,* in leaping from one mountainous wave to another, we snapped two wires. Wade kept right on with his wire dangling, thinking that it was less dangerous to fly on to Rangoon with his plane in that condition than to take any chance of descending in such a sea. But with two main stay-wires gone, we in the *New Orleans* had to taxi back to our moorings for repairs. However, we were ready to start again in a half hour, and proceeded to Rangoon through patches of drenching rain.

'At dawn we had been in Bangkok: just as the sun was setting we passed the golden Shwe Dagon Pagoda and the docks at Rangoon, alighting in a side stream near an old British army engineering camp.

'To make up for having had such good luck in getting away from Tavoy without breaking their plane, Lowell and "Les" got a thrill when they landed here at Rangoon. The current of the Irrawaddy is very swift and some one is drowned in it nearly every day. "Les" fell in as he was grabbing a mooring-buoy. Smith didn't happen to see what had occurred because he had his eye on a boat that had come near colliding with them. So he taxied off up the river, leaving "Les" to flounder about in his flying-clothes. But a moment later he missed him and rushed to the rescue, delicately maneuvering his plane so as to bring the pontoons close enough to enable "Les" to scramble on board.'

Here at Rangoon, only a short distance from where they had moored, the Fliers saw

'Elephants a-pilin' teak
'n the sludgy, squdgy creek.'

One old elephant, after putting down his load and starting off, glanced back. Seeing that the end of the log was not quite even with the rest of the pile, he gave it a final kick with his hind foot. When the evening whistle blew in the teak yard, every elephant dropped his load and trotted off, just as if these wise leviathans of the teak-piling business had trade-union rules about working overtime.

Instead of accepting the invitations of the millionaire Scottish teak kings, who wanted to put them up at their bungalows, the boys decided to stay at the old Royal Engineers' clubhouse, a few miles out of the city, where they could be nearer the planes.

'Whenever we recall our experiences in far-off Rangoon,' says 'Les' Arnold, 'we particularly remember the narrow escape we had from losing our commander, when Lowell took ill with dysentery; the collision of the *New Orleans* with a Burmese river-boat; the club life of the Europeans exiled out there; and the charm of the maidens of Burma.

'When dysentery hits a man, it usually lasts for weeks. Lowell, however, thanks to an English doctor, who insisted that he be moved to a bungalow where he could be kept quiet, in three days was ready to proceed. A Mr. Kemp was his host. This doctor said the attack was undoubtedly the result of Smith's having drunk that water from the dugouts of the Indo-China lagoon. Whatever the cause, thanks to a good constitution and careful nursing, he got right in record time.

'That first night in Rangoon, another ill-wind blew our way. We were sleeping off the effects of our nerve-racking flight across the Malay jungle, when a Burmese river-boat came drifting down the Irrawaddy on our planes. We had moored them well out of the main waterway. But the Burman at the rudder of this particular boat must have been asleep, or secure in the knowledge that his boat was heavier than anything on the river with which he was likely to collide.

'When the sailors from our destroyers guarding the planes saw this huge hulk, with its sail silhouetted above them, it was almost too late for them to prevent her from riding down all three Cruisers. The *New Orleans* happened to be the nearest plane in line. Realizing they had only a few instants in which to save her, one of the sailors clambered up the stern of the Burmese boat, clipped the

PAST THE GOLD-AND-JEWELLED SPIRE OF SHWE DAGON ON
THEIR WAY FROM RANGOON TO HINDUSTAN

FLYING LOW AND FAST OVER THE RICE BOATS OF THE IRAWADDY
DELTA ON THE WAY TO AKYAB

SUNSET — ON THE ROAD TO MANDALAY

UP THE SACRED GANGES PAST THE JUTE MILLS OF THE SECOND CITY OF THE BRITISH EMPIRE

LIFTING THE CRUISERS OUT OF THE HOOGLI RIVER AT CALCUTTA
IN ORDER TO CHANGE FROM PONTOONS TO WHEELS

helmsman in the jaw and took charge. The others in the
guard launch threw their frail cockleshell between the
plane and the oncoming Burman. A collision there was,
but thanks to the sailors it was only a glancing blow.
However, it smashed half the bottom left wing of the *New
Orleans* and made it certain that we should now be delayed for a number of days, no matter how Smith's attack
of dysentery progressed.

'While the repair work was going on, we took turns
motoring to Rangoon to see Smith and to purchase little
things that we needed. This gave us an opportunity to see
something of the life of the Burmese who lived between us
and the business section of the city. We also spent several
evenings at the clubs, the Gymkhana and the Pegu, where
the European throws off the "White Man's burden" at
night and attempts to forget that he is thousands of miles
from Pall Mall and Piccadilly.

'It is a life of languid hours, whispered scandals, waving
punkas, and clinking glasses, very bearable, no doubt, if
you are making your fortune out of rice or teak or tea.
But it was so hot that we were already getting out our map
of the world and calculating how many more days it would
be until we reached Iceland.

'Each afternoon, when the work on the planes was
finished, everybody would plunge into the large swimming-
pool that our English friends had made out there near
their headquarters. After a day of perspiring in that
steamy climate, it was certainly a relief to play water polo
for an hour or so. The clubhouse bungalow where we were
entertained was built high up in the air on piles, as a pre-
caution against snakes, scorpions, centipedes, and other
creeping and crawling things: it was very pleasant to sit
there with one's feet up on a long chair sipping a cool
drink after the labors of the day.

'The Burmese women intrigued us. With gay umbrellas,
bright-colored silk skirts, cute little white shirtwaists,
hair piled up in a black shiny coil and adorned with
frangipani blossoms, cheeks powdered with *poudre-de-riz*,

they looked like beings from another world. And yet they were very human, too!

'Like the Siamese, the Burmans are Buddhists, and there is a pagoda on every hill. The Shwe Dagon, the largest pagoda in the world, covered with gold from its base to its jeweled spire, is an unforgettable sight. We saw it first as we approached Rangoon, and the last view we had of this great Oriental metropolis, as we winged our way over the thousand waterways of the Irrawaddy, was again the golden "*ti*" of the Shwe Dagon glittering in the dawn.

'When the *New Orleans* had been repaired and we were ready to take-off, Lowell refused to stay in bed any longer and said good-bye to his miracle-working physician. So on Wednesday, June 25th, with not a breath of air stirring and the Irrawaddy smooth as glass, we left the land of teak and whackin' white cheroots. The *Boston* and *New Orleans* got onto their pontoon steps by following the waves left in the wake of an ocean steamer and then Wade flew down in front of us and let his pontoons ripple the surface for the *Chicago*.

'In finesse and delicacy of touch no airman has ever surpassed Leigh Wade. To take a heavy Cruiser down and daintily run its pontoons through the water so that they are barely an inch below the surface, and skim along like that for a mile, is the feat of a wizard. That's Wade!

'We saved quite a long distance by cutting straight across the Irrawaddy delta toward India instead of first heading west into the Bay of Bengal. Ahead of us lay the little seaport of Akyab, that has been a "hoodoo" to many flying men. Sir Ross Smith's supply ship with gasoline and oil had blown up not far from Akyab. MacLaren, the British world flier, had crashed there and been laid up there for many weeks. We had expected him at Rangoon before we left, for our destroyer had delivered his new Vickers-Amphibian a fortnight ago. But at Akyab, and over all this region, as much rain has been known to fall in a day as falls in a whole year in most parts of the United

States. It is, in fact, the rainiest part of the earth, as much as four hundred inches falling in a year. Owing to the perpetual downpour, MacLaren was delayed at Akyab until the day we left Rangoon, and we passed each other that day, without our seeing him.'

CHAPTER XXI

CALCUTTA — QUEEN CITY OF THE EAST

'The first two hours out from Rangoon,' says Lowell Smith, 'we cut across the delta of the Irrawaddy, over a low, green country of rice-fields, and the twisting branches of the great river. As we approached the Bay of Bengal, we encountered one of the heaviest rainstorms in our experience, the water lashing our faces and pouring in behind our goggles. We attempted to fly around it, but were unable to find any break in it.

'It was then that we missed McLaren. Not wanting to take any chances with his new plane, when he encountered the storm he landed in a little bay and waited for it to pass. He afterward told us that we had flown right over him. He heard the hum of our motors and even saw us faintly through the rain, but we saw nothing of him down there on the water.

'The rest of the flight to Akyab was uneventful. We landed at 2.20 P.M., hastily took on board a supply of gas, and were preparing to take-off again at once, but learned that the moorings were unsatisfactory at Chittagong. This meant staying overnight in Akyab.

'The British Commissioner and the few other Europeans entertained us at the club that night. The Commander of the American destroyer then at Akyab made a boast during dinner that we never allowed the weather to interfere with our schedule. "The boys will leave for Calcutta to-morrow morning at seven o'clock sharp," he said. "You can set your watches by them."

'"But what if it should rain?" asked the British.

'"Rain makes no difference to these chaps. When they set an hour for departure, they shove off on the dot, rain or shine, to the minute, like your Brighton express!"

'Of course this was pulling "el toro grande." As it

happened, a typical Akyab rain was drizzling down on us when we boarded the planes next morning. However, we decided that we would rather buck the monsoon than remain any longer in that nirvana for ducks. So at exactly seven o'clock we hopped off. Long afterward, we met the Commander of that destroyer, and he was profuse in his praise of our punctuality, saying he would never have been able to alibi himself to the Akyabites if we had not pushed off on time.

'After leaving Akyab I noticed that the rain seemed heaviest near the shore, so with the *Boston* and *New Orleans* following, I turned the *Chicago* out into the Bay of Bengal for fifteen miles. I then turned north, and an hour after we ran out of rain, picked up the coast, and came down at the seaport of Chittagong, near the mouth of the Chittagong River. Here we landed, refueled hurriedly, and at noon took-off for Calcutta.

'As on the flight across the forest of Malaya, so now we had a dangerous stretch ahead of us. The deltas of two huge rivers lie between Chittagong and Calcutta, the Ganges and the Brahmaputra, each of them about the size of the Mississippi. They join in central Bengal and then spread out like a fan. This dreaded delta region of backwaters is called the Sundarbans. Tigers infest the jungle parts while crocodiles slither through the ooze. A forced landing in these swamps would entail sending airplanes to the rescue, for searching parties in boats might hunt a month without finding you.

'We spent the afternoon scanning the landscape for stretches of water where it would be possible to alight in case of necessity. As soon as we picked out one, we would look ahead for another in order to keep some such spot always in sight. Visibility was perfect, and at 3.15 P.M., far ahead, we saw the smoke of a great city. It was Calcutta, eighty-two miles up the Hoogli water. A moment later we flew over village after village, on the outskirts of the second largest city of the British Empire.

'Calcutta from the air, with its countless mills and jute

factories, its mammoth docks, its rows of ocean-going vessels, handsome residential quarter and great common in the center of the city with a magnificent marble-domed palace at one end, is a most impressive sight. It certainly gladdened our eyes to see it.'

Arrangements had been made for the Cruisers to moor fifteen miles upstream from Calcutta, where there would be fewer river-boats to bother them. Even so, only quick headwork and footwork on the part of the three pilots enabled them to dodge in and out of the teeming traffic.

'The heat was even more oppressive than at Akyab,' says 'Les' Arnold. 'After Lowell had cut off the motor it seemed as though there wasn't a breath of air. Perspiration began to pour off us at once, and by the time we had fixed the planes securely for the night we were as wet as if we had fallen overboard.

'Turning the Cruisers over to the English river police, we went on board the launch of His Excellency the Governor of Bengal. All the way downstream, to the center of the city, people lined both banks and were packed on the decks of the river steamers. There wasn't much vocal enthusiasm, however, until we reached the European quarter. Here we were met by a throng of our own countrymen, together with many British, quite a few high-class Bengali people, and many strange types we had never seen before, all cheering and waving a welcome.

'Again, in the space of a few hours, we had flown from one world into another. Gone were the smiling maidens of Burma: in their place were women who drew scarfs across their faces and shrank away as we looked at them.

'At the Great Eastern Hotel, Smith, as our commanding officer, was given the bridal suite, consisting of two bedrooms, a bath, a little office, and a reception room. Fearing that he might get lonely in all of this regal splendor, he invited me to share it.

'Before we had an opportunity to wash, there was a knock at the door. In walked a bearded, barefoot native wearing a bulging turban, a long white coat reaching to his

knees, and skin-tight pants. Salaaming low, he asked
whether the masters did not desire a personal servant.
We looked at each other, and the more we thought it over,
the more the idea appealed to us. So we hired him on the
spot, and named him "Bozo."

'During our stay in Calcutta, "Bozo" was busily engaged in seeing to it that some other native pressed our
clothes, that still another washed our linen, that some one
else brought us suitable viands and refreshment. His
chief occupation was announcing visitors and salaaming
them in and out of our suite. When not actually in personal attendance upon us, he would park on his heels outside the door, and at the call of "Bozo" he was there in a
flash ready to carry out our commands. We were sorry
not to be able to take him along, for he would have added
an ornamental touch to our subsequent receptions — at
the Drake Hotel in Chicago, for instance.'

Here in Calcutta the World Fliers were confronted with
the prospect of languishing for many days unless they
could circumvent the hundred-degree-Fahrenheit Hindoo
philosophy of 'Why do to-day what you can put off until
to-morrow?' But Smith and company had lost too many
days flirting with the 'Willie-was' of Alaska to be in any
mood for lotus-eating in the 'City of Dreadful Night.'
They wanted to change from pontoons to wheels as quickly
as might be, and then fly across Asia to America, home
and beauty, with the throttle wide open.

But difficulties were many. The only real aerodome
of Calcutta is at Dum Dum, twenty miles distant from
Dalhousie Square. In between, the treacherous Hoogli is
even more densely crowded with shipping between Kidder-
pore and Howrah Bridge than the Hudson at Battery
Point or the Mersey at Liverpool. To dismantle their
planes, as was suggested to them, load them on trucks,
carry them overland to the British airdrome, and rebuild
them, would have occupied at least one month — or six.

They took a day to review the situation, during which

time they consulted with harbor officials, representatives
from the street commissioner's office, and naval experts,
made arrangements to bring the Cruisers back down the
river, land in the midst of the traffic, hoist them up with
a crane, roll them over into the Maidan, and make their
alterations right there in the heart of Calcutta.

The British coöperated, and even cut down some electric
telegraph and telephone wires and trees that were in the
way. But they thought it a risky undertaking, and it was
specifically understood that if the planes were wrecked
the responsibility would have to rest solely with the
United States Air Service.

Late that afternoon the Fliers went out to the famous
park in the heart of Calcutta, called the Maidan, where
they worked until dark over their cases of supplies and
spare parts, refusing various kindly suggestions to 'call it a
day' and take afternoon tea. When night came, they
loaded the cases into trucks, went to a garage where it was
light, and continued working until two o'clock in the morning.

Early next day they motored up the Hoogli to where
their planes were moored, and flew them down-river,
making a perfect landing near Fort William in the center
of Calcutta, in spite of the crowded waterway. The crane
hoisted each Cruiser out of the water, and in just three
hours the ticklish transfer was accomplished and they had
mounted the planes safely on wheels in the middle of the
Maidan.

'Not only were we delighted with the sportsmanlike
spirit shown by the British officials in Calcutta,' says
Commander Smith, 'but the enthusiasm of the sailors from
the American destroyers in port was almost overwhelming.
When a call for volunteers was made, every last man jack
fought for the privilege of helping us. If the World Flight
had done nothing else, it would certainly have stimulated
a fine spirit of comradeship between the Navy and the Air
Service.

'Flocks of natives gathered on the Maidan to watch us

THE STOWAWAY

CIRCLING OVER THE HOLY CITY OF BENARES

SHIPS OF THE AIR AND OF THE DESERT MEET AT ALLAHABAD
IN THE HEART OF ROMANTIC INDIA

IN INDIA WE DONNED SUN HEMLETS AND SHORT PANTS

READY FOR THE FINAL FLIGHT ACROSS INDIA FROM MULTAN
TO KARACHI

and it took fifty policemen to hold back the mob. Occasionally a fat bull would come over and lie down under one of the wings: they are sacred and should not be touched, but "Hank" twisted their tails for them when they got in the way until they bellowed with disgust and waddled off to more peaceful resorts.

'Several times, when we came out of the Great Eastern Hotel on our way to work on the planes, we met a sacred bull at the door, and Leigh says he saw a cow on the sidewalk in Chowringhee — Calcutta's Fifth Avenue — chewing her cud outside a Paris hat-shop.

'Among the thousands who visited us while we were preparing our planes were ash-covered fakirs, with withered arms and legs. Others were smeared with cow-dung and had diabolic-looking red-and-white Hindoo symbols on their foreheads and bodies. They were the most hideous-looking specimens of humanity that we encountered on the Flight.

'How the British or any one else can maintain a stable government in a land where millions wander about smeared with their sacred cow-dung is a puzzle to me.

'The American Legion post of India gave us a banquet and some of our fellow countrymen came a thousand miles just to wish us God-speed. We left the banquet fairly early, but from all accounts it was one of those things which improve with age, because next morning when we were going to work at six we met our hosts on their way home.'

On June 29th, after a small dinner with the representative of the Standard Oil Company in Calcutta, an accident occurred that came near causing another delay to the expedition. Smith and Arnold left at about 9.30 P.M. and Smith, in the darkness, stepped into a hole, and in falling struck the timber below the ground and broke his rib. Although he suffered intense pain all night he refused to believe that he had been injured. But Arnold called a doctor in the morning who discovered the fracture.

Next day while the other fliers were putting the finishing

touches to the planes, Smith remained at the hotel. Refusing to allow the flight to be delayed because of his injury, the following morning, Tuesday, July 1st, he was out on the Maidan at daybreak, ready for the flight along the course of the sacred Ganges and the marvelous plains of Hindustan, cradle of ancient civilizations.

CHAPTER XXII

ALONG THE GRAND TRUNK ROAD
WITH A STOWAWAY ON BOARD

UPON departure from Calcutta the quaintest episode of the flight occurred. A stowaway crawled on board one of the Cruisers and flew two thousand miles, from Calcutta to Karachi. Nor was this stowaway a cobra, centipede, or any other denizen of India that could easily hide in the plane. He was a full-grown man, and his presence was not discovered until the end of the first day's flight.

On account of the help he gave them in Japan and his contagious optimism, the Associated Press representative at Tokio, Mr. Linton Wells, had attracted the boys rather more than other newspaper men they had met on their travels. As far as Calcutta he had kept pace with them by train and boat, but in India he was supposed to relinquish his assignment to another 'A.P.' man. Linton Wells, however, was born an adventurer. For years he had roamed up and down the world, first with one newspaper organization and then with another — always turning up in the midst of exciting events. Rather than return to Tokio after 'covering' the flight to Calcutta, he decided to follow the fliers all the way back to America, even if it cost him his job — which it did.

How to keep up with the globe-girdlers was a difficult problem for him to solve. They were now cutting across continents far faster than he could travel except through the air.

In Calcutta, Wells made the important discovery that, after the substitution of wheels for pontoons, an additional weight of a hundred and forty pounds or so would make very little difference to the Cruisers. The pontoons weighed over half a ton, while the landing-gear with which they were now equipped weighed only a couple of hundred pounds. Moreover, the trip across India was to be made in three stages, on none of which was it to be necessary for the planes to carry their maximum load of 'gas' and oil.

So, unnoticed among the thousands who crowded the Maidan to watch the departure of the World Cruisers on the morning of July 1st, Linton Wells slipped into the baggage compartment of the *Boston*, with no impedimenta except a toothbrush and a pencil. A few minutes later the planes went roaring across the Maidan, over the Victoria Memorial, and headed across India.

The stowaway had plenty of room to stretch out inside the fuselage, but in order not to miss the sights he opened the trapdoor on the port side, stuck his head out a few inches, and watched the Bengal Club and the Ochterlony Monument fading into the distance.

For an hour they flew north along the Hoogli and then turned west. From then on, Commander Smith kept above the East Indian Railway and led the way across the plains of Bengal, Bihar, and Orissa, and the United Provinces, to the city of Allahabad near the junction of the Ganges and Jumna Rivers.

Dodging in and out of showers and racing ahead of the rapidly approaching annual monsoon storms, they plunged out of a cloud and saw far ahead a great bend in the Ganges, with a populous city extending for miles along the farther bank. This was Benares, the holy city, that was old two thousand years before Europe began to build by Thames and Tiber.

After circling over this city of ceaseless prayer where eight thousand Brahmin priests have conned the Aryan texts of our forefathers for unnumbered centuries, and have embarked, incidentally, on mental flights as daring as any physical adventure of the West, the American World Flight sped ever westward, until straight ahead they saw another metropolis, the city of Allahabad.

Six miles from the railway station, in the midst of a sunbaked plain, they circled over the field and descended with throttles closed, after having flown for six and a half hours since leaving Calcutta over more than 'twenty centuries' of history.

As Wade and Ogden climbed out of the *Boston*, whom should they see but Linton Wells oozing out of the tool compartment! With the perspiration rolling down their faces all three executed an Indian nautch dance. Nor was a word of criticism uttered to the first stowaway to 'hook a ride' on a world flight. On the contrary, Wells was greeted as a prodigal son. But a moment later they put him to juggling cans of high-test 'gas,' and from then on Wells had to work for his passage just like stowaways have to do at sea, only harder, for pouring 'petrol' into the hungry stomach of a Cruiser and cleaning and oiling the engine is as trying a task as nursing a teething infant.

Smith sent a cable to General Patrick asking whether it would be possible to take Wells with them. No reply was received — whether purposely or by mischance it is not necessary for the historian to speculate — until the fliers reached Karachi; by that time Wells had already flown two thousand miles.

As they roared across the airdrome at Allahabad, a long string of camels came trekking over the sun-baked plain. The excitement and curiosity of the drivers was only exceeded by the haughty disdain of their chargers. With the exception of Erik Nelson, none of the fliers had ever met a camel outside a zoo. So before 'servicing-up,' 'Jack' and 'Hank' coaxed two ships of the desert to kneel down while they climbed aboard for their first 'solo' flight on camel-back.

When their mounts started to 'take-off' and unfolded themselves with a series of fore-and-aft jerks, the surprised looks of the airmen brought shrieks of laughter from the spectators. After taxiing about the aerodrome at twenty miles an hour for some time, they both agreed that they would rather do fifty Immelmann turns in an airplane than ride the proudest camel of the proudest *sheikh*.

After spending the night in Allahabad they took off next

morning for Ambala, an important British military post not far from the Himalayas. To avoid the intense heat they flew at an altitude of five thousand feet.

Much of their way led over the Grand Trunk road, one of the oldest highways on earth, that has resounded to the tramp of migrating hordes and conquering armies ever since the early Aryans came down from the plateaus of Central Asia. Down this road came the hordes under Timur the Tartar, and the armies of Babar and the cavalry of the magnificent Moghuls. Over it, centuries later, marched the soldiers of England during the tragic days of the Great Indian Mutiny. And along this road the immortal Kim made his pilgrimage with the holy man from Tibet.

One wonders what Kim's Guru would have thought if some one had told him that, within a few years, men would come to India from a country over ten thousand miles away plunging from cloud to cloud above pedestrians at the rate of a hundred miles an hour. Probably he would have thought nothing of it, immersed as he was in matters outside this material age. The only internal combustion engine in which the *guru* would have been interested, was that inside himself, about which the West has still much to learn from the wise men of the East.

On this trip, the stowaway was no longer obliged to conceal himself in the tool compartment, for Ogden invited him to share his cockpit. Wells sat on six inches of seat, wedged against the dual set of controls. For six hours they sat jammed together, so neither could move.

'If it hadn't been that we were flying high enough to keep fairly cool,' says 'Hank,' 'and if it hadn't been for the glorious scenery of the snow-capped Himalayas, I believe I should have thrown Wells overboard. As it was, I was sorely tempted to feed him to the crocodiles in the Jumna.

'Our stowaway, like most beach-combers, made up in knowledge what he lacked in physical wealth, and told me stories about the country over which we were flying. At

Cawnpore, he told me of the terrible Indian Mutiny which raged sixty-seven years ago, this very month, down there beneath us in the plains. A hundred and fifty thousand Indian Sepoys, troops whom the British had trained, broke out in mutiny and bayonetted men, women, and little children. There were no airplanes in those days to fly across India in a few hours as we were flying, and thus bring help to a besieged garrison. Thus many a city fell to the mutineers. For example at Cawnpore, over which we were then sailing, three thousand Sepoys, with cannons, surrounded four hundred Englishmen and their wives and children out on that open burning plain that lay below us. For twenty-one days the little band held out. The native prince, who led the Sepoys, at last promised to send them safely down the Ganges to Allahabad if they would surrender. Starving and half dead from thirst, they accepted. But once he had possession of the English weapons, he murdered all the men and imprisoned the two hundred women and children in two small rooms, where he kept them for three weeks of horror, before finally deciding to kill them also. He gave orders for the women to have their throats cut, but his own soldiers refused to do this foul deed, so he hired butchers in the bazaar to hack them to pieces. Several times the butchers came out of the house to get new knives, having blunted the others. Finally it was all over, except that one little fair-haired boy, who had escaped the slaughter somehow, was running about in circles, stark mad with fear. Him they caught and killed also, and threw down a well with the other corpses.

'When the English retook Cawnpore they made the Indians lick up every drop of blood on the scene of the massacre.

'Nowadays a mutiny of this sort could easily be avoided by airplanes. The British realize this, because we discovered that they have nearly as large an air force here, in this one distant part of their Empire, as we have in the whole United States.

'Later, we passed near Agra. Wells drew such an alluring picture of the Taj Mahal, with its flashing fountains, its avenues of cypress trees, its flawless proportions, its latticework in marble and alabaster, and its exquisite mosaics of jewel-inlaid marble, that we thought his two days of flying might have gone to his head.

'Then ahead of us arose a city of pure white. It was Delhi, the dream of Eastern potentates since history began, and now the capital of the British Raj, and the headquarters of the new Indian Parliament, where for the first time in Indian history representatives of the masses have an opportunity to play a part in their own government.

'All around Delhi we saw the ruins of other cities — eight ancient Delhis, Wells explained to me — holding the history of all the peoples who have tried to grasp the sceptre of Hindustan before the British came.

'Shortly afterward we came in sight of Ambala and the hangars of the principal Royal Air Force station in India. Here we were welcomed by a great crowd of British fliers, and an enthusiastic brotherly welcome it was.'

BRITISH TOMMIES PUSHING THE OIL-SPATTERED NEW ORLEANS INTO A
HANGAR AT KARACHI AFTER THE THRILLING FLIGHT ACROSS THE
SIND DESERT

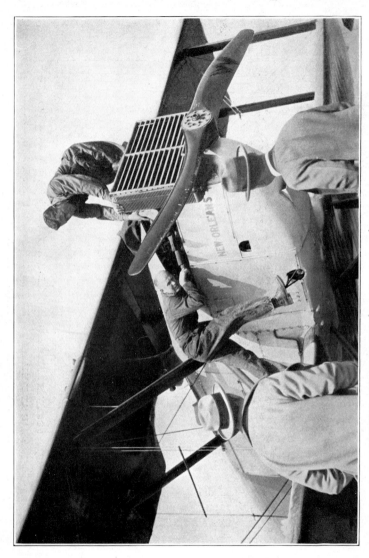

NELSON AND HARDING 'SERVICING UP' THE NEW ORLEANS

CHAPTER XXIII

ACROSS THE INDIAN DESERT
TO THE ARABIAN SEA

On the way to Ambala, the engine in the *New Orleans* developed a leaky cylinder. 'This accident might have caused us considerable delay,' says Erik Nelson, ' — if we had had to wait for a new part to be sent from our emergency supply depot at Karachi on the Arabian Sea. There was no welding outfit available here. But to our delight we found the British aviators in India were all using our Liberty motors — two thousand of them! And they swore by them too. This was gratifying, because European engines had long held first place in the aeronautical world. But since the War the Liberty–12 has come to the front.

'The British commandant at Ambala 'phoned to the machine shops at Lahore to have a new cylinder brought over by airplane. Unfortunately, the plane that was bringing it developed engine trouble shortly after leaving Lahore and was forced down near Amritsar. Leaving the remains of his plane on the outskirts of the Sikh city, and putting the cylinder under his arm, the badly shaken but otherwise uninjured pilot boarded a native bullock cart and caught a train which landed him at Ambala at three o'clock in the morning. It was no small favor that this British airman had done for us and we appreciated it more than we had words to express.

'Meanwhile, the Royal Air Force pilots in Ambala entertained us at their mess, and we had a particularly enjoyable evening, partly because it was not marred by a lot of unnecessary speeches.

'These lads were horror-struck when they saw us climb from our planes wearing the regulation leather helmets used in temperate climates, and they told us harrowing tales of how men went mad in the air as a result of the tropical Indian sun penetrating their skulls. While flying

along the Afghan frontier, where the Royal Air Force has a
patrol, they told us that pilots sometimes did insane stunts
that could only be accounted for by the sun. So not wanting to arrive in Baghdad crazy as loons, we were very
glad to accept their kind offer of specially constructed aviation sun helmets made for India. The Royal Air Force out
there is divided into two sections, A and B. At the time
of our visit, A section were taking their six weeks' shift on
the frontier, so the boys of B section broke into the store-
room belonging to their absent comrades in order to outfit
us with helmets. When we demurred, they said the men of
A flight would do exactly the same if the position were
reversed. So from then on, until we reached Northern Ara-
bia, we wore the helmets of the Royal Flying Corps. Those
pith topees are now among our most prized souvenirs.

'Early on the morning of Thursday, July 3d, we installed the new cylinder in my engine. After seeing that
everything was shipshape, we started west across the
northern rim of the great Sind Desert at nine o'clock.

'Leaving Ambala we crossed the rich "Land of the Five
Rivers" where the British are completing the largest irrigation project in the whole world. One result of these
ambitious canal cuts is that plagues are becoming rarer
and rarer. In railway mileage the British have also made
India the fourth country in the world, and when a plague
breaks out in one part of the country they rush trainloads
of grain to the stricken region. Another result of the one
hundred and fifty years of peace the British have brought
to this chaotic land, is that the population has increased by
one hundred million. Whether that is a blessing, I don't
know.

'Before reaching the desert, we flew over the native
state of Patiala, famous for the Maharajah's championship
polo teams. Polo of course, is a Central Asian game, and
was played here many centuries before it was even heard
of in Europe or on Long Island, although I was told in
India that nowadays Meadow Brook is considered the
Mecca of the game.

'While crossing Patiala we had climbed to six thousand feet to avoid the heat, when we suddenly ran into a sandstorm that completely obscured the earth as well as the railway line that we had been following. In order not to lose our way we descended to within fifty feet of the ground and then groped along a railroad.'

The sand whirled about them like snow, but so fine that it went through their clothes and filled their eyes, ears, noses, and mouths.

Although Commander Smith knew exactly where the flying-field at Multan should be according to his chart, the planes swept right on over the town in the blinding sandstorm. Thousands of troops had been placed in a single line, shoulder to shoulder, all the way around the landing field, but the airmen with their lacerated eyes had been unable to see them, while the soldiers on the ground, equally blinded, had heard the engines go roaring overhead without even catching a glimpse of the Cruisers. Flying back now over the parade ground, Smith dropped to just a few feet above the heads of the soldiers, circled several times and then made a perfect landing, followed by the other two.

'As we climbed out of our cockpits, Colonel Butler, the British officer in command at Multan, came over to us with his staff,' says 'Les' Arnold, 'and before even shaking hands he gave us each a tall glass of ice-cold lemonade. I have had many delicious and satisfying drinks in my life, but none to compare with that one in Multan.

'The thermometer that day in Multan — they ought to call it "Molten," by the way — had registered 120° in the shade before the sandstorm. Colonel Butler cheered us with the news that it was the hottest place in India. It certainly is the hottest place that any of us ever hope to visit in this world or the next!

'The officers stationed here wanted to entertain us and perhaps break the monotony of their well-nigh intolerable existence by throwing a big party. Smith's broken rib made it advisable for him to stay away, however, and

Erik and Leigh also needed as much rest as possible in order to be in shape for the flight on the morrow to the Arabian Sea. So Linton Wells, our aerial galley slave, "Jack," "Hank," and I were delegated to attend the function. It was a picturesque entertainment, served out of doors under soft lights. The tables were laid with fine damask and silver that might have graced the palace of King George himself. In the center were numerous valuable regimental trophies. Over us waved enormous punkas to keep us cool and drive away the insects that filled the air. Our hosts all wore their smart white "mess" uniforms, and their regimental band played near by. We liked these cheery chaps who guard the outposts of the British Empire and make merry in places they cannot help but loathe.

'We learned while at dinner that the regimental band had been due to leave for Waziristan five days before our arrival, but had been kept back in order to play for us. The bandmaster and his men were tall, fine-looking natives. When I called him over and thanked him on behalf of all of us, both for his music and for waiting five days to welcome us, he seemed much elated.

'The only untoward incident of the evening was when a lizard crawled up the leg of Jack's trousers, for he thought it was a scorpion or the deadly *krait* and danced like David before the Ark.

'The temperature hovered around 102°, 104°, and 106° until morning. Natives waved punkas over us all night long, but none of us got much sleep that night. We were up at daybreak next morning, the 4th of July, and were off for Karachi at six. On this trip we flew down the valley of the Indus River and across the Sind Desert. But this time we were lucky enough to miss sandstorms, several of which we saw on both sides of the valley.

'Everything went along well until we were about an hour out of Karachi, when the motor in the *New Orleans* decided to have a Fourth of July celebration on its own account and started to fly to pieces in mid-air. Looking

back, we saw spurts of white smoke pouring from Erik and
Jack's ship. Throttling down, we dropped back and flew
around the *New Orleans.* We could see oil all over the side
of the ship and had a fair idea of what had occurred.
The country over which we were then flying was open
desert. But instead of sand, the ground was baked mud,
which had cracked into gaping seams, so that if they had
been forced to land the plane would have been wrecked.

'Thirty-five miles or so to the east of us we knew there
was a railway line called "The Northwestern" which runs
from Lahore to Karachi. Erik signalled that he intended
to fly across and follow the railway in to Karachi, so that
in case of a forced landing they would at least be near to a
line of communication.'

The cause of the engine failure was never ascertained,
but what had actually happened was that one piston had
disintegrated and both exhaust springs flew out through
the exhaust stacks. Then two other cylinders went to
pieces. The exhaust valve broke the connecting-rod and
all the big pieces of the rod and wrist pin were thrown
through the bottom of the crank case into the cowling.
One of the flying chunks of metal tore a hole in the wing.
Another hit a strut. A third nearly hit Jack. By now the
motor was jumping up and down in alarming manner, and
the oil mist was pouring out through the open cylinder in
great clouds.

Erik first knew he was in for trouble when his motor
started slowing down. Both men were standing up in their
cockpits watching for fire. Throttling back, they descended in order to look for some possible place to land.
There was none. So Erik headed east, as has been explained, toward the railroad. When he increased the
revolutions of his engine, pieces of metal again started
shooting out of the exhaust pipes, one of which grazed
Jack's temple when he put his head out over the fuselage
looking for a landing ground.

It was all Erik could do, from then on, to keep the engine turning at 1100 revolutions a minute, which is just

enough to stay in the air without 'stalling,' for the normal rate is 1640 revolutions. All the rest of the way to Karachi, the motor kept rumbling and spluttering and oil came back in their faces at the rate of a quart a minute. Jack passed Erik a piece of cheesecloth every few minutes so that he could wipe the oil off his goggles. Smoking with vaporized lubricant and spattered with red-hot metal, the good old cruiser shivered and staggered and shimmied — and kept right on going. Every once in a while the motor stopped dead, but instead of 'freezing solid' it would grapple with its terrible cough and come to life again. At last Erik saw Karachi looming ahead and knew he had brought his ship safely through a serious crisis. Meanwhile the *Chicago* had sped on to locate the landing field, so that the *New Orleans* would not have to do any unnecessary maneuvering before coming to rest.

Nelson gave a remarkable exhibition of airmanship. First he would shoot down for five hundred feet or so to ease his engine when the temperature rose to the point where there was danger of the motor 'freezing,' then he would straighten out and use his throttle to bring the plane up most of the distance lost in dropping. Then he would shoot off again. For seventy-five miles he kept this up, until he successfully brought the *New Orleans* to the ground at Karachi, covered with oil from nose to tail and even dripping off the rudder, and punctured with holes. Over eleven gallons of oil were thrown out, much of it into the faces of Erik and Jack. It took them several days to get it out of their hair.

There was a large crowd waiting on the landing field at Karachi. One of the spectators was the American Consul, who stepped up to Lieutenant Smith with a cable from General Patrick. It referred to Linton Wells and was in reply to the cable Smith had sent. 'Request disapproved,' it read. But in the meantime, Linton Wells, the stowaway, had flown across India, and now has an adventure to his credit that he will remember long after the temporary inconvenience of losing his job with the Associated Press is quite forgotten.

CHAPTER XXIV

FROM KARACHI TO BAGHDAD
BY WAY OF PERSIA AND BALUCHISTAN

AT Karachi, the Fliers stayed just long enough to install new engines in their planes before venturing across the wild mountains of Baluchistan and Persia. These engines had been shipped from Calcutta to Karachi because the fliers considered it advisable to get through the monsoon belt of eastern India with all possible speed. If the seasonal monsoon storms had caught them in Calcutta they might have been delayed for weeks. The three pilots stayed with the Chief Commissioner of Sind, who had also acted as host to MacLaren, D'Oisy, Ross Smith, and most of the other famous airmen who had passed this way. Harding and Ogden were guests of the Collector of Karachi, who is the financial head of the local government, and to 'Les' Arnold fell the honor of being entertained by Major-General Cook, the General commanding the Army in that part of British India.

'That first afternoon when we arrived in Karachi — the afternoon of the Fourth of July,' says 'Les' — 'we were all much relieved to get down out of the air, but especially Erik and Jack whose engine had been flying to bits during that last hour on the way from Multan. We spent the rest of our national holiday out at the field where we worked on the planes until dark. I was so smeared from head to foot with oil and grease that when General Cook's Rolls-Royce, complete with chauffeur and footman, took me to his big white mansion I felt like the ragged urchin in the story books who dreams that he is a prince.

'As I whirled up the driveway through an avenue of palms I could see a crowd of men and women in spotless white sitting on the lawn. I was in my one and only suit of grimy overalls, so as soon as the car stopped I ran up the steps in order not to be seen. But with my face black from smoke and dirt and my overalls coated with grease, the General insisted that I must come right out to meet the assembled company. They were so charming, treating me as though I were a Knight of the Garter or a Commander of the Bath instead of a mere unwashed lieutenant, that I soon felt quite at ease.

'Karachi is the repair depot for the Royal Air Force in India. There are big shops here for the overhauling of motors, the rebuilding of wings, and the setting up of planes. In fact, it is one of the finest establishments of its kind in the world. The shops are well equipped, attractive, stucco and concrete buildings, and the entire depot was placed at our disposal. Although we accepted the assistance of a number of expert mechanics, who proved to be unusually competent and careful workmen, we did our own changing of motors and inspection.

'On the evening of July 4th, the Royal Air Force entertained us at dinner, and Commander Hicks held a banquet in our honor, and in a witty speech one of our hosts said he had seen all of the expeditions that had set out to fly around the world. He mentioned several British, a couple of French expeditions, Italian attempts in the course of which five or six planes were smashed, and a Portuguese expedition. He said they had all passed through Karachi, flying from west to east. "But you Americans," he added, "have the reputation of trying to do everything differently from any one else, and here you are flying around the globe in the opposite direction. However, you seem to have the right idea, for you have already flown farther than any of your competitors."

'As a matter of fact we had now flown exactly 12,577 miles since leaving Seattle, and our flying time had been 178 hours and 7 minutes. We still had nearly fourteen thousand miles to go.

'Monday morning, the 7th, we were called at three o'clock. General Cook got up at that unearthly hour to

PAST THE BAD LANDS OF BALUCHISTAN

ALONG THE SHORE OF THE GULF OF OMAN

have breakfast with me and escort me to the field. At
7.45, we taxied across the airdrome, flew over Karachi,
noticing the big docking accommodation which had been
built to enable it to become one of the principal grain-ports
of the world, and then we headed west toward Persia and
Baghdad.

'Of all the countries we passed over, Baluchistan turned
out to be the dreariest. Like so much of the rest of this
planet, it is under the control of the British.

'The more we see of the world the greater becomes our
admiration for the British. They are, indeed, a great
people. But the mystery is, where in the name of the
thirty million Hindoo gods of India do they find enough
administrators in their little islands to rule such an empire? A lot of Irishmen seem to hold high positions in remote corners of the earth. A marvelous race they are,
these Irish, even if they do throw bricks at each other
when they are at home. That story about the Irishman
who was shipwrecked on a South Sea Island and who said
"whatever the government of this island is, I'm agin it," is
all wrong. Instead of their being "agin it" they're running it — with the English helping them to be sure, and with
the canny Scotch bankers in the rôle of jute kings, teak
magnates, and oil capitalists to look after the financial side.

'Baluchistan is certainly the land that God forgot.
For hours and hours we flew without seeing a human being, or a tree, or even a bit of cactus. We looked down on a
desolate region made up of great gashes in the crust of the
earth. "A haggard land, forlornly spanned by mountains
lank and lean."

'As we flew across Baluchistan we thought of the
English flier who aptly described this region as "miles and
miles of damn-all."

'At last we could tell from our maps that we had crossed
into Persia and at 12.35 P.M. we descended at the little seaport of Chabar on the Gulf of Oman, merely to refuel and
take right off for Bandar Abbas and the land of dates.'

In 'The Arabian Nights' there is a tale of a Persian

prince who rescued his princess with the aid of a magic horse. By mounting this mysterious charger and turning a wooden plug, the horse was instantly transformed from an inanimate object to a winged steed that carried its rider wherever he wished to go. Whoever the writer was, and whether he read the future through a crystal glass or not, his dream was to come true. His magic horse has been reproduced even to the self-starter, corresponding to the wooden plug on the shoulder of that Arabian Pegasus.

The lone Englishman at Chabar, a Mr. G. A. Tomlinson who represented the Indo-European Telegraph Company, had consented to act as agent for the American airmen at this remote port on the Gulf of Oman and had arranged a supply of gas and oil and a gang of coolies to help refuel. Moreover, he had refreshments waiting for them at his bungalow. But the boys were so anxious to push right on to Bandar Abbas, that the consul had his wife and servants serve the lunch in the tent beside the planes. This was but one of many instances of thoughtful kindness which the Fliers met with in this part of their journey.

'At 2.35,' says Jack Harding, 'we took off again and flew for four solid hours over that rugged littoral. Beneath us were barren cathedral-like rocks, and canyons more desolate than any in Arizona.

'"A gorge sheered up in sandstone walls, and the caravans trekked betwixt;
'Twas as if the earth had gaped too far and her stony jaws were fixt."

'Away off to the north in the direction of Kirman and Seistan, where nomad tribesmen weave Persia's most exquisite rugs, a mirage followed us most of the way to Bandar Abbas. Instead of resembling water, it looked like a lake of quicksilver to me. When I half-closed my eyes I could imagine I was seeing almost anything from palm trees and camel caravans to ships at sea or the minarets of an Oriental city.

'"Phantom shapes before me were.
Caravans of silks and myrrh
Passing domes of gossamer,
While all the desert seemed astir.'

'It was on this flight across Baluchistan to Persia that we passed our halfway point, because on that afternoon of July 7th, when we landed at Bandar Abbas, Persia, at 6.40 P.M., we had flown 13,332 miles, or 160 miles more than one half the total mileage we were to fly in all. We had started at 7.45 in the morning from Karachi and, with the exception of the two hours we had spent refueling at Chabar, we had flown continuously for a distance of 775 miles.

'Although not a large city, Bandar Abbas, with the exception of Bushire, is the chief port of Persia. It is situated on the Strait of Ormuz which connects the Gulf of Oman with the Persian Gulf. The principal inland city which it serves is Kirman. Caravans laden with carpets, grain, tobacco, and cotton, come in every day.

'The only white people there are the few attached to the English and French consulates. The English consul put us up for the night in his home eight miles from the town, which really looked more like a fortress than a house and was surrounded by high walls.

'We were warned to stay away from the natives of Bandar Abbas as much as possible, because there was a cholera plague raging at the time. In fact many of the Persians had fled to the mountains to escape it.

'That night the few white people in Bandar Abbas dined with us at the British Consulate. The hit of the evening was the consul's little ice machine. Sad to relate, it was only big enough to make ice for just one round of drinks, and then for the rest of the evening they had to be cooled by evaporation, just as was done in the days of Omar Khayyám.

'Three of us slept in one house and three in another. Ogden, who happened to be bunking near me, woke up in the middle of the night with a maddening thirst. He tried to go back to sleep but his throat was too parched. So he got up and started prowling about in the dark. Finally, in the courtyard, he bumped into the wall of a well and, in feeling around, discovered a thatched lean-to where the earthen jars used in evaporating the water were kept. The rest of that night he spent in this hut, sleeping and drinking intermittently.

'At 3.30 A.M. on the morning of the 8th of July, we were up and on our way to the planes. The supply of gasoline had been sent here in two-gallon tins, and when you remember that we had to pour one hundred tins into each plane you can imagine what a long job it was. But we lined up the coolies like a fire-bucket brigade, and got through in time to get away at 5.40 A.M. We made a fast flight along the Persian Gulf to Bushire, arriving there in three hours and forty minutes.

'Most of the other airmen who have passed down this coast, including Poulet, the Frenchman who flew from Paris to the Dutch East Indies, and Ross Smith, Mathews, and Parer, had met severe sandstorms between Bandar Abbas and Bushire. Parer and McIntosh encountered the strange phenomena of a sandstorm blowing in from the sea! They ascended to over eighty-five hundred feet without being able to escape it, and finally had to fly away out over the Persian Gulf to get around the sand. Fortunately we were not troubled in this way, and saw nothing but wild, forbidding-looking country on our right, mirages along the horizon to the north, and to our left the waters of the Persian Gulf, where the galleys laden with the wealth of Ormuz and of Ind used to ply in ancient times.

'Perhaps the country we passed over between Bandar Abbas and Bushire was the most vicious we had seen. As Sir Ross Smith said after he had passed this way, it "appears as if a mighty harrow had torn down the mountain-sides into abysmal furrows. Fantastically shaped ridges and razorbacks rise precipitously from deep valleys devoid of vegetation and desolate of life."

'Looking down on Bushire it reminded us a little of far-off Manhattan Island. This seaport, which is the most important on the Persian Gulf, is built right at the end of a long narrow tongue of land, and just as in the case of New

York City every foot of ground is covered with streets and squares. As we flew over it from the desert, the morning sun glistened on the houses of white coral and sea shell, making it look twice as attractive from the air as it does from the ground.

'There is an American consul in Bushire, and as three of us had hurried away from Bandar Abbas that morning without taking time for breakfast we accepted his offer to send to the city for sandwiches. In the meantime we loaded up with another supply of fuel, and at 11 o'clock, despite the fact that the sandwiches had not arrived, we took off for Baghdad.

'Approaching the Shatt-el-Arab, where the conjoined waters of the Tigris and Euphrates carry the silt of Iraq into the Persian Gulf, we saw the dark-green date-gardens of Basra, nestling under a haze of heat. Half the dates consumed in the world are shipped from this port and all along the river-front, as far as Ezra's tomb, these gardens form a setting to the gleaming water, like a green ribbon with a silver thread in its center, coiling across the desert sand. To our left lay the marshes of Nasiriyeh, to our right, more lakes and great irrigation cuts hewn by the civilizations of long ago, fading into the purple of the Persian foothills. Straight ahead lay the ancient river, leading to Baghdad.

'Ezra's tomb is marked by a mosque, some huts, and a landing ground. It is supposed to be the site of the Garden of Eden, and as a sweltering "Aussie" said of it: "Old man Adam must have been as balmy as a gold-panner to stay in those ruddy date groves until the devil turned him out."

'At Amara, we passed a straggling village where General Townshend won his clever "regatta victory" against an overwhelming force of Turks, by embarking his army in boats and attacking over flooded ground which the enemy had deemed impassable for infantry.

'At Amara the date cultivation ends and the desert is just a flat dun plain stretching away to an horizon which may be mirage or reality — the airman cannot tell which. Below him is the winding Tigris, with occasional villages, infrequent horsemen, and sometimes a string of barges. Beyond are the immensities of the desert, which somehow lift up the heart to a sense of the majesty of the Creator.

'The Tigris here becomes more serpentine than the maziest dance of a Delhi nautch girl, first taking a right angle bend one way and then the other. At the second corner lies Kut-el-Amara, where an ill-fated British Army was besieged. The British offered the Turks $10,000,000 to be allowed to march out with their arms, but the bribe was refused. All around are the mounds of ruined cities and a modern network of entrenchments which figured in the struggle.

'Down the Shatt-el-Hai is the modern village of Hit and the ancient mounds of Babylon, the mighty, whose name, after all these years, is still a synonym for splendor. Here came the captive children of Israel and here Baltha-zar parked Daniel in the lions' den — now all is sand!

'An hour out of Baghdad, at a corkscrew corner before the straight reach which leads to the City of the Arabian Nights, we saw the famous arch of Ctesiphon, a triumphal gateway hulking up into the desert and visible for miles around. It was here that Townshend was defeated in his first dash for Baghdad; a disaster avenged a year later when Maude's cavalry chased the flower of the Ottoman army into Kurdistan and beyond.

'And now, against the westering sun, the minarets of Baghdad began to appear. The Tigris had turned to molten gold in the sunset. A river-steamer struggled up through the sand-banks, past green suburbs where Sinbad and the slave girls feasted! A magical city it seemed, in the soft evening light.

'At 5.55 we landed at the British aerodrome. Another lap of the long journey was over and another chapter in our lives was closed.'

CHAPTER XXV

ACROSS THE ARABIAN DESERT
FROM BAGHDAD TO CONSTANTINOPLE

PLACES and people are rarely as they seem and Baghdad is no exception to this rule. Haroun-el-Rashid never ruled over a city as beautiful as the pseudo-Baghdad of Hollywood, Aladdin never extricated himself from difficulties as gracefully as Fairbanks, and no antelope-eyed princess was ever more alluring than Anna May Wong: in short, Baghdad in the cinema, or as seen from the air, is very different from Baghdad in the sand. From the former vantage-grounds it is still a dream place, whereas from the latter, terrestrial standpoint it is only an Arab city of mud huts, full of British troops and town-bred Bedouins. The old glamour is far to seek. Certainly the boys did not recapture any romance, being too busy with their real-life story of Liberty-12's and charts of Asia.

A big detachment of the British Royal Air Force is stationed here, for King Feisal is perched rather insecurely on his throne, surrounded by wild races that will not submit tamely to any man's rule. With the Air Force at his back, however, he can collect his taxes and administer his government within cruising distance of the capital, provided the planes are always ready for action.

All the British pilots, many of them 'aces' of wide experience, were of course keenly interested in the American World Flight. A big dinner had been arranged for the boys at the R.A.F. Mess, to show them that it was still possible to have a good time in the city of the Thousand Nights and a Night, even though Caliphs and Circassian slaves were lacking. But after their long day's flight from Persia, and with the promise of an equally arduous journey on the morrow, to Aleppo, they decided to turn in early.

'Just as we were getting ready to leave Baghdad, on

July 9th,' says Erik Nelson, 'the battery on the *Chicago* went dead, so it wasn't until 11.15 that we got under way and headed west toward the Euphrates. It was a gorgeous day, with perfect visibility. The golden domes of Kazemain Mosque against their dark green background sparkled in the sunlight as we flew over the irrigation channels of former kingdoms.

'Before reaching the Euphrates, we passed over a mound said to be the tomb of Nimrod the "mighty hunter." Many of the mounds are from three thousand to six thousand years old, and archæologists have already discovered tablets giving the names of more than a hundred kings who ruled here before the time of Abraham. Surely this must be the most fascinating spot in all the world for the explorer.

'These mounds of Mesopotamia, cities lost in centuries of darkness, and now in the midst of desert inhabited by nomad Arabs, gave us more food for thought than any region we flew over on our way around the world. There is no doubt but what Iraq was once the center of civilization, a land teeming with people and crowded with mighty cities. One of these days, if the British succeed in carrying out their irrigation schemes, the desert will bear again a rich harvest, as in the days of Nebuchadnezzar.

'On this flight across the North Arabian desert to Aleppo, we saw scores of "sand devils" whirling about the desert. They seemed to travel at great speed and reminded us somewhat of the pictures of waterspouts that we used to see in our school geographies. They made the air extremely "bumpy," but the stimulus of the desert air at five thousand feet, the great panorama of desert that spread out before us on every side, and above all the fact that we were well on our way now to the accomplishment of our task, contributed to render that day's flight particularly enjoyable.

'Sixty miles south of Aleppo we encountered a big sand devil that looked like a mountain moving towards us. Climbing to six thousand feet we got well above it. The

BRITISH AVIATORS PATROL THE SKIES ABOVE THE TRADI-
TIONAL HOME OF ADAM AND EVE AND ABOVE THE WATERS
OF THE PERSIAN GULF

THROUGH THE TAURUS MOUNTAINS ON OUR WAY FROM ALEPPO TO THE GOLDEN HORN

top of that storm was at about four thousand feet, and the sun shining down on the whirling white particles gave it an appearance of a colossal spinning-top.

'Leaving Jerablus on our right, we headed directly towards Aleppo. At 5.15 p.m. we were in view of a collection of flat-roofed houses that looked even larger from the air than Baghdad whence we had come. In the center, on a high hill, was a citadel with crumbling walls and the minarets of an ancient mosque — Aleppo, city of Saladin and Cœur de Lion. Here also Allenby's cavalry smashed into little pieces the already broken army of the Turks, retreating from the Holy Land.

'To-day Aleppo is ruled by the French, who have a mandate over Syria. Nine miles north of the city we came down on the French airdrome. Here, as in Mesopotamia, we found a country that is controlled almost entirely by squadrons of airplanes.

'The French officers were all out to welcome us, and the first thing they insisted upon doing was to drink our health in some wine of special vintage which they had saved for the occasion. Then we worked until dark, spent the night in the principal hotel in Aleppo, and were up at dawn, ready to start for Constantinople. With the Bosphorus only a day's flight away, we felt that victory was in sight.

'On the morning of July 10th, we motored down from the Syrian Hotel to the French aerodrome beyond the north wall of Aleppo. It was just at dawn, and this picturesque metropolis of two hundred thousand people which lies midway between Orient and Occident was just coming to life. Camels were burbling and complaining as their drivers loaded them. Merchants were on their way to the bazaars, and nearly every other native sat astride a diminutive donkey. "It was like a scene from a comic opera," said Wade.

'Many of the people we passed were swarthy fellows with fierce mustachios. To make the picture all the more incongruous and full of color, each wore a tall red fez, and a long

Mother-Hubbard of many colors, like Joseph had on the day his brothers chucked him into the well. On his feet were red slippers, with upturned toes dangling in the dust.

'To see one of these pompous business men of Aleppo joggling along on his little Syrian ass was quite enough to put all of us in a good humor for the day.

'Just at six o'clock, as the sun came up over the rim of the desert, we took off for our six-hundred-mile flight across Asia Minor. It was a glorious, sparkling, desert morning, with perfect visibility. As we circled around before leaving this ancient capital of the Saracens, I couldn't help but think of all the historic lands that lay spread out around us.

'To the east, whence we had come, lay the traditional birthplace of the human race. Beyond was Armenia, oldest home of Christians, who claim that their Eucharist is sanctified by bread baked in the same manner and with the identical leaven used at the Last Supper. Ahead, stretched the mountains and plains of Turkey, with all their terrible and tremendous legacy of history.

'We passed over miles of cultivated lands near Aleppo, and then we came to another stretch of desert. Far below a long camel caravan was proceeding in the direction of Urfa, the ancient Edessa and the scene of a terrible massacre of Armenians during the War.

'Below us passed many another caravan. When the airplane comes into its own, as it is sure to do within a few years, one wonders what will become of that most picturesque of men, the desert Arab. Journeys that take him two months can now be made by airplane between sunrise and sunset. Within a short time, planes will be so cheap that even the Bedouin sheik will own one, or several. Then the day of desert raids and racing camels will have passed, because the sheik with his swift pursuit planes will be able to overtake and wipe out his enemy within a few minutes. Both the British in Mesopotamia and the French at Aleppo told us that the Arabs were extremely interested in flying developments. When taken up in a plane the average sheik keeps begging the pilot to go higher and faster.

'Long before this, we had already become convinced that the airplane is destined to have an immense influence on the peace of the world. The speed with which men will fly from continent to continent will bring all peoples into such intimate contact that war will be as out of date as the cuneiform inscriptions of the ancient civilizations that the shadows of our Cruisers were passing over.

'Forty minutes north of Aleppo we crossed the Amanus Mountains and passed just to the left of the city of Aintab, where in 1638 the Crusader Knights of Saint John made one of their last stands against the Turks, and where to-day is an American girls' school.

'Turning a little to the east, we headed toward the main range of the Taurus Mountains and flew a bit to the right of Tarsus, birthplace of Paul, who was Saul.

'We crossed the snow-capped Taurus by the route of the Berlin–Baghdad railway. These mountains are from seven thousand to ten thousand feet high, but the passes we used — one of which was so narrow that our wing-tips had hardly a safe clearance — were not more than five thousand feet, an altitude sufficient, however, to give us our first taste of real cold since leaving the Kurile Islands.

'Leaving the northern water-shed of the Taurus behind us, and the relics of German engineering works planned to assure *kultur* for the lands of Mohammed, we flew over the many-minareted city of Konia, capital of the dancing dervishes, and the notorious rock of Afium-Kara-Hissar — the "black opium city" where thousands of Allied prisoners languished amidst the poppy fields of Anatolia. By one o'clock we had traversed the rich home-lands of the Turk and had come within sight of the glorious blue waters of the Sea of Marmora. In a few minutes we knew we would be flying over Constantinople and landing for the first time in Europe. Less than a week ago we were in India, and the day before yesterday in Persia!'

CHAPTER XXVI

FLYING OVER THE WITCHES' CAULDRON
FROM CONSTANTINOPLE TO VIENNA

OF all the expeditions that attempted the World Flight, the American was the only one to use the historic waterway of the Bosphorus from Asia to Europe. The others followed the route by Greece, Crete, Egypt, and on to Baghdad, for the Turks were not enthusiastic about the idea of foreign airplanes flying over their country, the World War being a too recent and too bitter memory.

'Having given Shanghai, Hongkong, Bangkok, Rangoon, Calcutta, Delhi, and Baghdad the " once over," ' says Smith, 'we came to an even more wonderful sight — Constantinople from the air. Our first glimpse of the Sublime Porte, as it is aptly named, was an inspiring spectacle. It was an ideal flying day, with visibility so perfect that we could see more than a hundred miles in every direction, southward across the corn-lands and poppy-fields of Anatolia, westward to the plains of Troy and the equally epic battle-grounds of Gallipoli, and eastward, past the twin fortresses that frown on the silver streak of the Bosphorus to the Black Sea, where the Argonauts of old sailed out across the Euxine. Ahead lay Scutari, on Constantinople's Asiatic shore, then a blue strip of water across which two more cities rose up, pink and white and ethereal with their spires and cupolas, from the shipping of the Marmora — Pera, to our right, and Stamboul to our left, with the massive mosque of Sancta Sofia bulking in the foreground — the whole being Constantinople. Between Pera and Stamboul twisted the aureate and glittering Golden Horn, crowded with caïques and lateen-sailed boats and crossed by two pontoon bridges.

'We turned left at Seraglio Point, over the gardens which were once the most closely guarded in the world,

when the Sublime Sultanas lived here, watched over by a
corps of Abyssinian eunuchs. For some ten miles, we flew
down the shores of the Marmora, past crumbling suburbs,
and the ruined ramparts of the city, whence Crusaders
looked long ago, with their eyes turned toward the land of
morning and Jerusalem of their hearts' desire, until at
1.40 P.M. we reached the attractive aerodrome of San
Stefano.

'Admiral Bristol, our ambassador to Turkey, Lieutenant
Halverson, who had made the advance arrangements in
the countries over which we had just flown, Major Carlyle
Wash, who preceded us across Europe, and a number of
our other fellow countrymen, were waiting for us. But it
was only by chance that they were out at San Stefano.
Due to the inefficiency of the telegraph in that part of the
world, the messages we had sent from Baghdad and Aleppo
had not reached them.

'After working from two o'clock until four-thirty, we
drove to Constantinople. There was nothing special to do
that night because no one knew we were coming, so we
enjoyed ourselves thoroughly doing nothing for a change.

'The lobsters here are great, more delicious even than
our own from Newport! Epicures told us that they are
the most succulent in the world, except during the five
nights of the full moon, when Mr. Lobster goes "goofy"
and eats things that don't agree with him, probably owing
to some change of light on the sea-floor. As to the caviare,
luscious-fresh from the Black Sea, it costs only a dime a
dish! What do you think of that?

'Over in Pera, they drink champagne mostly — at
least so it seemed to us. The night life in the clubs run by
Russian refugees would make the Alabam' in New York
look like a Sunday-School picnic. Some of these dyed-in-
the-wool, rolled-below-the-knee, boyish-bobbed Slav aristo-
crats were washing dishes and peddling cigarettes. All
honor to them for working for their living. We have often
been asked — why, I don't know — which of the countries
we flew over contained the most beautiful women. Our

World-Flight beauty-experts, of whom we carried three, one in each rear cockpit, give these Slav brunettes an honorable mention. But "Les," "Hank," "Jack," and all of us give first place to the American girls we met in Shanghai, and second, to the American girls we met in Vienna — always excepting certain American girls in America, of course. We don't claim to have been able to make a very exhaustive study of the problem, however, owing to want of time, not to want of will. The Burmese, for instance, merited more research than we were able to devote to them, while the beauties of Bucharest, London, and Paris require more than an afternoon of study: the fact is, the world is a large place, and although it will undoubtedly grow smaller as flying progresses, the feminine temperament will remain mysterious long after most other things are solved.

'According to our original schedule, we were supposed to spend four days at Constantinople. But we were anxious to reach Paris by Bastile Day, which was only four days away, and then hurry on across the Atlantic. We would have taken-off for Bucharest next morning if it hadn't been that the Turkish officials were anxious to inspect our Cruisers. They very hospitably asked us to stay a week, but when we explained that we had been flying from eight to ten hours a day, working until after dark on the planes, and getting up before dawn nearly every morning, in order to get around the globe as fast as possible, they agreed to look them over next day. They came, they saw, and they charmed us by their pleasant manners. Courteous people, the Turks, and their officers as smart as any we met on our travels.

'This one day's delay gave us a further opportunity for rubber-necking around Constantinople. We had heard that the Mohammedan ladies of Turkey had discarded their veils. This is true, and very pretty some of them are, with their pale complexions and lustrous eyes, and lashes very carefully treated with *kohl*, but it is noticeable that their hair, considered by the Turks to be woman's chief beauty, is still hidden from view. The purdah has gone, but bobs, jazz, and auto-parties have not yet assumed any significance in the "hanoum's" life. Yet she demands the best of everything in the matter of dress, shoes, and scents. When a rich Turkish lady goes out shopping with her attendant *cavass*, carrying a roll of Turkish paper pounds, she is little different from her sister turned loose on Madison Avenue. Her husband, however, instead of fretting himself to death over bills and overdrafts, merely takes another cigarette and mutters " *Allah verdi!* " — "God will provide!" When things get too bad, he will pledge the rents from his Anatolian property to some Armenian, for several years in advance.

'In Pera, the polyglot Levantine predominates — a common type the world over. Indeed, the Grande Rue de Péra, with its electric lights and fashionable shops, would not appear to be under Turkish rule at all, were it not for the stalwart traffic policemen who marshal the trams and flivvers. These men are Turks, and they give one some idea of what fine fighting material still exists in Turkey, in spite (or because?) of all her wars. Sometimes, too, you see a typical Ottoman peasant who has strayed into his own capital like a lost soul, with his huge trousers and a sash full of daggers. The Lazz from the Black Sea is another fine physical type. Fair-skinned and handsome, they are reputed to be terrible villains in spite of their good looks: their hobby being massacring Armenians. They would certainly be bad men to meet in some of the twisting lanes of Galata, or the dark docks, where the underworld lives and thrives with more immunity in Constantinople than anywhere else on earth.

'Certain quarters of the city are exactly like the "Little Italies" and the "Ghettos" of the United States, only older and lousier. Here live Jew and Greek and Armenian and Syrian, speaking their own languages and worshiping their own gods, people of every nation and yet of no nationality, who pay lip-service to the Turks while relieving them of any surplus cash they may happen to have — which isn't much, these days.

'Behind the Pera Palace Hotel where we stopped for tea, there is a quaint old Mohammedan cemetery, from which you can see the Golden Horn, winding up to the Sweet Waters of Europe. Across the sapphire stretch of the Horn is the Turkish quarter of Stamboul, whose minarets rise proudly into the blue sky, like lifted spears, as if in token of the militant basis of Islam.

'On our way to the mosque of Sancta Sofia we passed a curious specimen of the old régime — a specimen, by the way, for which there is still a small but high-class clientèle. He was an Abyssinian and had been prepared as a child by a special process for the harem. This one was six feet tall, with the singularly broad, flat shoulders which are the characteristic of these unsexed creatures. What stories he could have told, if he would, and we had had time to listen, of the secrets that never pass the walls of harems — of lovers surprised and lovers disguised and sultanas strangled and thrown into the Bosphorus — real life romances that even the most hardened reader of our Sunday supplements would find scarcely credible!

'The mosque of Sancta Sofia is surrounded by many burnt-out districts, where people are living in rags amongst the ruins, in terrible straits for food and shelter. What they do when winter comes, I can't imagine. The well-to-do Turkish quarter, on the other hand, is fascinating for its scrupulous cleanliness and sequestered, old-world air. An occasional rickety cab or wobbly flivver rolls along its vine-trellised alley-ways. Otherwise all is still, save for the veiled ladies — for custom dies hard and they are not all emancipated by any means — pattering out to market, and men strolling about with long cigarette holders in their mouths, or large amber necklaces in their hands. These necklaces, by the way, correspond to the European walking-stick — something to twirl and play with while walking.

'Inside the great mosque, once the pride of Christian Byzantium and now one of the chief glories of Islam, we saw wide, quiet spaces, fluttering doves, rich carpets on the flagstones — in short, an air of strength and serenity

THE WORLD FLIGHT COMMANDER (IN SWEATER) WITH LIEUTENANT
LESLIE ARNOLD, HIS COMPANION, AND THE SHIP IN WHICH THEY
GIRDLED THE EARTH

UP THE VALLEY OF THE DANUBE AND ACROSS THE RICH PLAINS OF
HUNGARY ON THE WAY TO BUDAPEST

which was very impressive. As a place of worship it is
truly magnificent in its proportions and its exquisite
simplicity. Armed men came in, put their weapons in
front of them and dropped on their knees to pray, like
knights of the Middle Ages. High on one of the walls is
the red imprint of a great hand — said to be the hand of
Mohammed II, conqueror of Constantinople, who rode
into the then Christian Cathedral of the Divine Wisdom,
over the bodies of its slain defenders, and ordered the
massacre to cease. Tradition says that the hand will dis-
appear when the Kings of Christendom again hold Mass
here, but it looks as if a good many crowns and thrones
must perish first!

'We spent a quiet evening, writing letters and getting a
much-needed rest. With 15,282 miles to our credit when
we left Asia behind and entered Europe, we now had
11,000 miles ahead to go, for Europe, the Atlantic, and
North America still remained to be crossed. Next morning
— July 12th — we were up at dawn as usual. At 6.55 A.M.
we took-off from San Stefano, turned for a last look at the
crumbling walls of old Byzantium, the gay glitter of the
Golden Horn, the pleasaunces of Pera and the narrows of
the Hellespont where Leander staged his cross-channel
swim: then we headed for Thrace and were soon over the
tangle of trenches which guard Constantinople from the
north. Here were ruined villages, fields pock-marked with
shell-holes, mounds of barbed wire and other scrapped
equipment — all the ugly relics of the ambitions of many
nations to rule in this key-city by the Bosphorus. Near
Adrianople, where so much blood has flowed, there were
signs of considerable military activity, for the Ottoman,
while engaging with the enthusiasm of an expert in various
diplomatic parleys, never forgets Mohammed's advice to
"Pray to God, but also watch your camel." He is a two-
fisted fighting man, as well as no mean negotiator, and if
any one ever tries to take his country away from him, he
will find that the Turk has a heavy punch behind his
placid exterior.

'Ahead of us now lay the Transylvanian Alps, connected in our minds with were-wolves, vampires, and passionate gypsy music.

'For some reason our telegrams from Aleppo and Constantinople had failed to get through to this kingdom of ghosts and enchantment, so not a soul was waiting for us when we landed at Bucharest shortly before noon. We telephoned to Colonel Foy, the American Consul, and then went to work refueling the planes, much relieved at not having a crowd around us for once. Two hours later, the Colonel dashed up in a car and explained that he thought we were still thousands of miles away in southern Asia.

'It was a disappointment to us to find that the Queen of Rumania and her beautiful daughters were not in Bucharest. Far away in Burma, Jack Harding had read in the Rangoon "Gazette" that the rumored marriage of the Prince of Wales to a Rumanian princess had fallen through. This had sort of set Jack thinking and naturally we had done nothing to discourage him. So it was a shock to find that the princesses were away at their country seat. However, next day, we received a message from Her Majesty, sent down by special courier from her summer castle in the Transylvanian Alps, inviting us to spend the week-end with her. Very reluctantly we had to send our regrets, explaining that we were hurrying around the world. Later on, we added, we hoped we might have the opportunity of accepting Her Majesty's gracious hospitality. So you see how close Jack came to living happily ever after!'

That night, an impromptu dinner was given in honor of the Fliers by some of the foreign colony in the Rumanian capital. There were many in attendance and the picturesque uniforms of the Balkans added color to the occasion. During the evening, the Chief of the Rumanian Air Service came in. He had hurried down from the summer capital when he had heard of the arrival and apologized on behalf of the Rumanian Government for not being able to give them a real Rumanian reception on such short notice.

'We found Bucharest to be a clean, snappy-looking city,

with sidewalk cafés just like Paris,' adds 'Les,' 'and it was full of beautifully gowned and attractive-looking women, accompanied by dashing cavaliers. We were particularly impressed with the Rumanian Air Service and found that this small Balkan State had more airplanes ready for service than America!

'The plumbing arrangements in our hotel were very — Balkan. We all had separate rooms and Erik and Leigh were by themselves at one end of a corridor. Erik tried to turn on the water in his room, but nothing happened. Then he went into Leigh's suite, to try his luck there. The result was the same. However, when Erik went out, he neglected to turn off the faucet. An hour afterward when Lowell went into Leigh's room, he found it like a lake, with the chairs floating about. But there lay Leigh sound asleep not even dreaming that he was in danger of being drowned. Lowell called the hotel attendants, who baled the water out with buckets, but Leigh slept right through it all and never knew that anything had happened until we told him next morning.

'Sunday, July 13th, we were up at 3 A.M., and off for Budapest at 6. The sun was just coming up over the lagoons and marshes of Dobrudja as we taxied across the landing-field of the Franco-Rumanian Aero Company and flew over the great plain of the province of Wallachia, which is one of the principal granaries of the world.

'From the farming country around Bucharest we flew almost due west until we reached the Danube where it flows through the Transylvanian Alps. Following upstream, we passed through a wild mountain gorge and, shortly after reaching the plains of Serbia, we saw the spires of a city just ahead. A moment later we were flying over Belgrade, at the junction of the Danube and Save. Here at the foot of Mount Avala lay the famous city that for many years was the capital of Serbia, and is now the metropolis of the ambitious new State of Jugo-Slavia.

'We hadn't arranged a stop at Belgrade and, as we had plenty of fuel on hand and our motors were running perfectly, we continued right on up the Danube, crossed the border from Jugo-Slavia into Hungary, flew over the rich Hungarian plains and after six hours and fifty minutes in the air landed at Budapest. As you know, there are two cities here instead of one, Buda, on the right-hand side, clings to a mountain, and Pest is spread out over the beautiful Danubian plain to westward.

'The Hungarians, or Magyars as they call themselves, are proud people, and we stopped in their great city to pay our respects to a nation that has supplied America with so many hundreds of thousands of citizens. A great crowd had been at the field to welcome us, but about ten-thirty in the morning one of those curious rumors, that cannot be accounted for, ran through the throng to the effect that we were not coming. So when we reached Budapest at 12.50 P.M., all but a few had gone home.

'We stopped for less than two hours, just long enough to partake of an exceedingly delicious luncheon, and pay our respects to the Hungarian officials; then climbed back into our cockpits and were off again for Vienna at twenty minutes past two.

'In exactly two hours we crossed from Hungary into Austria and found ourselves looking down on the bulwark of Western civilization against the Turkish menace of the Middle Ages, the capital of old Austria-Hungary, and seat of the once mighty Holy Roman Empire, now defunct. Especially noticeable was the Ring-strasse, the famous boulevard of Vienna, two miles in circumference, that has taken the place of the old walls.

'When we reached the aerodrome, we saw a big crowd in front of the hangars. To our surprise they turned out to be mostly Americans, more of our own countrymen than we had encountered anywhere else in the world. And the manner in which they welcomed us took us right back home.

'The men wore horn-rimmed glasses and "plus fours," the women carried guide-books and kodaks. "Say, boys, do yuh mind if we take a coupla snapshots?" they shouted. It was good to hear them.

'As soon as Mrs. Ebenezer Plunkett from Xenia had finished snapshotting us in front of the "prop," Mrs. Babcock, president of the Ladies' Aid Society of Muskogee, would ask us to pose in front of the tail. This over, we heaved six sighs of relief and started to "service-up." But before we could begin Mr. Jim Whozis, visiting the Old World to prepare a lantern-slide lecture to deliver before the Lion Tamers of Pocatello, would sing out: "Say, son, do yuh mind if my missus shoots you talkin' to me? 'Attaboy, just like that."

'Kodaks to the left of us. Kodaks to the right, front, and rear. It looked as though we were not going to be able to get our planes ready for the next day's flight to Paris. So Smith finally announced that if they would all line up with their picture machines, we also would line up and then they could get us all with one volley. But in spite of this, until dusk, and indeed long after, for the amateur photographer is not particular about lighting conditions, the kodaks clicked.

'We reached the city shortly after seven o'clock and were taken for a quick drive around the old Imperial Palace of the last of the Hapsburgs, Franz Josef. Here he had reigned for sixty-seven years, longer even than Queen Victoria. On his ill-fated house had hung a strange curse. His beautiful wife was assassinated. His children went mad or were killed in terrible ways. His heir-apparent, the Archduke Ferdinand, and the Princess Sophie of Hohenberg, were killed by that epochal bomb at Serajevo. He lived to see his Empire, in his eighty-sixth year, become a vassal of the Kaiser. He died knowing that Austria-Hungary was doomed. Now out of the ashes of his Empire have arisen three vigorous and ambitious young republics: Hungary, Czecho-Slovakia, and Austria.

'Austria to-day is a tiny state of 30,000 square miles — hardly half as big as Ohio. The total population is less than seven millions, and a third of them live in Vienna.

'We motored rapidly around the Ring-strasse, with its attractive shops, magnificent palaces, and famous opera house; then we were taken to the Imperial Hotel. Shortly after dinner we went to bed.

'Our rooms were each about the size of the ballroom in an American hotel, more suitable to courtiers of Louis XIV than to lieutenants from the U.S.A. The parlor of the quarters Lowell and I occupied measured about sixty by forty feet, and had a twenty-foot ceiling from which hung a chandelier with five hundred lights. The bedroom was about as large, and we had twin beds, each on a raised dais, draped with silk canopies. The mattresses were so soft that we sank right down almost out of sight.

'Next morning four visitors and the six of us had breakfast in our private parlor. Although there were ten of us, we only took up a bit of one corner. They served us bowls of raspberries and cream, and it was almost worth flying around the world to eat them. I couldn't help thinking of those long days and nights in the traders' shacks on the Alaskan Peninsula and in the Aleutian Islands, where we made our beds on boxes to keep the rats from running over us, and where Smith had fed us on "eggs Vienna."

'The bill for our breakfast amounted to three million, seven hundred and fifty thousand kronen. Just the toast alone, without butter or jam, if paid for with kronen at pre-war value, would have cost us fifteen thousand dollars!

'Lowell had promised us in India that if we could gain an extra day and get to France twenty-four hours ahead of schedule, we could take a holiday in Paris. But instead of gaining one day, we had gained four, with Paris just a day's flight ahead. So we left Vienna in high spirits.'

CHAPTER XXVII

ADVENTURES IN PARIS AND LONDON

'WE took-off from Vienna at five-fifty on the morning of July 14th,' says Leigh Wade, 'and thirty minutes later plunged into heavy rain and flew through dark skies all the way across Austria and Germany. The gloom seemed somehow appropriate, symbolizing as it did the feelings of these people of Central Europe who are paying so heavily for the part their autocratic leaders forced them to play in the World War. Occasionally we dived through banks of fog that lasted for ten or fifteen minutes. There are many high mountains between Vienna and Paris, and the flight was a very hazardous one. The rain and fog drove us down to the river, and often we shot around sharp bends and kicked rudder just in time to avoid crashing unannounced into a castle. For several hours we followed the winding course of the Danube, flying against a stiff head wind that held us down to fifty miles an hour.

'When we were above the Black Forest, we suddenly shot out of the fog and gloom, and there in front of us, glistening like quicksilver, lay a river famous in story and song:

"'Der Rhein, der Rhein, der Deutscher Rhein
Wer soll des Strömes Hutter sein?"

'It had thrilled us to fly over the great rivers of the East — the Yangtze-Kiang, Mekong, Irrawaddy, the sacred Ganges, the stately Indus, and the historic Tigris and Euphrates. Then had come the blue Danube and now the wonderful Rhine. What noble streams our eyes have seen! That very day we saw also the Seine, and two days later the tiny Thames with its mighty cargoes. Last and best of all were the bluffs and gorges of our own Hudson, the long reaches of the Mississippi, the wild Colorado, and the glorious Columbia.

'On account of the head wind, we were running short of fuel. Six hours and a half had elapsed since we had left Vienna. But just ahead of us we saw the slender spire of Strasbourg Cathedral. Passing low over the city and its famous bridge, we came down on the outskirts of the capital of Alsace.

'We stayed here in Strasbourg only just long enough to load up with supplies of "gas" and oil and took-off again at 10.20 A.M. without visiting the city. We now cruised over picturesque little Alsatian villages; then, as we crossed the mountains into France proper, we saw ahead of us a city that I knew like my own home town of Cassopolis. To "Les" Arnold also, its churches, gardens, parks, and "hotel de ville" looked very familiar. It was Nancy, charming Nancy, innocent victim of so many night raids by fleets of Gothas that its inhabitants ceased to count them.

'From here all the way to Paris, "Les" and I were sailing in an airway we had used many times before — skies once flecked with white puffs from bursting "archies," and echoing day and night, with the scream of projectiles on their mission of death.

'Turning north from Nancy we flew over the famous Saint Mihiel salient where the first American army to visit Europe fought its first great battle under the leadership of its own generals. From Nancy all the way along the old Hindenburg Line, the earth was still scarred by the War, but most of the fields were green now and leaves grew on the trees, not as in the nightmare days of 1918, when birds, beasts, and vegetation had been blown away by the guns.

'Past Verdun we flew. Looking over the edges of our cockpits we saw the graves of those gallant Frenchmen who said, "THEY SHALL NOT PASS!" and stood like steel while wave after wave of a mighty army spent itself against their devoted ranks. Then on to the Argonne Forest. It seemed difficult to realize that it was in these same skies that Ball, Guynemer, Bishop, Fonck, Nungesser, and our own Eddie Rickenbacker and Frank Luke, and thousands more of our fellow airmen — and many

LIEUTENANT OGDEN WAVING THE TRICOLOR OF FRANCE AS THE
BOSTON TAXIED ACROSS LE BOURGET AERODROME ON
BASTILE DAY

PARISIANS WELCOMING THE FLIERS AT LE BOURGET

WHEN THEY LANDED ON THE OUTSKIRTS OF PARIS, NELSON AND
OGDEN WERE STILL WEARING THE KNEE PANTS THEY HAD PICKED
UP IN INDIA

WADE AND NELSON IN A JOVIAL MOOD, READY FOR THEIR
HOLIDAY IN PARIS

equally gallant enemy airmen also — used to dive down,
spitting tongues of flame, to send their adversaries crashing
to destruction. Our thoughts were with them as we turned
west toward the valley of the Marne, for we realized that
it was by their efforts that what we were doing now had
been made possible.

'I was thinking of my pals, who had fought their last
fight here, for La Belle France, when Ogden pointed to a
fleet of airplanes approaching us. I'll admit that my heart
skipped a beat or two, while I brought myself out of my
reverie and remembered that it couldn't be Richthofen's
Flying Circus. Instead, it was a fleet sent out to escort us
to Paris.

'Fifty miles from the city we caught our first glimpse of
the familiar Eiffel Tower and farther to the right the white
dome of the Church of the Sacré Cœur, on Montmartre.
When we arrived over Paris, the boulevards were packed
with people. We circled round several times and it was
easy to pick out the landmarks familiar to every doughboy.
There was the Seine, with its famous bridges, and all the
fine buildings that line the left bank from the Île de Cité to
the Tomb of Napoleon. Now we were above the Trocadéro
and the Eiffel Tower, and then to our left we saw the Bois
de Boulogne with its charming landscapes. There also was
the Champs-Élysées, with the Arc de Triomphe at one end
and the Garden of the Tuileries at the other. From our
vantage-point in the sky, the obelisk in the Place de la
Concorde, Napoleon's column of victory in the Place Ven-
dôme, and the winged statue on the site of the Bastile,
looked no larger than toothpicks. After circling above the
spires of Notre-Dame, the low dome of the Opéra, and the
vast wings of the Louvre, we flew directly above the Arc
de Triomphe and dipped in salute to the Unknown Soldier
whose grave is there.

'It was the afternoon of July 14th, Bastile Day, and
thousands of people were cheering and waving flags when
at five-fifteen we taxied up to the hangars at Le Bourget.
An hour passed before we could get a chance to do any

work on our planes because it took that long for us to shake hands with the many high French officials and foreign diplomats who had come out to greet us.

'During that hour on the outskirts of Paris we met more generals, ambassadors, cabinet ministers and celebrities, than we had encountered in all the rest of our lives. There were so many of them that we couldn't remember their names, despite the fact that they were all men whose names are constantly in newspaper headlines.'

Andrée Viollis, in *Le Petit Parisien* of July 15th, tells of the arrival in his vivid style:

The American World Flight wanted to celebrate with us, in our capital on our national holiday, hence its arrival yesterday ahead of its original schedule which called for a stop at Strasbourg. A great crowd had assembled to do them honor at the airport of Le Bourget. Indeed some enthusiasts had waited there since seven o'clock in the morning.

Flying in a perfect triangle above us, the great planes come, with the sunlight glinting on their wings. One by one they drop to earth with the light grace of a dragon-fly. Slim khaki figures emerge from the cockpits — one cries, 'Just in time for tea!' Then Smith asks who are winning in the Olympic Games. Wade lifts his goggles with a placid air. Nelson pulls off his helmet, watches the camera-men, and then, with a full-throated laugh, takes a kodak and shoots back in return. Congratulations, speeches, glasses of champagne. The heroes, with Generals Niessel and Dumesnil, pose for posterity before the news-reel men and press photographers.

There are cries of 'Vive la France!' and 'Vive l'Amérique!' But where are the heroes? They have vanished. 'Feeding their horses,' some one explains. And in fact, the Fliers have left the throng, and with a gesture that is simple as it is symbolic, they are wiping down the engines to which they owe a part of their glory.

'After we had refueled,' Wade continues, 'we were whirled to a hotel in the staff cars of the French Aviation Service, given a few minutes in which to clean up, had an American dinner in our rooms while dressing, and then were ushered into a box at the Folies Bergères.

'Dead tired after having flown more than ten hours

that day, as soon as we had made ourselves comfortable in the box, we promptly fell asleep. The whiskers of the Assistant Cabinet Minister, who was sitting near me, bristled with astonishment at my behavior: I know they did, because he gave me a nudge in the ribs during a particularly spectacular scene. I opened my eyes, looked at him and then at the celebrated Folies, who were prancing along a runway out over the heads of the audience. "Huh," I said, too tired to take interest, and then went back to sleep. The Paris newspapers commented on this and *Le Matin* said: "If the Folies Bergères won't keep these American airmen awake, we wonder what will?"

'When we returned to our hotel that night, we printed the following notice and put one on each door:

PLEASE DO NOT WAKE US
UNTIL NINE O'CLOCK TO-MORROW MORNING
UNLESS THIS HOTEL IS ON FIRE;
AND NOT EVEN THEN
UNLESS THE FIREMEN HAVE GIVEN UP ALL HOPE!!

'Until now, the fastest time made across Europe and Asia was when Lieutenant D'Oisy flew from Paris to Tokio. The newspapers had been full of the marvelous speed he had made. But in flying from Tokio to Paris, we had clipped two days off D'Oisy's record.

'Moreover, from the time we had left Southern California, we had not had a single holiday. This is how we rested in Paris:

'At ten o'clock we went to the Arc de Triomphe and placed a wreath on the tomb of the Unknown Soldier. Then we started on a round of official calls, visited the President of France, attended a private luncheon and various ceremonies, went to two teas, and finally banqueted until midnight.

'Nevertheless, we did enjoy our day in Paris thoroughly. For instance, what could have been more delightful for six lieutenants than the luncheon at which we were the guests of General Pershing? As lieutenants in the army he had seemed about as far from us as the Dalai Lama of Tibet. But there in Paris he put his arms around us, told us funny stories, and proved himself a genial host and a regular fellow!

'We also met President Doumergue and liked him. Of course we had only expected to stay at the Élysée for a few minutes. But he kept us an hour, and just when we were ready to leave he said: "I am going out to meet the athletes and delegates to the Olympic Games. If you can spare the time I would feel highly honored if you would meet them also."

'So we went along and stood next to the President as he reviewed the athletes from all over the world. Afterward he said he wished to decorate us with the Legion of Honor. But Smith, in thanking him, explained that our Government would not permit us to accept foreign decorations unless it was possible to get special consent from Congress. So in place of the Legion of Honor he presented us with autographed pictures of himself, which we value very highly.

'The banquet that night was held at the Allied Club and was attended by a great crowd of military "brass hats," and other dignitaries. But we found all of these big men exceedingly easy to talk to. That seems to be one of the attributes that goes with success and high attainment.

'Next morning we went out to the airdrome at Le Bourget and prepared for the hop across the English Channel. With this flight we were to leave the mainland of Europe, and start on the most hazardous part of our journey — from Europe to North America.'

'The era of transport by air is not coming some day in the future. It is here!' says Erik Nelson, pilot of the *New Orleans*. 'Those who doubt it should have been with us at Le Bourget airdrome the morning we left Paris for London. Passenger planes were leaving for London, Brussels, Amsterdam, Lyons, and Marseilles, every few minutes.

Others were pulling out as punctually as "The Twentieth Century" from New York, or the "Olympian" from Chicago, while travelers were having their tickets punched for Amsterdam with the same bored expressions that you might see on the faces of commuters waiting for the Garden City express at Pennsylvania or the San Francisco-Oakland ferry.

'The airdrome at Le Bourget had been especially decorated in our honor. Colonel de Geys, Chief of Staff to the Under-Secretary for Aviation, Major Carlyle Wash from the American Embassy, and a number of prominent officials were there to see us off. A few moments before the time for departure, the airdrome crew rolled back the doors of the hangars and trundled our planes into the open, as nonchalantly as the brakemen on the "B.&O." might shunt a few cars. We stepped into our cockpits, warmed up our engines a bit, said au revoir to our kind hosts, and at exactly eleven o'clock we were on our way to Trafalgar Square.

'A Pathé camera-man was flying alongside us in his own plane and ground off several hundred metres of celluloid as we crossed the Channel. Three French military planes also flew with us for forty miles as an escort of honor.

'At eleven o'clock, to the second, we left with two air liners for London. Back in the year 1066 they say it took William the Conqueror a year to get his forces from France to Hastings. It took us three hours and seven minutes to fly from Paris to London and, as everybody knows, this is a daily routine experience for many people. We were considerably delayed by head winds, or we should have made the distance quicker.

'It was rather a hazy day, and before Paris dropped out of sight we encountered a great cloud-bank. We kept climbing in order to get above it, and all the rest of the way we flew at an altitude of about seven thousand feet. For nearly an hour we were above a sea of clouds that cut us off from the world below, so that it seemed as though we were somewhere far out in space, like a meteor going from one solar system to another.

'If it hadn't been for the American tourists riding in the luxurious enclosed cars of the two planes speeding alongside, we should have had nothing at all to remind us of our connection with Mother Earth. But as it happened we did have a pleasant reminder. The tourists kept waving at us, and "Hank," who is an adept at aerial sign language, kept up a running conversation by means of expressive gestures with a smart and apparently voluble "flapper" in the French express plane nearest us — voluble with her big eyes, anyway — as we sailed from one cloud-peak to another.

'When we landed outside London, we discovered that all the passengers on board the two commercial planes were Americans. The "flapper" hustled off with a severe chaperon in a Rolls-Royce and was seen no more. Then we made another discovery. Although commercial aviation has advanced far more rapidly in Europe than over here, eighty per cent of all the passengers carried on the Continent are Americans, so it seems we support aviation better in the Old World than we do in the New.

'On our way across the Channel, the clouds had parted once or twice, just enough to enable us to catch a glimpse of angry seas lashing against Cape Griz Nez and Dover. We shed a Hollywood tear as we saw them, out of sympathy for the poor travelers wallowing in the steamers below. There we were, never uncomfortable for a moment, happy as birds, and reveling in scenery as grand as the views from the tops of the Alps. Within a few years, these cross-Channel ships of horror, where you are given a basin with your deck chair will be as obsolete as the galleys of the Phœnicians.

'What Europe is doing in commercial aviation, we Americans will also be doing soon. And when we take up flying as seriously as we should, and as systematically as we certainly shall, passenger planes will cross Montana, Vermont, Arkansas, Texas, and Indiana, with the same regularity as trains now travel on the "Big Four," the Milwaukee," or the "Lackawanna." In fact, I expect to return to Chicago in a few years to find the newspapers waging an editorial campaign on behalf of the unfortunate aerial strap-hangers. And if Chicago hasn't her long promised subway by then, she may not need it after all.

'After reaching the coast of England, the clouds became thinner. We looked down through rifts and caught fleeting glimpses of the Cinque Ports, Canterbury, and the Roman road called Hare Street.

'Shortly before two, on the afternoon of the 16th of July, our eyes were gladdened by the sight of the city from which one fourth of all the human beings on earth are ruled, one of the oldest cities still inhabited by man and, strangely enough, the center of the newest experiment in world-government, the British Commonwealth of Nations.

'Much to the surprise of some of the boys, London was not enveloped in fog. Several of them thought that landing here would be like coming down in the dark. Without stopping to give Westminster Abbey the "once-over" or to see whether London Bridge was still falling down, we dived over Croydon, the airport of London, where planes leave every hour for all parts of Europe.

'When we stepped out of our cockpits at seven minutes past two, we were mobbed by photographers, and autograph collectors, for the crowd had broken through the police lines. But in ten minutes the "bobbies" had the mob corraled, and one of the first to welcome and congratulate us was Mrs. Stuart MacLaren, wife of the British world flier.

'The heads of the Royal Air Force entertained us at luncheon there on the airdrome and then took us to the R.A.F. Club, a palatial institution on Piccadilly. That evening, we were the guests of the heads of the British Air Ministry. The British, be it noted, have a special Cabinet Minister who devotes all his time to aviation, because they have long ago realized that their Air Force is of paramount importance. It was at this dinner that Leigh Wade nearly

disgraced us all. In fact I believe you will agree with me
that he actually did. It was at the table and on one side
of Leigh sat a dignified general and on the other sat Lord
somebody. Well, with a knife in one hand and a fork in
the other, Leigh fell sound asleep — and snored. Nor was
this his first offense, for you will recall that he had done
the same thing at a dinner after one of our long flights in
the Kurile Islands. But folks insisted on entertaining us,
so listening to Leigh's imitation trombone solo was the
price they paid.

'Next morning we drove back to Croydon and hopped
off northward at eleven-fifteen on our way to the famous
seaport of Hull, whence so many early navigators and explorers, not forgetting Robinson Crusoe, set sail in the
past.

'It was a delightful day, so we took a hurried glance at
the Tower of London, Saint Paul's, the Houses of Parliament, Buckingham Palace, and a few other landmarks,
including the Bush Building in the Strand: then we crossed
over the British Empire Exhibition at Wembley and flew
on with the Great North Road a ribbon of white below.
On the way, we frequently passed airplanes traveling from
one part of Britain to another. When they would spot us
from a distance they would fly up close, look us over, wave
a "cheerio," and then continue on their way.

'As we sped north, our way led across a corner of industrial England. We saw mills, iron and steel works, coal
mines, potteries, and a thousand manufacturing concerns.
It reminded me somewhat of flying over Pennsylvania from
Pittsburgh to Altoona, only there was more smoke and
dinginess over a smaller area. A thirty-mile breeze was
tickling our tail, however, and we soon passed over the
Black Country, as they call it, to the green and smiling
shire of Lincoln, with the Wash to our right, where King
John lost his laundry.

'Boston — old Boston from which our forefathers came
— is here, a little way over our starboard fuselage, and
Lincoln Cathedral is ahead, set high on its hill and girt with

'SO THIS IS PARIS?' A BIRD'S-EYE VIEW OF MONTMARTRE FROM A WORLD
CRUISER

'We circled around over Paris several times before descending on Le Bourget Aerodrome.'

ALL THE WAY ACROSS THE ENGLISH CHANNEL, OGDEN
WIGWAGGED SOFT NOTHINGS TO A FLAPPER IN A
NEIGHBORING PULLMAN PLANE

LOOKING DOWN ON THE FLAGSHIP OF THE SCUTTLED GERMAN
FLEET AT SCAPA FLOW

lawns that look from the sky like emeralds mounted in rubies and diamonds. Five hundred years of loving care has gone to make these strips of greensward, and surely the time has been well spent. On again, with a rising wind astern, over the wold-country and verdant pastures and yellow corn and meadows of purple vetch, the colors all blending into the haze of English summer and producing a lovely harmony, as if professional landscape gardeners had laid out those tiny, tidy acres.

> '"By blowing realms of woodland
> With sun-struck vanes afield
> And cloud-like shadows sailing
> About the windy weald,
>
> '"With the great gale we journey
> That breathes through gardens thinned,
> Borne on the drift of blossoms
> Whose petals throng the wind."

I still remember this flight across great little England, as something that pulls the heart-strings, I hardly know why. We flew for two hours and ten minutes from Croydon to Brough, near Hull, and during that time we had seen something of the country — or *felt* something of it — which the tourist afoot can but gradually realize. This, indeed, is the wonder of flying: in a couple of hours you may achieve a feeling-realization of what Shakespeare meant by his stately lines to "this England." Wizard as he was, it probably took William half a lifetime to figure it out: but up in the air one saw at once that England was just what he said — a "*jewel set in the silver sea.*"

'At one-ten we landed at the airdrome of the Blackburn Aviation Company, where arrangements had been made for us to stay, while we installed new engines in the planes and fitted them with pontoons for the Atlantic flight.'

CHAPTER XXVIII

FROM HULL TO SCAPA FLOW

Now that the World Flight had completed two thirds of its course, General Patrick and his advisers in Washington were anxious to eliminate every possible risk of failure by stationing destroyers along the route from the Orkney Islands to Labrador. Ahead, lay the most dangerous lap of the journey. Airplanes had never been to either Iceland or Greenland, and the Fliers were sure to encounter skies heavy with fog there and seas full of icebergs.

Originally, no plans had been made for the United States Navy to patrol this area, but as Smith and Company had broken all records in their flight across Asia and Europe and had made up seventeen days of lost time, arriving ahead of schedule in England, the Navy offered to coöperate. While Admiral Thomas P. Magruder was getting his ships in position, the airmen had thirteen days of comparative leisure in which to prepare their planes and themselves for this last and greatest exploit.

'Another reason for our delay in England,' explains 'Les' Arnold, 'was that our advance officers did not anticipate our great speed across Asia and Europe, and had encountered a great deal of trouble in finding supply bases and in landing the supplies in Iceland, Greenland, and Labrador. For instance, Lieutenant Crumrine had not yet arrived in Iceland, and Lieutenant Schultze was on his way to Angmasalik, Greenland, with gasoline and oil, on a ship from Denmark. There are few places on the planet so hard to reach as that icecap of the earth which is quaintly named Greenland.

'When we landed at Brough,' says 'Les,' 'the officials of the Blackburn Airplane Company placed their plant at our disposal. The place had once been a British training center, but since the War the Blackburns had taken over the whole establishment, including up-to-date machine shops, landing fields, hangars, workmen's quarters, officers' club, and everything that goes with a thoroughly modern aviation depot.

'We were given comfortable quarters, a special table in the club hall, and the free run of the works. Everything that men could do, the Blackburn people did for us. The younger Blackburn, Norman, stayed with us all the time and was our "man Friday." We dubbed him the "Duke of Brough" and the name evidently suited him, because all the men in the shops started using it, so that before we left, Norman Blackburn was known up and down the Humber as "'Is 'Ighness the Dook." Nor was ever a man more deserving of the title, for he was a noble host.

'We had landed on the Blackburn airdrome on the afternoon of July 17th, and before dark we had all three motors ready to lift out. The following night we were scheduled to dine with "My Lords and Ladies" at a great banquet in London, and, as by that time we were about as well equipped with clothes as the head hunters of Borneo, Smith ordered me to sprint up to London, home of sartorial perfection, and assemble a few spare parts for our wardrobe. Escorted by Major Howard C. Davidson, of our Embassy, who assured me he knew all the narrow streets where the best "West End" tailors hide, I set forth, armed with a shopping list and the family purse.

'From morn to dewy eve, I milled around between bankers, tailors, hatters, and bootmakers. Of course, the only establishments we patronized were those with signs outside reading: "Bootmakers to the Late Emperor Menelik" or "Haberdashers to the Dowager Empress of China," etc., etc. Evidently unless you can advertise that you deal with royalty — whether "late" or living doesn't matter— you might as well put up your shutters and buy a barrel organ. Why wouldn't it be a good idea to introduce this system into America? Think how effective it would be to advertise in the *Saturday Evening Post* that you are pajama-maker to the Imperial Wizard of the K.K.K. or plumber to the Grand Master of the Knights of Pythias!

'Late that afternoon, Smith and Wade joined me in London. Erik, Jack, and Hank decided to keep right on working on the planes and visit London later in the week, when we in turn would remain at Brough.

'The banquet that night was a regular high-hat spiel-fest, with Lords and Earls and Dukes accompanied by their Ladies. It was held at the Savoy Hotel, a place famous for its American jazz band. When we arrived, we went into a side room and were corraled along with a lot of people who kept talking away politely about the weather until a major-domo, with a walrus mustache and all dolled up like a musical comedy potentate, came cruising in and announced that the show was on.

'As we went down the hall, we could see past this crimson-coated "bozo" to a huge crowd in the room we were headed for. Right away, we knew what was going to happen. The "bozo" stepped forth, threw out his chest and bellowed in a voice that silenced the multitude:

'"Left-tenant Lowell H. Smith."

'Leigh and I tried to sneak in with Lowell, so that we shouldn't have to go through the same ordeal all by ourselves. But the "bozo" kept a wary eye on us. Amid tumultuous applause, Lowell walked across the floor with every eye and every eyeglass trained in his direction.

'Then came the turn of "Left-tenant Leigh Wade," and again I tried to seep through. But you couldn't fool the "bozo" in the red coat. So I had to go in and meet my fate alone, just like my brave companions. Once in a lifetime for a stunt like that is enough: just like going to the electric chair. But hot dog! — my heart bleeds for the Prince of Wales!'

Smith sat in the place of honor between the Minister for Air and the Chief Air Marshal of the Royal Air Force. 'Les' Arnold sat between Lord 'Teddy' Grosvenor and the American Ambassador. The former was to have had

charge of the British seaplane racing team that was sched-
uled to compete with the U.S. Navy planes for the
Schneider Cup in Baltimore. But an accident befell the
British team and the race was called off.

The boys were greatly impressed by the professional
toastmaster, he of the red coat, who stood behind the
celebrities at the speakers' table and introduced them in
stentorian tones. Many brilliant speeches were made, not
only praising the American airmen for what they had accomplished, but also for the help they had given Major
MacLaren. Finally the announcer roared out the following terrifying request:

'Your Excellency, my Lords, Ladies and Gentlemen,
pray silence for Left-tenant Lowell H. Smith, Commander
of the American Round-the-World Flight.'

Lowell Smith made one of his usual exceedingly brief
speeches that apparently appealed to the British, because
it was devoid of all frills. He ended by proposing a toast to
Major MacLaren.

Although the Prince of Wales did not attend this function, he happened to be dining upstairs at the Savoy with
a party of friends, and when the banquet was over he sent
word to the Fliers that he would like to meet them. So
they were escorted to his suite and there had a chat with
the Prince, who told them that he expected to visit America shortly and hoped to be on Long Island to greet
them.

After the banquet that night, the Fliers were taken on a
night trip around London by the American newspaper correspondents, caught a train back to Brough next morning,
donned their overalls, and resumed work on their planes.

While completing their work at the Blackburn plant the
managers of the establishment kept out all visitors in order
that the boys might not be bothered. The British are great
autograph collectors, and scores of people used to wait at
the gates of the Blackburn plant for the American airmen
to pass in or out. The boys did their best to dodge them,
but they agreed among themselves that whenever any one

was smart enough to catch them, they would at once grant his request.

On July 22d an accident occurred that might have had a fatal result. 'We were taking off the landing-gear and putting pontoons on the *Chicago*,' says Smith, 'and in order to do this we used a crane and a heavy chain to lift her up on the "dolly." As we had to get right in under the plane to do some work while it hung suspended in the air, we first tested the chain. It stood a strain of six and a half tons, and as the plane only weighed two and a half, we naturally thought it more than strong enough.

'We had to work in a cramped position, so several of us took turns. A moment after we had crawled out, the chain broke, and the plane crashed to the floor. Why it took a notion to break at that particular moment, we don't know. But we got a bit of a kick out of seeing those two and a half tons fall where we had been just a few seconds before. Of course, it was nobody's fault. It was just one of those things that occur without one's being able to prevent them. The pontoons were badly damaged, so we had to take them off and put on new ones. Fortunately, there was another set, the ones that had been sent from America for Major Martin's *Seattle*.

'Having heard so much about the English "Pub" and how different it was from the old American saloon, we decided to have a look at one before flying on to Iceland. The "Duke of Brough" volunteered to chaperon us on such an expedition, and took us to a famous inn at Brough, where ruddy-cheeked fishermen were sitting around drinking ale. On the walls are racks of long-stemmed clay pipes. You take one that hasn't been used, smoke it, write your name on it, and hang it back on the wall. For ever after it is yours, and they told us that no matter how many years should elapse, upon your return you would find your own pipe there. The walls are stacked with them, and their owners are those sturdy, ale-drinking, pipe-smoking sailors, slow of speech but kind of heart, who have made Britain mistress of the seven seas. Their sons apparently are seeing to it that she is not outstripped in the air.

'We each took a long white clay and smoked it with our "pint of bitter," signed it, and hung it with the hundreds of others on the walls.

'Admiral Magruder had by this time arrived in the Firth of Forth with his flagship, the *Richmond*. Instead of going up to review our plans with him, I turned over my notes and drawings to Major Davidson, who had come up from our Embassy in London, and he went to Edinburgh to confer with the Admiral, while I remained to continue working on the planes.

'On July 23d, we had been invited to a garden party at Buckingham Palace as the guests of the King and Queen. We should have been delighted to have gone, but were expecting word from Admiral Magruder every day advising us that Navy arrangements were complete to Iceland, in which case we should start at once. So we stayed in Brough and continued working on the planes.

'Our time at Brough was an interesting experience, although of course we were worried about the weather in the Arctic and extremely anxious to get through the ice when it was possible to fly by way of Greenland. Out in the country where we were, the ozone-laden breezes blowing in from the North Sea were a superb tonic after our experiences in Asia. And the food was wonderful — marmalade and oatcakes for breakfast, and "cuts off the joint" for lunch and dinner: two things the English cook well, if nothing else, are their superb sirloins and their Southdown mutton. We enjoyed being at Brough so thoroughly that, outside of the one trip each of us made to London, we had no desire to go anywhere, until preparations were complete for us to fly to the Orkneys.

'Late on the afternoon of July 24th we were driven to the home of Mr. Robert Blackburn, head of the airplane factory where we were doing our work. This was on the outskirts of the city of Leeds, some forty miles away. Leeds is a city larger than San Francisco, and another of

England's great industrial centers. General Branker, the Air Vice-Marshal of England, arrived at the airdrome just as we were leaving, and accompanied us. This little holiday gave us a glimpse into the life of the wealthy English country gentleman of whom we had heard so much. Nor is there any doubt but what they really do know how to get a lot of enjoyment out of life. '

'Mr. Blackburn's home was a rambling, English country mansion, with enormous rooms, cozy dens, an aviary, conservatory, tennis lawns, and putting greens. Near by were kennels for the hounds used in fox-hunting. By the way, to call these noble animals that chase the wary fox by the common or garden term of "dog" is about the worst blunder a foreigner in England can make. When being shown the precious hounds, you look wise and say, 'A nice, even-looking lot! Plenty of bone and breeding, what?' This shows you to be a person of discrimination.

'On our way back to the plant next morning we drove through the quaint streets of York, and stopped a moment to see the Cathedral, where the second Archbishop of the Church of England has his See.

'On Monday, several of us went to Hull, visited the place where the ill-fated British dirigible fell into the river, killing thirty-five British and American officers, and spent the day buying heavy clothing for the flight to Iceland. Tuesday the 29th we devoted to cleaning up the final details, with the expectation of "hopping off" next day.

'Wednesday morning, July 30th, we were up at four o'clock, launched the planes down the runway into the Humber, and took on a load of "gas" and oil. There was a low fog hanging over the coast, so it was not until ten-fifteen that we got away. With the *Boston* and *New Orleans* close behind, I headed the *Chicago* out over the North Sea.

'North of Montrose, the clouds had kept forcing us down until we could go no farther, so we climbed up over them and for an hour we flew without so much as seeing a glimpse of heather or the banks and braes of bonny Scot-

ONE FOR ALL AND ALL FOR ONE

Left to right: Leigh, Erik, 'Les,' 'Hank,' Smith, and 'Jack'

THE WIFE OF THE BRITISH WORLD FLIER CONGRATULATES
THE AMERICANS AT CROYDON AERODROME
Left to right: Ogden, Arnold, Harding, Smith, Wade, Nelson, Mrs. MacLaren

BOBBIES HOLDING BACK THE CROWD WHILE WADE SIGNS HIS
NAME FOR THE THOUSANDTH TIME

SIGHT-SEEING IN THE ORKNEYS

SMITH, ERIK, AND LEIGH PREPARING FOR THE
FLIGHT TO ICELAND AND GREENLAND

land. But I did see a Scottish castle that caught my fancy. It was built on a promontory jutting right out into the sea. On three sides were sheer cliffs with the waves from the North Sea pounding against them, and on the land side was a high wall. When I'm a millionaire, I shall buy it. What little we did see of Scotland fascinated us. All the way 'round the world we had encountered Scotsmen — hard-bitten, clear-thinking Empire-builders. They are scattered more widely even than Jews and whether they are beach-combers or "burra-sahibs," they are always the same canny, blue-eyed children of the "land o' cakes."

> '"What though on hamely fare we dine,
>   Wear hodden gray an' a' that;
>   Gie fools their silks and knaves their wine,
>   A Man's a Man for a' that!"

'Our longest water hop on this flight was for eighty miles to Dunkensberry Point. From there we flew on to Scapa Flow, where the Germans surrendered, and then scuttled, their fleet. We were now in the Orkney Islands, the place where some of the British and American fleets based throughout the final years of the World War. At the northern edge of Scapa Flow is Houten Bay, where the British had a war-time airplane base, near the fishing city of Kirkwall, which we decided to use. The U.S.S. *Richmond* waited for us just outside the little bay.

'At last we were on the edge of the North Atlantic, all set for the adventure ahead.'

CHAPTER XXIX

THE FLIGHT TO ICELAND AND
THE SINKING OF THE BOSTON

'THERE was so much fog hanging over the Orkneys and Faroes the day after our arrival at Scapa Flow, and the ships stationed between us and Iceland reported such bad weather, that we had to give up all hope of flying that day,' says Jack Harding. 'There wasn't anything we could do about it, so we decided to take a launch and cruise about among the half-submerged hulks of the scuppered German Fleet.

'With some naval officers and newspaper correspondents we landed on the derelict *Hindenburg*. We climbed up the masts and from the tops of them looked down through the clear water and saw every part of the German Dreadnought. There were two great guns on the stern. Leigh walked out on one, while "Les" and I balanced ourselves on the other. Then we made a bet with Leigh that he couldn't jump across to where we were. Leigh is always ready to take a dare, and he almost made it. But he fell into the sea, clothes and all, and had to be hauled out.

'The Orkney Islands are nearly as far off the beaten path as the Aleutians on the other side of the world, and they are in about the same latitude, away up near the sixtieth parallel. Who the original inhabitants of these islands were, no man seems to know. But when the Vikings came from Scandinavia in the eighth century, they found the ruins of an ancient civilization here in which stones weighing from four to eight tons had been used. Ever since the eighth century the Orkneys have been inhabited by descendants of Norsemen. The islanders use peat for fuel, for there are practically no trees. The majority make their living catching herring, cod, ling, and lobsters, while the Orcadian women are world-famed for the shawls and sweaters they weave during the long winter nights. In Kirkwall, you can buy a Fair Isle jersey for from six to ten dollars, which would cost six times as much in America.'

'It was not until Saturday, August 2d,' continued Arnold, 'that the weather cleared sufficiently to warrant our attempting the hop to Iceland. At 8.34 A.M. we set out by way of the Faroe Islands. Hardly ten minutes out of Kirkwell we ran into thick fog. Although we came down as low as five feet off the water, we couldn't escape it. Then it cleared for a moment and we plunged into a heavy rain squall: beyond, we again met fog. Climbing up to about twenty-five hundred feet, we got above both fog and rain. Looking around for the others, we saw the *Boston,* but there was no sign of the *New Orleans.*

'For twenty minutes we circled round wondering whether Erik and Jack had flown on or whether they had met with an accident and fallen into the water. Lowell finally decided that the safest thing to do would be to turn back and report at Kirkwall, so that the destroyers could start a search. If Erik and Jack were actually lost, and if we flew on to Iceland, the boats might hear nothing of the accident for six or eight hours, until we reached our destination. If, on the other hand, they had passed safely through the fog, then a report would be sent back to us as they flew over the Faroe Islands and we could follow next day.

'So we turned back and hunted for the cruiser *Richmond,* which we knew to be following along our course. But in the fog we missed her. As we flew over the city of Kirkwall, where Major Davison from our Embassy was stopping, we dropped a message bag in one of the streets so that he could telephone to the wireless station and have the news sent to the *Richmond* and other boats. Then we returned to our moorings at Houten Bay, and landed.

'A few hours later, we learned that the *New Orleans* had been sighted passing over the Faroes, and at six that night the *Richmond* returned to the Orkneys. A little later the following wireless message came through from Iceland:

> Got into propeller wash in the fog, went into a spin, partially out of control, came out of it just above water. Continued on, landing at Hornafjord. All O.K.
>
> NELSON

'We were overjoyed at hearing they had got through to Iceland. Later, we learned that they had had a narrow escape.'

Erik Nelson tells the story of their flight:

'After losing sight of the *Chicago* and *Boston* in the fog, the weather became so thick that we could see nothing six inches from the cockpit. But we felt ourselves being jerked and thrown about and knew that we had got into the propeller wash of one of the other ships. This threw the plane out of control, and once one loses equilibrium in a fog, it is very difficult to regain it. With fog everywhere there was no basis of comparison and it was difficult to tell whether we were flying north, south, east, west, up or down. An instant later, my instruments indicated that we were descending in a spin at great speed.

'Finally we managed to straighten her out. Not a minute too soon. As we pulled level, we shot into a clear spot, and from then on we were lucky enough to be able to fly under the fog until we were entirely out of it. Once clear, we flew back and forth for a time, hoping the other planes would show up. When they failed to appear, we climbed higher, and after flying for three hours over another fogbank we saw something black jutting up through the clouds. It was Sydero Island.

'Twenty-five miles farther on, the fog ended abruptly, the sky became perfectly clear, and straight ahead we sighted the smoke of the first destroyer we had encountered. Gliding down, Jack wrote a note asking them if they could give us any news regarding the other planes and requesting them to verify the direction of the course ahead of us. We flew right across the bow of the destroyer, but the first message bag fell into the sea. The second time we had better luck, and a moment later we had our signals, as well as the news that no other planes had passed that way.

'Proceeding on our way, we passed the cruiser *Raleigh* and then encountered another fog belt that hid the sea all the rest of the flight to Iceland. This prevented us from even seeing whether there were any more boats patrolling for us or not. As we neared the coast the weather cleared again, and right ahead we saw the tiny village of Hornafjord, surrounded by somber mountains and great glaciers. As soon as we had moored the plane (we had descended at 5.37 P.M.), we hurried ashore, where we found some of the naval men from the *Raleigh* who had been left there to rig up a temporary radio station. Here we waited for the *Chicago* and *Boston* to join us.'

Anxious to catch up with the *New Orleans* that had reached Iceland after their miraculous escape from death in the fog, the other boys were up early next morning. From the appearance of the sky at Kirkwall it was an ideal day for flying, and at 9.30 the *Chicago* and *Boston* took-off from Scapa Flow, and amid the cranking of movie cameras, the shrill whistles of steamers, and the cheers of Orkney fishermen, they were off again for Iceland.

'There was a stiff breeze on our tail and we were clipping off a hundred miles an hour,' says 'Les' Arnold. 'Leigh always flew at our right, keeping the *Boston* a few yards astern of us, so that I could easily check his position.

'But at eleven o'clock I glanced round and the *Boston* had vanished. She had been in her usual place just a moment before. So we looked around to the left and there we saw Leigh and "Hank" turning back, heading into the wind, and gliding for a landing on the ocean.

'We, of course, turned immediately, circled as close as we dared, and watched them land. In spite of a long swell and mountainous waves, Leigh brought her down perfectly. Flying low to get her signals, we saw oil on the water and all over the plane.

'Leigh signaled frantically for us not to land. Because of the swell he figured that if we came down beside him we should never get off again, and then we should both be helpless in the middle of the ocean. But we did hate to leave them sitting out there in that remote part of the North Atlantic. However, after circling round once or twice we headed off on our course and flew with the throttle wide open to the nearest destroyer, which was over a hundred miles away, near the Faroe Islands.

'As we passed over the Faroes we saw a telegraph line, which we followed around Sydero Island until we came to a village where we dropped a message. A bit north of the Faroes we picked up the *Billingsby*. But before we reached her, Lowell had written two notes, each identical, describing Wade's mishap, the peril he and Ogden were in, their exact location, time of landing, and the condition of both sea and wind, so that the naval officers could estimate how far the wind might blow them in the interval before a rescue could be effected.

'The first note we put in a message bag and dropped on the *Billingsby*, but she was making fully twenty knots and I missed her deck by several yards. We had only one note left, and every moment was precious. It was imperative that this one should get to the destroyer, so I tied it to my one and only life preserver. When I dropped it this time, I again missed the deck, but a sailor dived overboard and fished it out of the sea.

'The note ended with a request that if they understood our message and were ready to start at once to the rescue, they were to give us three blasts from the whistle. We circled around, saw the captain seize the message, read it, and run across the deck. A moment later we saw three long streaks of steam coming from the whistle, and almost at the same moment clouds of smoke poured from the funnels, and the destroyer shot ahead like a greyhound whose leash has been slipped. Never have I seen a vessel jump into high speed so quickly. Later we learned that she had traveled so fast she burnt all the paint off her stacks.

'As she raced through the sea at thirty-one knots, the captain wirelessed to the cruiser *Richmond* and the latter immediately started to the rescue also, at a speed of thirty-three knots.

'We now returned to our course, and from here on to Iceland flew through light rain and fog. In order to see the water, we had to fly fifty feet off it for over three hundred miles. But the wind was still with us and we continued to average a hundred miles an hour. Through mist and rain we flew over the cruiser *Raleigh*, and, although he had no way of checking our compass course, Lowell piloted us right in to Hornafjord. After we had moored alongside the *New Orleans*, Erik and Jack pitched in and helped us "service-up," while crowds of Icelanders came out in rowboats propelled by funny-shaped oars.

'There on shore, in a large fisherman's hut, with a background of grim mountains, a smoking volcano, and five glaciers, we anxiously waited for news of Wade and Ogden.'

Leigh Wade, in describing the misfortune that befell the *Boston*, declares that everything had seemed ideal for a quick trip to Iceland until the moment that the accident occurred. Their trouble came like a bolt from the blue.

'All of a sudden I noticed the oil pressure going down. In a few seconds it dropped to zero. So there was nothing to do but land at once. Our altitude at that moment was approximately five hundred feet, so I had no difficulty in turning and landing into the wind.

'When we reached the water, I discovered how deceitful the sea is when you are above it. At five hundred feet it had looked fairly smooth. But when we landed, we found it so rough that the left pontoon nearly wrapped itself around the lower wing, and snapped two of the vertical wires.

'At first I thought the oil tank had burst and let the entire supply drop out. But it was still full. So we knew that our trouble was due to the failure of the oil pump. This meant that our repairs could not be made at sea.

'Smith and "Les" were circling around us, and I was afraid that they might land and crack up also. That was why we signaled so emphatically for them to stay in the air. We indicated to them that our engine had failed, that our repairs could not be made at sea, and that they should go on.

'The first thing we did, after they had left, was to fasten the anchor to the bridle and heave it overboard. We hadn't been bobbing up and down on the waves for many minutes before we discovered what a nasty business it is to be in mid-ocean on a fragile plane with the waves hitting her at right angles. Soon we both grew dizzy. But we realized that unless the vertical wires were repaired, the ship might not ride out the sea until help arrived. So we managed to crawl onto the wing and get them fixed. Then, climbing back into our cockpits, we settled down for a little rest, "rocked on the bosom of the deep," as the song says.

'Our oil pump could hardly have picked out a more remote spot in which to let us down, for we were just about midway between the nearest points from which help might come. Knowing the approximate locations of both the *Billingsby* and the *Richmond*, Ogden and I decided that the very earliest we might expect help would be late in the afternoon. Of course, if fog settled down over us, there would be no telling when we should be picked up. So we decided not to drink our meager supply of fresh water, and not to eat our emergency rations until driven to do so by hunger.

'It was exactly 10.56 A.M. when we landed on the water. Two hours went by, during which time we saw no living thing, not even a porpoise — only those cold, gray swells that kept us from having a moment's peace.

'The first sign of life was a seagull. "Hank" remarked that we surely must be near land or the bird would not be

FRESH FROM THE TRIUMPHS OF THE
PACIFIC, WADE LITTLE DREAMED
OF THE TROUBLE HE WAS TO EN-
COUNTER ON THE WAY TO ICELAND

WADE AND OGDEN AWAITING RESCUE IN THE NORTH ATLANTIC

THE SINKING OF THE BOSTON

WHEN ERIK NELSON GOT THROUGH THE
FOG AND FLEW ON TO ICELAND HE HAD
AMPLE REASON TO SMILE

AT REYKJAVIK THE NEW ORLEANS WAS LIFTED OUT OF THE
WATER AND OVERHAULED IN THE STREET OF ICELAND'S
CAPITAL CITY

SUPPLY SHIPS THAT LEFT FUEL FOR THE FLIERS ALONG THE
COAST OF GREENLAND

there, but I assured him, sadly, that gulls fly many hundreds of miles out to sea.

'Nevertheless, it was comforting to have that lone gull around. As we drifted about, the waves would carry us away from it, but when we had gone about fifty yards, it would hop off the water and moor beside us again, as if it also wanted friends in those bleak solitudes.

'I urged "Hank" to get a bit of sleep, because I knew we might have to take turns watching all through the night. So he curled up in his cockpit while I kept a lookout. About two o'clock, away off to starboard I saw a wisp of smoke. Shouting to "Hank," I crawled out on the top wing and waved a sheet of canvas, while he fired flares with the Véry pistol. Although this boat remained in sight for half an hour, and although we signaled frantically all that time, our efforts were in vain and she sank below the horizon without seeing us.

'Up to this moment our spirits had been high. We had felt sure that it would not be long before a boat would pick us up. But now we realized that a ship has to be fairly close in order to see a speck such as we were, bobbing about on twenty-foot waves. A drizzly rain and fog started closing in on us from the northwest and the wind was picking up fast. So we began to wonder just what our fate was going to be. Never in our lives had either of us felt so lonesome, so helpless. Had we been in mid-ocean in a rowboat, it wouldn't have been so bad because then we at least could have kept our bodies warm and our minds occupied by rowing.

'Although the rain and wind were coming from the north and west, we knew they might shift any moment. So, of course, it was impossible to tell where we might drift. It had been our custom to cut our maps into strips and roll them so they would be easy to handle in the cockpit as we flew. They were large scale, and whenever flying over thoroughly explored regions showed every village, mountain, stream, or other landmark. The strip we had along on this hop to Iceland included nothing but the

Orkneys, the Faroes, and the eastern end of Iceland. So we could only make a rough guess as to how far we were from the nearest mainland.

'We now did a thing that caused the rest of the fellows afterward to dub us the world's greatest optimists. "Hank" climbed out of his cockpit, hung on to the edge of it with one hand, opened the tool compartment, and ferreted out a very small-scale National Geographic Society map of the world which we had carried all the way with us. On this map we measured off the distance we were from the coast of Norway, and calculated that with favorable winds we might possibly exist until we drifted to those shores, providing, of course, that we could keep the plane intact that long.

'But within a very few minutes after we had come to this satisfactory conclusion, the weather changed for the worse. The sea became increasingly choppy, and it looked as though the wings would dip under the waves and buckle up at any moment.

'Hour after hour went by. The gull left us. There was nothing now but the expanse of water all round us and the gray bowl of the Arctic sky. We said very little, but we did a lot of thinking. I saw in imagination the faces of my relatives and intimate friends.

'Finally I saw something real — another wisp of smoke away on the rim of the horizon. This time we were determined that it should not get away from us. Yanking one of the wooden supports from the back of the fuselage, we attached a strip of fabric to it and with a few tacks improvised a flag that was lighter and easier to wave than the heavy canvas we had used in vain earlier in the afternoon.

'"Hank" climbed out on the upper wing with it and started wig-wagging furiously. We wondered whether the ship would turn out to be the cruiser *Richmond* or merely a passing fishing boat. Fortunately, it was headed in our direction, and as it drew nearer we saw that it was a trawler.

'But in order to make quite sure that it saw us, I got out the flares, and also fired a few shots with our rifle while

"Hank" kept on wig-wagging. You can't imagine the feeling of relief when we saw that they had noticed our signals and were coming toward us.

'The trawler proved to be the *Rugby-Ramsey*, and as she came alongside at three-thirty, somewhat to our amazement her skipper shouted out:

'"Do you want any help?"

'"Well, I should say we do!" I replied.

'"What kind of help?" asked the old fisherman.

'"Throw us a tow line," said I.

'But there was such a stiff wind blowing by now that it was extremely difficult for us to talk back and forth. We shouted to them to come astern and throw a line overboard on floats, so that we could drift along and pick it up without danger of colliding with the trawler. But instead, they attempted to come closer and toss us the line. Of course, they were not aware of the speed with which our light plane was drifting. A moment later, as they wallowed in the sea, we rode up to the crest of a wave and the whole of our fuselage was suspended over their stern. We yelled for them to push us away, but fortunately, as we both bobbed up out of the trough of the wave, we were carried one way and the trawler the other.

'The captain of the trawler then saw for himself how to pass us the line. This time he attached it to a float which he threw over and towed around in a circle until he dragged it near enough for "Hank" to fish it out of the water.

'By good luck we had come down near the course that is taken by fishing boats plying between the Orkneys and Faroes. The latter islands were the nearer, so the trawler attempted to tow us toward them. But each time the trawler went up on a wave, she seemed to stand still and at these moments the *Boston* would swing round and head into the wind according to the natural instincts of a plane. Then, when the trawler would shoot off from the crest of the swell, the poor old *Boston* would get a jerk that would make her shiver from nose to tail. Frequently the pontoons would be yanked right under the water.

'After a half-hour of this, the trawler found that she wasn't making any headway, so they stopped towing and simply stood by awaiting the arrival of one of our destroyers. In a little while the *Billingsby* arrived and we cast adrift from the *Rugby-Ramsey* in order to pick up the destroyer's line. Then a few minutes later the *Richmond* raced up. Again we switched over, and in transferring to the Admiral's cruiser one of our wings dipped under a wave and the ribs of the trailing edge popped like the crackle of a machine gun.

'Pulling alongside the *Richmond*, we drained off all the "gas" and oil, to lighten her before attempting to hoist her to the deck. The sling was dropped down from the crane, and, after attaching it, we went aboard in order still further to lighten her. Our spirits were high again. We foresaw no difficulty in the way of hoisting the *Boston* on board, and of then returning to Kirkwall for repairs.

'The signal was given and I can recall the feeling of joy that swept over me as I saw our beloved plane rising off the water. Then the crash came. The tackle was wrenched loose from the main mast, and the plane fell. Fortunately all the sailors had cleared away from underneath and no one was injured. Our task now was to keep her afloat because the fall had broken the pontoons. Men went aboard at once with veneer, fabric, and "dope" to make emergency patches while others operated the bilge pump. We took everything loose off the plane, such as baggage, tools, and spare parts, and also decided to disassemble her by sawing off the wings and pontoons before attempting to hoist the fuselage onto the deck.

'But fate was against us. The wind had been increasing in violence and it soon became impossible to work on the plane. She tossed so violently that it looked for a bit as though the men on her were going to lose their lives. One of them did get carried overboard, but two of his companions seized him before he had been carried away. Then they all returned to the cruiser, and we saw that our only chance was to attempt to tow her to a lee shore in the Faroes and disassemble her there.

'After we came on board the *Richmond*, the officers urged us to have some food, as we had fasted all day. But we were too anxious about the plane to be interested in anything else. However, they brought coffee to us on deck, and it bucked us up a lot.

'As we started to tow her, "Hank" and I remained astern to watch. We had very little hope that in such a rough sea she would be able to stay afloat until reaching the Faroes. We watched in silence until nearly midnight, and as she had survived the gale so far we decided she might pull through and went below.

'There were many newspaper men on board and they realized how we felt about our accident, and not one of them bothered us with a single question that night. It was very decent of them.

'Shortly after five o'clock I was aroused and told that the plane had capsized. This had occurred after the front spreader bar had broken loose and allowed the pontoons to come together. All of the tanks had been left open in the event of just this sort of thing happening, so they would fill with water and cause the plane to sink instead of drifting about as a menace to shipping.

'When this occurred we were within a mile of land — so near and yet so far! Alas, we were forced to abandon her, and at 5.30 A.M. we cut the tow lines, bade farewell to our friend who had carried us so far round the globe, and headed for Iceland with heavy hearts.'

CHAPTER XXX

FROM ICELAND TO GREENLAND
EIGHT HUNDRED AND THIRTY–FIVE MILES
OVER THE ARCTIC ICE–PACK

WHEN Smith received Wade's wireless that the *Boston* had gone down after all efforts to save her had failed, there was mourning at Hornafjord, for the boys knew how 'Leigh' and 'Hank' were feeling after coming twenty thousand miles round the world and then losing the *Boston* through no fault of their own. They realized also that nothing but blind chance had prevented the accident happening to one of them. In England, where they had changed motors, Wade and Ogden happened to be the first to get their plane ready to install the new engine. Four new motors lay there on the floor of the Blackburn aircraft factory, and as luck would have it Wade selected the one that failed. Just where the weakness developed will never be known, but the probability is that the oil pump shaft broke, thus preventing the oil from circulating.

. . . .

'There are no hotels in Hornafjord, so Lieutenant Crumrine, the advance officer, had rented a fisherman's bunkhouse for us to live in,' says 'Les' Arnold. 'Blankets and canned food had been provided. But the cruiser *Raleigh* was anchored twenty-five miles offshore, unable to get in on account of shallow water, and her commander sent a number of men to stay with us, cook our meals, help us refuel, and keep us in touch with the world by means of a portable radio.

'The night of August 4th we spent a few hours at the home of the leading citizen, listening to Mr. Danielson's six flaxen-haired daughters, dressed in native costume, sing old Icelandic songs. They were all charming, but we were thinking far too much about "Leigh" and "Hank"

to enjoy ourselves as we should have done. Next morning
at 9.12 we got away for Reykjavik, the capital of the island. Although the run was only about two hundred and
ninety miles, we had to buck such a stiff head wind that at
times we were barely creeping through the sky, and at one
point we had the strange experience of flying through a
dust storm away up here where we had only expected to
encounter snow. We followed the coast line most of the
way from Hornafjord to Reykjavik, but on account of
clouds of vapor we missed seeing many of the volcanoes
for which Iceland is famous.

'However, it was far from being a monotonous trip, for
we passed many glaciers, and saw along the rocky shore-
line scores of wrecked ships piled up by the angry seas
that lash this coast.

'What amazed us chiefly were the well-tilled fields over
which we flew. It seemed as though we surely must be
flying over Europe. Those neat farms with their crops
and grazing cattle failed to fit in with our preconceived
idea of Iceland, but the truth is that one's preconceived
notions about the Arctic are frequently wrong. Being in
the course of the Gulf Stream, Iceland enjoys a climate
rather like that of Scotland.

'As we approached Reykjavik, a few minutes after two,
we could tell at a glance that we were going to be out of
luck if obliged to come down in the outer harbor, for no
plane could survive such seas as were sweeping in from
the somber Atlantic. Our buoys had been placed in the
shelter of an immense breakwater, and by clever handling
on the part of Lowell and Erik the planes were landed in
this sheltered area among the hundreds of boats that had
taken refuge there. Crumrine was waiting in the outer
harbor for us and was surprised to see us land in such a
small area.

'Along the breakwater wall the population of Reykjavik, some twenty-five thousand people, were waiting to
give us a lusty welcome. Not many minutes after we had
moored, in steamed the *Richmond* with our unlucky com-

panions, Wade and Ogden. They immediately put off in
a launch and joined us on the dock while we were being
welcomed by the Prime Minister of Iceland. Poor old
Wade put his arms around Lowell and his eyes filled with
tears. Although we were overjoyed at seeing them again,
there were lumps in our throats as we thought of their
hard luck and the fate of the *Boston*.

'The Prime Minister drove us to a beautiful residence
which he said was to be ours during our stay in Reykjavik.
Next day, however, in spite of this hospitality, we felt
obliged to move in to the hotel near to the beach, where
we could keep an eye on the planes and be ready to dash
out to them at a moment's notice. In addition to our two
air cruisers there were five American men-of-war in port
with some twenty-five hundred sailors on board. So we
were responsible for a veritable American invasion of Iceland. Up to this time, according to the inhabitants, no
Yankee warship had ever visited them. So crowded were
the streets and docks with our sailors, and so numerous
were the newspaper reporters who roamed about looking
for news stories in likely and unlikely places, that Reykjavik seemed just like a New England port during maneuvers.

'Next day, while waiting for wireless reports from Advance Officer Le Clair Schultze, regarding the ice along the
coast of Greenland, we wandered around the town. We
had expected to find it a village of natives. On the contrary, we found that we were in a city inhabited by people
of Scandinavian descent; a modern city with well-paved
streets attractively illuminated by electric-light clusters.
Instead of igloos of ice, we found good hotels, banks,
clubs, and shops. Instead of eating blubber, the inhabitants sup in cafés. Instead of spearing seals for sport,
they patronize a *palais de danse* and the movies. Under
these circumstances we thought we might celebrate our
first Icelandic evening with a haircut and manicure. Lo
and behold! the versatile manicurists chatted with us in
English! And on our way back to the hotel we had to

OVER 'GREENLAND'S ICY MOUNTAINS'

LOCATELLI'S ILL-FATED MONOPLANE

AFTER THREE DAYS AND FOUR NIGHTS ADRIFT, THE SEARCHLIGHT OF
THE RICHMOND PICKED UP THE ITALIAN PLANE

The rescued Italian aviators were Lieutenants Antonio Locatelli, Tullio Crosio,
Giovanni Branni, and Bruno Farcinelli

THE CHICAGO AND THE NEW ORLEANS MOORED IN THE ICEBERG-INFESTED HARBOR AT FRED-
RICKSDAL JUST AFTER COMPLETING THE LONG AND HAZARDOUS FLIGHT FROM ICELAND TO
GREENLAND

ESKIMO AWAITING THE ARRIVAL OF THE FIRST AIRPLANES EVER TO VISIT
GREENLAND

watch our step to keep from being run down by taxis, just as if we were in Paris or New York.

'The people, because of their Norse origin, have blue eyes, and the girls of Iceland are simply stunning: the bear's growl of nifty flapperism. No "parkas" and "mukluks" for them — their styles come direct from the Rue de la Paix and the Rue Royale.

'Since our return to America, friends sometimes ask whether we didn't suffer away up there near the North Pole. To which our answer is, "Yes, we suffered, for in all Reykjavik there wasn't a single solitary brunette!"

'Of course Erik was in his element. He talks Swedish and Danish with the same ease and enthusiasm as English, and the Icelanders seemed to appreciate the fact that one of our number was Viking-bred, like themselves. And the way that boy went svenskaing about was a joy to behold!

'As to the climate, it was delightful. Up there on the edge of the Arctic Circle there is less snow and ice in winter than in St. Louis or Denver. In the future, when asked to name some place to escape the rigors of a Chicago winter, we are going to suggest as a substitute for Florida or California that they try Iceland!

'The island is affiliated with Denmark. Although the Prime Minister receives his appointment direct from Copenhagen Iceland has home rule and is virtually independent, except that the King of Denmark is also King of Iceland. One of the first functions we attended was a luncheon which the Prime Minister gave for Admiral Magruder, his staff, and the six of us. We at first felt uncomfortably conspicuous at this gathering because we were the only ones unable to attend in uniform. We had to appear in the working togs of the cavalry of the clouds, and our breeches and khaki shirts, which were a distinct blot on the landscape in the midst of all those naval officers in their resplendent full dress. But we had a rollicking good time and voted Iceland a great success.

'While we were in Reykjavik a forty-foot boat, the

Leif Erickson, arrived with four men, a Swede, an Englishman, and two Americans. They were attempting to
follow the original route taken by Leif Erickson centuries
ago when he crossed to North America. We found them
an interesting and picturesque quartette of adventurers,
and we all went down to see them off when they sailed
away in their cockleshell for the coast of Greenland. On
our return to America, we learned that they got as far as
the west coast of Greenland but that no one ever saw or
heard anything of them afterward. However they were resourceful men and we haven't yet given up hope.

'Our thirteen days in Iceland were irksome in one respect: we were anxious to get on. But we kept receiving
adverse reports from the *Gertrude Rask,* the Danish boat
on which Lieutenant Schultze was trying to land our supplies of gas and oil on the coast of Greenland. First we
heard she was stuck in the ice about forty miles from
Angmasalik. Later we received a wireless from Schultze
saying that she was fast running out of coal.

'We had arranged an elaborate system of checking the
weather between Iceland and Greenland. Every hour,
both day and night, we received radio messages giving the
barometric pressure, temperature, wind-velocity and direction, and also the condition of the sea. We made up large
charts on which we recorded all of these reports, and in
this way were able to trace the direction and speed of
every storm. Smith, Nelson, and Crumrine were constantly on the job, ready to seize any opportunity for the
Flight to proceed. But so far as the coast of Greenland was
concerned, our chance to get to Angmasalik never did
come.

'All this time we were going over every inch of our
planes, making sure that they were in shipshape for the
long jumps ahead. We cut down weight to bare essentials,
even leaving out many tools and abandoning all clothing
except what we had on.

'Admiral Magruder and Smith held a conference about
this time and decided to send the cruiser *Raleigh* recon-

noitering to see whether some other harbor on the east coast of Greenland might do. Wade, who, of course, knew our requirements, went along, and there were also two small scout planes on the *Raleigh*.

'Our next message from Schultze said that the *Gertrude Rask* had finally broken through the ice and reached her destination. This was a great relief to us and somewhat surprised the newspaper men, who had become decidedly pessimistic and were laying wagers that the Flight would have to be abandoned. I believe that only the Washington *Star* correspondent, out of all the reporters, still had faith that we would finish the trip.

'The original plan had been to fly direct across the Atlantic from Iceland to Angmasalik. The distance was about five hundred miles, and except for the last fifty or seventy-five miles over the Greenland ice belt we would have had open ocean under us. From Angmasalik the plan was to make a second five hundred mile hop, over sea and ice-fields, skirting Greenland as far as Ivigut, away around on the western coast. This had been decided upon in Washington, where it was known that supply ships usually could get through the ice-field toward the end of August. But 1924 turned out to be a very bad year for ice.

'Although Schultze had wirelessed that his supply ship had at last crept through the seventy-mile ice belt, he had added that it would be impossible for us to alight on the water in the harbor at Angmasalik owing to the drifting bergs that would be sure to wreck the shell-like pontoons of any plane.

'Meanwhile the *Raleigh* had radioed that she was bucking fifty-mile gales en route to Greenland in search of another harbor on the east coast, so we gave up all hope of finding any base on the nearer side of ice-bound Greenland and laid plans for a far longer flight, around to Fredricksdal, eight hundred and thirty-five miles distant on Davis Strait, facing Labrador. It was a long chance, more dangerous even than an attempt to fly straight across the Atlantic in one leap from France or England, because we were entirely off the line of steamship travel in case of trouble, we were in the region of fogs and gales, and we were on the edge of the Arctic in the land of ice. But it was our only chance now unless we abandoned the Flight and let the newspaper men win their bets.

'In the meantime, on August 11th, the advance agent of an Italian Flight had arrived, and shortly after midday on the 16th, Signor Locatelli, a former lieutenant in the Italian air service, an ace with a brilliant war record for bravery and daring, and a member of the Chamber of Deputies in Rome, arrived in Hornafjord from the Faroe Islands in a super-flying boat, a sister to the two planes to be used later by Amundsen and Ellsworth on their attempt to reach the North Pole. On August 17th, while Admiral Magruder's squadron was getting into position between Iceland and Fredricksdal, Locatelli reached Reykjavik. We were much impressed by his business-like, twin-motored monoplane with its all-metal hull. It appeared to be the most efficient plane for long-distance flying that we had ever seen, and Lieutenants Locatelli and Crozio and their two assistants were dashing fellows.

'The following morning we were up before dawn, out on the planes, waiting for favorable wireless reports. At ten o'clock fairly good news came, and at ten-fifteen we taxied to the outer harbor and attempted to take-off. There was not a breath of wind, but the swells were so great and the planes were so heavily loaded with fuel — more heavily than ever before — that we were unable to rise. The propeller on the *New Orleans*, struck by a roller, snapped in two. A wave hit the *Chicago* and ripped loose the front spreader bar. Both planes had a great many wires loosened while careening over the combers, so we were reluctantly obliged to return to our moorings.

'At dinner that evening, Lieutenant Crumrine, the advance officer for us as far as Iceland, a man noted for his quiet manner and his desire to keep in the background, astonished us, as well as the Icelanders, by appearing in the main café wearing a flaming red shirt. He told us

he was " going Bolshie" if flying conditions didn't improve.

'On the night of the 19th of August, we entertained the
Italian crew, and Smith invited them to fly with us so they
too could have the protection of our American cruisers and
destroyers. Locatelli of course was delighted and immediately accepted.

'We worked all the next day, and it was not until 2.30
A.M. on the morning of August 21st that we finally finished
repairing our planes with the spare parts which the *Richmond* had just brought back to us. She had started for
Greenland with them on board. As we were returning to
the hotel, a sheaf of radiograms was handed to us announcing that weather conditions were at last favorable. So
without a moment's sleep or rest that night, we climbed
into our cockpits and at 6.55 set out for Greenland on the
longest and most hazardous "hop" of all, a flight that was
to overshadow all previous experiences on our way around
the world.

'As a result of Lowell's invitation to Locatelli, the
Italians took-off with us. Their plane was totally different
from ours. In addition to being heavier, it was much faster.
Locatelli did his best to fly with us, and for a time kept
circling and stalling in order to do so. But this apparently
grew irksome to him. He knew that, if all went well, he
could get through to Greenland several hours ahead of us.

'So he finally shot past us, and the last we ever saw of his
big speedy monoplane was when it vanished over the
horizon ahead. When we reached Fredricksdal, after one
of the most trying experiences of our lives, we discovered
that Locatelli was lost.'

Strung out between Iceland and Greenland, about one
hundred and twenty-five miles apart, were five American
ships, the cruiser *Richmond*, with Rear-Admiral Magruder
on board, the cruiser *Raleigh*, and the destroyers *Barry*,
Reid, and *Billingsby*. Captain Lyman A. Cotton, in com-

mand of the Admiral's flagship *Richmond*, described this
stretch from Iceland to Greenland as 'the longest and
most difficult leg of the trans-Atlantic flight':

Eight hundred and thirty-five statute miles across an ocean
covered by ice and beset with fog and cold, it was truly a flight
to test the skill and courage of the hardiest aviator. As the
Chicago and *New Orleans* swept by the *Richmond* close enough
to the bridge for every feature of the aviators to be recognized, it
made a lump come in one's throat to realize how fragile were
these man-made ships of the air and how many miles of restless
waters lay ahead of them before they reached Fredricksdal.

'We realized when we passed over the *Billingsby* this
time,' says Smith, 'that it would be good-bye to her. So
we flew low in order to wave to our old friends, and we were
cheered to find that the sailors had painted "GOOD
LUCK" in huge white letters on the deck. Perhaps the
telling of this sounds prosaic, but to us, out there in the
middle of the North Atlantic on the most dangerous leg
of our World Flight, such encouragement from our Navy
friends made an impression that looms large in our
memories even now. Next we passed the *Barry* with Wade
and Ogden on board en route to Pictou, Nova Scotia.
Displayed from her yard were two flags. This was a
signal to notify us that there was dangerous weather ahead.
But it was too late to turn back now. Nor was there any
place to park out there in the Atlantic midway between
Iceland and Greenland. There was nothing we could do
but carry-on and trust in Providence and our Liberty
motors.

'For the first five hundred miles we had flown through a
perfect sky, but, shortly after passing the *Barry* with her
danger signals, we plunged into fog and rain and wind.
And the farther we flew the denser grew the fog and the
greater became the velocity of the wind. This is an un-
usual combination, but as luck would have it we encountered both.

'We were forced to fly close to the water on account of
the fog. But even then it was so thick that we flashed over

the *Raleigh* without seeing her. Seventy-five miles out from Greenland we struck the first floes. As we neared the coast, the ice increased until we were flying over a seemingly endless expanse of fantastic bergs of every size and shape. Some looked as high as the Chicago Tribune Tower or the Woolworth Building. Had we seen them under different conditions the sight, no doubt, would have inspired us. As it was, they were terrifying, because we never saw them until we were right upon them. We had to fly as low as thirty feet off the water in order to keep our bearings at all, so you can just imagine the close shaves we had while playing tag and leap-frog with those icebergs!

'The presence of all these bergs and so much ice made the fog even more dense than before. We were traveling along at a speed of ninety miles an hour, and could see only between a hundred and a hundred and fifty feet ahead, so use your own imagination as to how soon a plane traveling at that speed could use up the distance that we could see, and then try and figure out how little time was left us to sight a berg ahead, decide which way to turn, and then execute the maneuver. Three times we came so suddenly upon huge icebergs that there was no time left to do any deciding. We simply jerked the wheel back for a quick climb, and were lucky enough to zoom over the top of it into the still denser fog above. Here we were completely lost and unable to see beyond the "prop" and wing-tips. Blindly we would grope and feel our way downward, hoping against hope that the little space we should eventually descend into just above the surface of the water would be clear of ice for a great enough distance to enable us to glance around, size up the situation, and get set for dodging the next one.

'We are often asked why we didn't fly above the fog. Excellent idea! — except for the following reasons: we did try to climb out of it, but the fog apparently had no ceiling, while, with the extra heavy load of gas and oil we were carrying, about eight thousand feet was as high as we could go. Moreover, some of the mountains along the Greenland coast rise to eight and ten thousand feet. So had we climbed to our limit there still would have been plenty of room for us to crash into the top of one of those mountains just as Major Martin had done in Alaska. So our best bet was to keep low, just above the water, where the fog was thinnest and where we had at least a Chinaman's chance of seeing what was ahead and of then dodging it.

'But finally what we feared would happen, did happen. Diving through a small patch of extra heavy fog that was clinging close to the water, we emerged on the other side to find ourselves plunging straight toward a wall of white. The *New Orleans* was close behind us with that huge berg looming in front. I banked steeply to the right while Erik and Jack swung sharp to the left. "Les" shouted, "Hold on, God," and I'm sure I did some rapid praying myself. Both left wings seemed to graze the edge of the berg as we shot past it. And in far less time than it takes to tell it the two planes were lost from each other.

'But neither of us dared circle around and look for the other. When you are in a fog, traveling at ninety miles an hour, don't ever start looking for anybody in an airplane, because you are likely to find him much sooner than you like!

'I headed the *Chicago* in toward shore. Erik, as we learned later, turned out to the sea, making a wide circle of thirty miles or so before swinging back on the course. From then on we saw nothing of each other and neither knew but what the other had crashed into that floating mountain. But we had no time to think of anything but our own problem right then. Things were happening fast—faster than they had ever happened in all our lives.

'For another hour we dodged icebergs and shadows that fairly seemed to leap at us out of the fog. Suddenly, instead of the white ghostlike shadows of the icebergs we had been passing, a dark patch loomed up in front of us. That was encouraging, because we knew it must be land, and we knew that at last we had reached the mainland of Greenland. The next hour was the most exciting of all. First, we

THE ESKIMO WHO CAME OUT TO MEET US IN THEIR KYAKS HAD NEVER SEEN AN
AIRPLANE BEFORE

OUR ESKIMO FRIEND WHOSE NAME SOUNDED LIKE 'I-SUCKA-MUKLUK,' WHO LOOPS THE LOOP IN HIS BOAT

CHILDREN OF THE LAND OF THE MIDNIGHT
SUN, FAT AS BLUBBER AND WITH FACES
LIKE BASKET-BALLS

JACK AND HIS ADOPTED GREENLAND FAMILY

THE ARRIVAL AT IVIGTUT, GREENLAND

would dodge a white shadow, and then a black one would suddenly loom up on the opposite side. Once in a while, when concentrating all our attention on a particularly ominous-looking patch of cliff to our right, we would instinctively feel something sliding by the wing on the left. Turning quickly we would be just in time to see a ghostlike berg that we had missed by only ten feet or so, melting into the gloom. Perhaps it was a sudden icy draft from the berg, like the cold hand of death, that would cause us to turn our heads.

'Until our eyes ached we peered in our vain effort to pierce the blanket of fog and see what we were hurtling toward. We were flying a compass course and keeping as near shore as possible. Finally we reached Cape Farewell, the southernmost tip, and, after heading north up the west coast for a few miles, we ran out of the fog into a short stretch of clear weather, just enough to give us a glimpse of "Greenland's icy mountains." And what a glorious sensation it was to see sunlight again after those nightmare hours in the fog!

'However, our troubles were not over. Up ahead we saw a layer of fog lying absolutely flat on the water, but only extending to a height of about fifteen hundred feet. In this instance it was impossible to get under it, although we should have preferred doing so in order to keep on the lookout for Fredricksdal. So from then on we flew above clouds, racing from one tumbling mass to another and with a row of ice-capped peaks jutting up through the fog on our right. It was only by means of these peaks that we could check our course, for the remainder of Greenland, as well as the sea, was totally obscured.

'Finally, we arrived over where, according to our charts, we thought Fredricksdal ought to be, and watched anxiously for an opening in the clouds. We circled around several times, and then the All-Wise Providence, who had already spared our lives a dozen times on this day's journey, parted the clouds for us so that there was a shaft of light extending down to the sea. Far below we spied a boat emitting clouds of black smoke. We knew she must be the Danish coast guard cutter, the *Island Falk,* sending up smoke signals for us, because there was no other ship in these waters. Her guns were firing and her whistle was blowing, but, of course, we could hear nothing above the roar of our Liberty.

'Throttling down, we spiraled through the providential cloudrift and landed alongside her at five-thirty in the afternoon. Finding that we were away out at the mouth of a fjord where the water was exceedingly rough, we taxied several miles up the fjord between the snowy mountains, and climbed out of our cockpits where we had been strapped for those eleven hours that had seemed like eleven years. We were busy mooring when a Danish officer came alongside in a launch and asked where the *New Orleans* and Locatelli's plane were. We told him we didn't know, and that we had lost them in the fog. Then we set about our work of refueling and inspecting the plane, routine work that we invariably got cleared out of the way immediately after landing from each flight. Neither of us said a word about Erik and Jack, but we were thinking of little else. So narrow had been our own escape that it seemed hardly possible that Providence could bring them through in safety also. We simply couldn't see how any one could be as lucky as we had been.

'But forty minutes later, we heard the welcome hum of a Liberty, which meant that Erik and Jack were arriving. Imagine how glad we were to hear that old familiar sound in the sky! It sounded like a hymn of triumph. No choir of celestial angels could have sounded half so beautiful. For ten minutes or more we could hear the *New Orleans* circling around above the fog, hunting for Fredricksdal just as we had hunted. Suddenly they, too, spotted the same cloudrift that had guided us, and down they dropped. In landing, they nipped the top of a big wave and slightly damaged one pontoon. But a mishap like that after all we had passed through on our eight-hundred-and-thirty-five-mile flight from Reykjavik seemed about the most inconsequential thing in the world. We had made Fredricksdal; we had completed the first flight from Iceland to Greenland; the Atlantic and Pacific were crossed; success was now in sight, for just across Davis Strait lay North America!'

CHAPTER XXXI

THE RESCUE OF LOCATELLI
ADVENTURES IN GREENLAND
AMERICA AT LAST!

HURRYING ashore after the arrival of Nelson at Fredricks-dal, Smith sent a wireless to Admiral Magruder informing him that Locatelli apparently had not passed Cape Farewell and that in all probability he had gone down in the fog.

When the Admiral received this message, he flashed orders to all his ships to search the region from Iceland to Greenland. Meanwhile, Smith arranged with the Danes to send fleets of natives in their kyaks to comb the fjords from Cape Farewell north toward Angmasalik and to look for the Italian fliers in the ice-pack.

Nothing had been seen of Locatelli's monoplane after it had passed from sight into the haze to westward of the destroyer *Barry*. The Italians had been in the air when they crossed longitude 39 degrees west and that became the eastern limit of search. The ice-bound shore of Greenland was, perforce, the western limit of endeavor for ships and the line of flight was naturally the axis of the zone in which they might have fallen. Taking into account possible drift by wind and current, a belt forty miles wide on each side of this axis was thought by the Navy to be the area in which it could reasonably be hoped to find the missing monoplane. The problem, then, was one of locating a tiny floating object in an area of approximately twelve thousand square miles. All these plans for rescue were based upon the assumption that Locatelli had been forced down eastward of Greenland. Had the Italians crashed on land, only one who has seen the myriad peaks of this glacial region can realize the slender chance that they would have had of life.

The destroyers *Billingsby* and *Reid* had been obliged to steam back to their usual stations in European waters because they barely had enough fuel to get them back. This left the *Barry* and the cruisers *Richmond* and *Raleigh*. But the *Barry* also was almost out of fuel, and the two cruisers were but little better off.

Where Locatelli had disappeared was one of the most remote regions of all the seven seas. Not only were there no ordinary trading vessels plying these waters, but even whalers did not come here. So only three ships, all short of fuel, could hope to find the *Dornier-Wall* in those twelve thousand square miles of angry sea — if indeed it were there at all.

Fortunately, both cruisers carried small airplanes, and whenever the fog cleared away these scouts would go up to sweep the ocean with their binoculars. By night, the ships kept their searchlights flashing, the *Raleigh* scouring the ice-infested waters to the north of Cape Farewell, and the Admiral's flagship searching the seas to southward. It was heart-breaking work, for the fog kept constantly closing down and they were rapidly running out of fuel. As the unsearched area grew smaller, the flame of hope burned dimmer.

The quest lasted from the evening of August 21st up to the evening of the 24th: by that time only one hundred miles of sea remained for the *Raleigh* and *Richmond* to cover.

Captain Cotton, skipper of the flagship *Richmond*, tells us what happened on that eventful night:

'Midnight. Cold, and cheerless. The *Richmond* ploughing through the trackless sea one hundred and twenty miles east of Cape Farewell, Greenland, searching for a tiny object bearing four human lives, lost now for three and a half days. A momentary flicker of light on the horizon ten miles away. The *Richmond* turns and speeds toward the spot, throbbing with her hundred thousand horsepower. A red star, fired into the air, lights up our decks with lurid light, as officers, men, correspondents, and camera-men rush up on deck half-clad, hair disheveled, with heavy overcoats and trailing blankets hastily thrown around them. An answering star from the darkness ahead. Can it be that the lost are found? Can it be? Our search-lights feel along the horizon, groping over the hostile sea that is loath to surrender its prey. The light touches a small object, bobbing about like a cork on the water. All eyes are strained toward the plane, through moments of tense silence. How slowly it seems to draw near! The beams of our searchlights catch it again as it rises to the crest of a breaker, and this time we see the red, white, and green rudder of the Italian monoplane. One, two, three, four — the crew are all visible now. All are alive and safe!'

We can imagine with what a sense of triumph Captain Cotton rang down the 'Stop' signal to the engineers, when success thus crowned his efforts after eighty hours of search. The *Richmond* pulls up, with a surge of water from her reversed propellers, not ten yards from the *Dornier-Wall* and is greeted by a veritable salvo of Italian. A line is tossed from ship to plane. (Locatelli subse-quently said, 'This line was like the first thread connecting us with life again.') Helping hands are extended, for two of the crew are so exhausted that they have to be lifted limply on board in nets. Movie-men crank their machines in the light of the aurora borealis which is dancing its strange reel in the Arctic sky. There under the northern lights, on the *Richmond's* deck, stand Locatelli and his crew, heavy-eyed, and utterly spent, but safe. For three long nights they have kept their watch with Death in a sea-swept cockpit: now they are in the world of men again.

Personal effects are passed up from the wrecked mono-plane. Her tanks are punctured. She is set on fire, cast adrift, passes astern, flares up, and sinks in a thousand fathoms of water. Silence once more on the *Richmond*, ex-cept for the purring of the radio as it tells the world of the drama's ending, while the lights of the North, heedless of earth's affairs, poise 'above the Polar rim like a coronal of flame.'

Locatelli had landed in the fog through which the American fliers had continued to Fredricksdal, for the simple reason that he was afraid of running into an iceberg or a mountain in the blind weather. Theoretically, his scheme was feasible, for his monoplane was a better sea-boat than the lighter American biplanes, but practically it was a mistake. His intention had been to alight on the water and await clearer weather. But, in landing, he had seriously damaged his engine-carriers. Further, instead of clearing up, the weather grew rougher and rougher, break-ing first the ailerons of the *Dornier-Wall* and then the stabilizer, and finally the elevators. Having done its worst, the sea abated somewhat and the fog lifted, but by that time the Italian ship was too badly wrecked to fly.

'Perhaps we, better than any one, can appreciate how Lieutenant Locatelli and his companions felt,' says Leigh Wade, 'both at being rescued after drifting for three days in an icy sea and on seeing the destruction of their plane. Had the *Richmond* missed seeing that light on the night of August 24th, they would have passed on to the next section of the lane, the Italians would have drifted into an area already searched, so that no one would have ever known just what fate had befallen Locatelli and his gallant men.'

Out of the wreckage of the monoplane, Lieutenant Locatelli carried his country's flag, which he presented to Admiral Magruder. Later on, when he met the American pilots in Boston, after mutual congratulations, he said that in his opinion the navigation of the *Chicago* and *New Orleans* through that terrible and blinding weather was an epochal feat which will mark a point in the history of air navigation. Nor is the historian inclined to dispute Locatelli's opinion. Smith and Nelson, Arnold and Hard-ing, remained in the air for eleven hours of intense nervous tension during this long flight through fog and storm.

By the time they reached Fredricksdal, they had been without sleep for forty-two hours. Surely no adventure over earth or air or water has ever called for more grit than this! The stamina of clean-living men, the nerves of steel that are only won through peril often faced, the cold-blooded courage of those to whom duty is more than death and the enthusiasm that follows an ideal in spite of every obstacle — such qualities did the pilots bring to their task. That they triumphed is not their victory alone, but belongs, like Lincoln's life, to the ages. While this land breeds such boys, the spirit of young America shall conquer more than the earth.

'Raw fish, seal blubber, and Arctic birds constitute the bill of fare of the native Greenlanders of Fredricksdal,' says Erik Nelson. 'They are good-natured, cheery people, and, thanks to the Danish Government, they are still practically free from the taints that usually come with the white man.

'Although they have a few rifles, ammunition is so expensive that they depend almost entirely on their ancient hunting spears, which they hurl with amazing accuracy. When an Eskimo wants a new suit of clothes, he simply goes out and spears it. But the thing that amazed us most was the clever way they manipulate their tiny boats. They are the frailest little things I ever saw, but in the hands of the Eskimo they are thoroughly sea-worthy. The native fastens himself in his kyak, ties a skin round his waist to make the boat waterproof, and then the kyak seems to become a part of him. He can roll up-side down, and go through all sorts of evolutions that are utterly impossible in any other craft.

'Chunks of ice floated by all day long from their parent glaciers to the sea, and a heavy blanket of fog hung so low that flying was impossible. While we were working on the planes, we saw a huge berg tumble over. It was hardly a hundred yards away, and when this mountain of ice commenced to wobble, and then turn and roll, we sat there

FROM GREENLAND TO LABRADOR

AN HISTORIC MOMENT: THE CHICAGO AND THE NEW ORLEANS
ARRIVING AT ICY TICKLE, LABRADOR

FLIGHT COMMANDER LOWELL SMITH WAS THE FIRST TO SET
FOOT ON AMERICAN SOIL

ADMIRAL MAGRUDER CONGRATULATES THE FLIERS UPON THEIR
SUCCESSFUL CROSSING OF THE ATLANTIC

Left to right: Smith, Arnold, Admiral Magruder, Nelson, Harding, Captain
Cotten of the cruiser Richmond

SMITH AND NELSON ENJOYING GRIDDLE-CAKES AND COFFEE
AT MERE POINT, MAINE

HIS DREAM COME TRUE: GENERAL PATRICK STARTING OUT TO
MEET THE RETURNING WORLD FLIERS

The General earned his wings and became a full-fledged pilot at the age of
sixty

SMITH SIGNING THE AIRPORT REGISTER UPON ARRIVAL AT BOSTON

spellbound. It tossed and splashed for fully five minutes before it reached an even keel.

'On Sunday, August 21st, we discovered to our dismay that our Eskimo guards had let a few cakes of ice drift against the *Chicago's* pontoons during the night, so that they were punctured in two places. While the rest of us set to work pumping them out, Smith took off his clothes, plunged into the icy water, and hurriedly put on emergency patches.

'Although we had landed at Fredricksdal, our regular supply base was one hundred and fifty miles farther up the west coast of Greenland, at Ivigtut. There the cruiser *Milwaukee* awaited us with supplies for the journey to Labrador. The weather had been reported fine at Ivigtut that morning, so, in spite of rain and fog at Fredricksdal, we took-off at five minutes to eleven, the morning of August 24th.

'It was quite a tricky take-off, too, for we had to dodge in and out between the icebergs. But we made it, and for two hours flew along the bleak coast of Greenland, encountering winds that reminded us of the "Willie-was" of Alaska. Nearly every time we rounded a mountain, a terrific gust would strike from the shoulder of a fjord and knock us all over the sky.

'When we landed alongside the *Milwaukee*, shortly after one o'clock, the first person to greet us was Lieutenant Clayton Bissell, who had acted as advance officer for us along the Alaskan coast. Bissell was the first friend from home whom we had met previously on the Flight, and it was a great joy to encounter him here again.

'He had constructed a runway on the beach, so we pulled the planes up, out of the way of the floating ice, and tied them down. Then we jumped in a launch and went out to the cruiser, where the whole crew was mustered on deck to welcome us as we came on board.

'Realizing that we had only one more long water jump ahead of us, we decided that we had better eliminate as much risk as possible by changing engines again. During the days we spent here at Ivigtut, it rained most of the time, but we worked out in the open and paid no attention to the weather, for we had long ago grown accustomed to such trifles as being soaked to the skin.

'Whenever the wind died down, the air would be filled with billions of tiny gnats. They were the most troublesome brutes you ever saw — worse than tropical insects. They flew into our eyes, up our noses, buzzed in and out of our ears, and we had to talk with our lips shut, to keep them from swarming into our mouths. In fact they were so bad that we finally couldn't work at all until we got some netting draped over our heads and tied around our necks. It seemed odd to find all these flies in the Arctic, but the Danes told us they were always troubled with them during the short Greenland summer.

'Ivigtut is farther from civilization than any place we had yet visited. It lies at the head of a fjord and is surrounded by wild, rugged mountains. Our planes were beached right at the base of a cliff that rose sheer and smooth, as though polished by stone-masons, to a height of forty-five hundred feet. The peaks all round us were capped with ice, and down every valley ran a glacier from which great chunks cracked off every few minutes and floated down the fjord to join the millions of others in Davis Strait. It was still summer in Greenland and hundreds of cataracts came tumbling down the steep mountains. The ground, wherever not coated with ice, was covered with a layer of moss from six inches to a foot in depth, and with each step we took, we sank down into it as though walking on a pile carpet. Such was the scene of the last and barrenest of the emergency repair depots we established.

'Ivigtut consists of an Eskimo village and a mining camp. So far as I know, it is the only place in the world where cryolite is found in commercial quantities. It is a mineral made up of fluorine, sodium, and aluminum. Each spring, the Danish firm that has the mining concession sends up about one hundred and fifty husky men to Ivigtut and supplies them with living quarters, clothing, food, tobacco, and drink. They are unable to spend a cent in Greenland, so each miner goes back to Copenhagen in the autumn with a great thirst for gayety and a bank-roll that enables him to satisfy it.

'Life gets a bit monotonous for these cryolite miners, during their working season, so it was a great event for them when we turned up. The night of our arrival, the *Milwaukee* invited the whole Danish colony on board. After dinner, movies were shown on deck. Although it rained all through the exhibition, the miners sat there in the drizzle roaring with laughter over a slap-stick comedy.

'Next day, while waiting for the weather to clear, several of us went trout-fishing. This was the first opportunity Smith had had of using the rod and line that had been presented to him by friends in Seattle. The fishing was marvelous, and he christened his rod by catching forty trout in less than two hours.

'Back at Fredricksdal the Danish officers on the Coast Guard cutter *Island Falk* had asked us to tell them when our birthdays were: August 28th was the auspicious occasion of "Les" Arnold's seeing the light. So the skipper of the *Island Falk* passed the good news along to the miners. That night a feast was given in honor of "Les." These unmelancholy Danes of Greenland never miss an opportunity of celebrating. If a boat comes in, they have a party. If a boat goes out, they do the same. And a birthday provides them with excuse for a regular jamboree. After much good cheer and drinking of healths, in which we joined with the necessary caution, we attended another movie-show on the deck of the *Richmond*. The sky was perfectly clear, and in addition to the show on the screen we had a show in the sky. Those northern lights are the most uncanny things in all the world. They just whip across the sky, noiselessly and luridly, lighting up the deck and the gaunt mountains and the glittering bergs. It was an unforgettable evening, watching the movies to the cosmic flicker of these Arctic solitudes.

' " And soft they danced from the Polar sky, and swept
　　in primrose haze;
And swift they pranced with their silver feet, and
　　pierced with a blinding blaze." '

As would naturally be supposed, Erik Nelson was very much at home among the Norsemen. He tells us a little of the history of this land from which the Vikings of the air, having exchanged the dragon-prowed boats of the past for the winged skiffs of the present, were now setting out, as their prototypes did of a thousand years before, to find the fertile shores of America.

Originally Iceland was colonized by a group of Norsemen who objected to paying allegiance to their King, Harold Fairhair. So fifty thousand of them — if history does not exaggerate — set their prows toward the sunset lands of adventure. Landing in Iceland, they settled there. Their sheep and cattle flourished, they raised hay, and their boats carried on a trade with Norway, Denmark, and the British Isles.

･ They also developed a literature which antedated that of France, Germany, and England. We learn from their sagas how a party of settlers was driven across to Greenland in a storm. They survived the winter of A.D. 875 and returned home the following spring, when the ice broke up. A hundred years later, Erik the Red explored this unknown land where the settler Gunnbjorn had wintered. After sailing for three years in and out of the Greenland fjords, he decided to establish a colony near the southern end of the island where he had discovered a fertile plain.

And now Erik — pioneer real-estate promoter — conceived the bright idea of calling the country Greenland. So successful was he that the following season he embarked no less than twenty-five shiploads of settlers, with promises of good hunting and fat seals, and other residential amenities. Eleven of the ships struck icebergs and went down before reaching the promised land, so their passengers were not disillusioned. What the others said on reaching Greenland is not recorded in the sagas.

Then Leif, son of Erik the Red, followed in his father's footsteps. He was a picturesque but thoughtful Viking, and one of the few 'hard-boiled' sea-captains whom the priests had converted from the wassails of Valhalla to the rites of the Roman Church. *'Leifr var mikill madhr ok sterkr, manna skoruligastr at sja, vitr madhr ok godhr hofsmadhr um all hluti,'* says the saga recording his virtue: to wit, 'Leif was a large man and strong, of noble mien, wise and temperate in all things.' After taking a few priests to Greenland, he sailed south to see if he could find another town-site proposition as good as his father's. Strange to relate, he found a better one, nothing less than North America! Furthermore, he made a good start by naming the country Vineland, in an appeal to the well-known Nordic taste for good cheer. Then Nemesis overtook him. Before he could launch his Greenland-wide publicity drive for colonizing America, he died and his scheme collapsed. What he would have done, with his inherited resources and his personal talent, is one of those byways of history into which the present narrator, with facts and deeds to chronicle, may not stray, however pleasant the path.

Our Odyssey nears its end. The boys were 'all-set' to follow in the footsteps of Leif the Lucky. On the night of August 30th, fair weather reports were wirelessed from Labrador. The fliers rose at 4 A.M., warmed up their engines, and made ready to take-off.

'It was at 8.25 on the morning of August 31st,' says Smith, 'that we left Greenland on the flight that was to land us on American soil. From the fjord at Ivigtut we flew over Davis Strait and five miles from shore ran into a fog-bank. However, we knew that the weather was clear on the Labrador side of the strait, so we calculated that the fog would not last long. After thirty minutes' flying, we came out of it near an iceberg the size of a mountain, that had been reported to us, and had perfect weather for the greater part of the way.

'Occasionally we would pass through a bit of fog or a shower, but it never lasted for more than a few minutes.

When it was clear, we could see the Navy patrol boats for thirty miles, although they could never spot us until we were almost on top of them, owing to atmospheric conditions.

'It was good flying weather and all was going well when the cold hand of Failure suddenly tried to claw us down. We were two hundred miles off Labrador when this happened. Our motor-driven gasoline pump failed, and five minutes later our wind-driven pump also gave out, making it necessary to turn on the reserve tank, containing fifty-eight gallons of gas, or enough for over two hours.

'I throttled down and shouted to "Les" that our one hope of maintaining the supply in the reserve tank and making shore lay in the "wobble-pump," which is installed in all the planes for just such an emergency and is manipulated by hand. "Les" was already stripped to the waist. He laid hold of that handle and pumped with it for dear life.

'I watched the overflow with a blessed sense of relief. "Les" has the strength of a lumberjack, otherwise he could never have done what he did. For nearly three hours he pumped without pause or intermission, supplying life-blood to the engine, while I flew on greatly worried about the loss of oil that had smeared the side of my ship. Nelson signaled me about this shortly after leaving Greenland, and I was praying for it to hold out. Only the fact that I had put in more than usual, because it was a new motor, enabled us to reach shore, with tank practically empty.

'An hour out from Icy Tickle, our destination on the Labrador coast, we ran into a forty-mile wind that cut down our speed and made things even worse for "Les," who by that time was lathered in sweat like a Tia Juana two-year-old, and almost "all out." But he stuck to the pump. It is wonderful what guts will do for a man — and the sight of his native land over the starboard fuselage!

'We reached Icy Tickle, at 3.20 P.M. on August 31st,

after a 560-mile flight lasting six hours and fifty-five minutes. So that was that. We were in America.

'A launch came out from the *Richmond* and took us ashore after we had moored. We had landed after our travel, like the Pilgrim Fathers, on a large rock, but I'm afraid our first actions were not as edifying as theirs. We were just too darned happy for words.'

CHAPTER XXXII

FROM ICY TICKLE TO BOSTON

ALTHOUGH 'Les' Arnold had been able to celebrate the Flight's arrival at Icy Tickle by a step-dance, and said nothing about the condition he was in until the official formalities were over, at the end of that time he nearly collapsed from muscular exhaustion and heart-strain. The naval medical officers took him in hand, had him massaged, and sent him to bed.

Many of the newspaper men had been waiting for over a month to 'cover' the arrival of the World Flight on North American soil. After having told each other all the stories they knew, their restless minds demanded diversion. Their only excitement had been one night, when the wind howled so as to drown the rattle of the 'bones' and the familiar jargon of *'Come on, seven, baby needs new shoes!'* and suddenly a gust of exceptional violence blew in the door of their hut and disclosed the breakers licking up to the stack of gasoline drums which had been piled on the beach to await the arrival of the Fliers. Into the teeth of the storm rushed the journalists, and for a few hours they had work and to spare in salvaging these drums. But once the high-test 'gas' was saved, they had to return to their game, or invent new means to while away the long northern twilights. So along about the second week in August they devised and had inscribed a brass tablet commemorating *August the 31st* as the day of the arrival of the World Flight. This plate was finished and set up nearly a week before Smith and Nelson actually moored at Icy Tickle, and is proof, if proof were needed, of the uncanny gift of the modern reporter, who is always ahead of the fleeting hour. Another pastime of the fraternity was to write 'advance stories' describing the adventures of the airmen in detail: these articles were sent by boat to their news-

UPON ARRIVAL AT BOSTON WITH STILL ANOTHER THREE THOUSAND
MILES TO GO

THE PRINCE OF WALES AWAITING THE FLIERS AT MITCHEL FIELD

ARRIVING OVER NEW YORK CITY

THE ARRIVAL AT MITCHEL FIELD

papers all over America, together with a special code, so
that the right story should be released for publication
when required.

Article number one described the arrival of both planes
at Icy Tickle. Article number two told of one airplane
being lost at sea and of one lone and battered World
Cruiser fluttering down in Labrador after a battle with
Arctic storms. The third story was a harrowing account of
disaster having overtaken both planes on the way across
Davis Strait and of the arrangements being made to search
for the wrecked Fliers. So, when the *Chicago* and *New
Orleans* appeared in the sky above Indian Harbor, the
pressmen simply radioed the code-word 'codfish' to their
offices where the three stories had already been 'set' by
the linotype operators and only awaited the editorial
'O.K.' Before, therefore, the pontoons of the World
Cruisers had touched the waters of Icy Tickle, the great
presses of America were already rolling out this tale of
achievement at the rate of two hundred thousand copies
an hour. Thus is history made!

After they had spent a little while ashore, the officers of
the *Richmond* took the airmen out to the Cruiser, where
the crew was already assembled on deck. Admiral Magruder then read the following message from the President:

Your history-making flight has been followed with absorbing
interest by your countrymen and your return to North American
soil is an inspiration to the whole Nation. You will be welcomed
back to the United States with an eagerness and enthusiasm
that I am sure will compensate for the hardship you have undergone. Your countrymen are proud of you. Your branch of the
Service realizes the honor you have won for it. My congratulations and heartiest good wishes go to you at this hour of your
landing.

                                        CALVIN COOLIDGE

From the Secretary of War came a radio to each member
of the Flight, congratulating him on his 'bravery, hardi-
hood, and modesty.' 'More particularly to you as leader
of the Flight,' added the Secretary of War to Smith, 'I

desire to say that your courage, skill, and determination have shown you to be a fit successor to the great navigators of the Age of Discovery. The Air Service, the War Department, and the whole country are proud of you.'

Not having had any food since early morning, the Fliers were as hungry as wolves by this time. So a special dinner was prepared for them at five o'clock. An hour later, they dined again in the officers' mess. Then at seven came word that the Admiral wanted them to sup with him.

That night they crawled into their bunks with laden stomachs but light hearts, knowing that a few short flights now would carry them to the great cities of their homeland.

'After a long night's sleep, we celebrated our return to America by working all day on the fuel pumps and fixing up the oil leak that had nearly let the *Chicago* down on the way over from Greenland,' says Nelson. 'Tuesday morning, September 2d, we were up at dawn, and, although weather reports from Labrador were far from favorable, Smith decided to get away from Icy Tickle as quickly as possible.

'At 11.10 A.M. we bade farewell to our frigid friends the icebergs, and at noon cut across a narrow peninsula with scrubby pines, which were the first trees we had seen since leaving the British Isles.

'Two hours and fifty-five minutes from Icy Tickle, just after passing Cape Charles in Belle Isle Strait, we encountered our old enemy, fog. Belle Isle Strait is said to be the foggiest stretch of water in the world, and the day we passed, the weather was living up to its reputation: the farther we flew, the thicker it grew. In spite of the fog, there was a huge swell running, and we were flying so low that it looked as if our pontoons would slap the water sometimes. Once a black object was borne up toward us with incredible speed on the crest of a wave and then sank out of sight again in the sea-trough and fog. It was all over in a second, but had we been thirty-five feet closer we should have crashed into that steamer's bridge. What her captain said, I wouldn't care even to guess. No doubt he was an old salt, familiar with every sound on the Labrador coast, from the bellow of a bull-moose to the voices of his trawler friends. But a couple of 400-horse-power World Cruisers zooming across his nose may have left him dumb, with his rich vocabulary paralyzed.

'Although not quite so bleak as Labrador, this part of Newfoundland was also grim and rockbound, with a fringe of spray some fifty feet high from the angry sea. We passed almost as many wrecks as we had seen off the coast of Alaska. At one place we flew over a big iron steamer impaled on a sharp rock, and farther down we saw a derelict British cruiser.

'When the fog abated, the wind rose and we had to buck a stiff head wind, so that it took us four hours and fifty-six minutes to fly three hundred and fifteen miles from Icy Tickle to Hawkes Bay, Newfoundland. This bay, by the way, should not be confused with another of the same name farther north on the Labrador coast.

'After spending the night on board a destroyer we took-off next morning, September 3d, for Pictou, Nova Scotia, four hundred and thirty miles nearer Boston. For half this distance we flew down the west coast of Newfoundland. I counted the miles off one by one because each brought us nearer and nearer our goal. From Cape Anguille, near the southern tip of Newfoundland, we made an hour's flight across a sparkling sheet of blue water which is named Cabot Strait after the brothers who preceded us across the Atlantic four centuries ago. Then on over Cape Breton Island we flew to the smiling orchards and fishing villages of "Evangeline-land."

'Several miles from our destination we were met by a Canadian Royal Air Force plane whose occupants waved us an airy salute and then escorted us to Pictou. As we circled over the harbor at 5.40 P.M. we saw Wade's new plane, the *Boston II*, that had been sent up to Nova Scotia by General Patrick in order that "Leigh" and "Hank" might make the rest of the flight with us. Every whistle in Pictou was tooting its shrillest and the shore was lined with cheering Canadians when we taxied to our moorings. Wade and Ogden were the first out to meet us and with them were our friends Lieutenants MacDonald and Bertrandias, the officers who had ferried the *Boston II* from Virginia to Nova Scotia. "Les" and MacDonald had been "bunkies" at various aviation camps around the U.S.A. since 1917, so they were overjoyed at seeing each other again.

'Here we were to get our first taste of the reception that was to follow us now all the way back to Seattle.

'After fueling up, we were taken ashore, ushered into autos, and paraded through the streets behind a band of Highlanders, and thousands of school kiddies and civilians. The streets were decorated with bunting and flags, and at every corner was a big sign reading "Welcome World Fliers." To the skirl of bagpipes, we were hoisted up on a platform, around which milled the population of Pictou. After a few feeble oratorical flights on our part, we proceeded to a lobster party. MacDonald told us of his experience in buying the ones served to us. When he called at a fishmonger's, he had asked the price and been told he could have a dozen for fifty cents. So he came back with a dollar's worth — twenty-four crimson young crustaceans, all for one lone simoleon! If you are a lobster-lover, Pictou is your Paradise.

'All next day it was windy and rainy. Fearful lest we might get bored, the Pictou Chamber of Commerce sent the Scotties to cheer us up with their bagpipes. In the evening we were taken aboard the Canadian destroyer *Patriot* to another lobster banquet, and initiated life-members of their mess.

'That night we turned in early, but we were all far too thrilled with the prospect of reaching Boston on the morrow to do much sleeping.

'We took-off at 11.15 A.M., turned west along the coast of Nova Scotia, and then took the shortest land crossing to the Bay of Fundy. Just south of St. John, New Brunswick, we encountered fog again. It grew so thick that when we passed the boundary between Canada and the United States we were skimming just off the water, dodging rocks and little islands. Visibility was nil. We attempted to climb over it and to get around it. But we were taking chances, and Lowell decided that it was not worth while attempting to push through and risk a tragedy so near our goal. So, turning back a few miles, we came down in Casco Bay, off Mere Point, Maine, in a sheltered cove that was an ideal place for an emergency landing.

'Some of the most hospitable people in New England have their summer homes along the shores of this pictur-esque bay, and as soon as they discovered who we were they came out to us in motor-boats, carried us ashore, and did everything to make us comfortable. Commander Peary, of North Pole fame, wisely selected this as his haven of rest between Arctic expeditions.

'We all remembered the mere passing interest which the American public had taken in the remarkable flights from New York to Nome and return, to Porto Rico and return, and the non-stop flight from New York to San Diego. After all, the receptions given us in foreign countries were accorded us mainly because we were representatives of the Air Force of the United States of America who had been entrusted with an important and somewhat spectacular mission. So as we winged our way down from Greenland we simply took it for granted that our countrymen would look upon our flight much as they had looked upon the others, and little did we dream that what in some respects was to be the most thrilling part of our journey still lay before us.

'We were out on the planes early Saturday morning, September 6th, and, although reluctant to leave our new friends and such a charming spot as Casco Bay, we were anxious to reach Boston and then push rapidly on to the Pacific Coast, our final goal. A very stiff head wind sprang up just as we were about to take-off, and we found that we needed more gas to ensure our getting to the Boston airport. This had to be brought from Brunswick, the nearest town, and it was nearly noon before a supply arrived by truck.

'Meanwhile ten De Haviland planes, led by General Patrick, and Lieutenants Streett and Brown, of the World Flight Committee, had flown up to meet us and escort us in. When they saw us lying on the water, they broke formation and each in turn dived down and waved to us. By holding up a funnel and pointing to the gas tanks, we let them know what was delaying us.

'Seeing those planes filled with our old friends gave us a great thrill. After circling over us for a while, they flew to Old Orchard, Maine, landed on the beach, and waited until they saw us coming.

'The trip to Boston was uneventful. As we circled over the historic Harbor and Bunker Hill, we saw a throng of people evidently waiting for us at the landing-field. Although we couldn't hear a thing owing to the roar of our motors, we could see fire-boats spouting fountains of water, streaks of steam shooting up from factories, ocean liners, tugs, and ferryboats, and puffs of smoke coming from the warships beneath us, firing 21 guns salutes.'

'The first thing that happened when we stepped ashore at Boston,' says Smith, 'was that some one shoved a radio microphone in front of me. I looked at it dumbly and then asked: "What am I supposed to do with this?" Of course the "mike" was turned on, so these were my first words to the American public. Then General Patrick, or somebody, explained that Mother and Dad were out in Los Angeles "listening in" and that I was supposed to make a little speech. I simply said: "Hello, folks, I'm glad to be home," and let it go at that.

'About the next thing I can recall was seeing a very beautiful young lady burst through the crowd, throw her arms around Erik, and give him a smack on each cheek and another on his bald head. None of us, including Erik, knew who she was. At any rate, she was not the girl whose photograph had been the mascot of the *New Orleans*.

'After receiving the greetings of our Chief, who had sent us forth to explore the airways of the earth, we were greeted by the Governor of Massachusetts, the Mayor of Boston, the Assistant Secretary of War, the Corps Commander, and any number of other officials. Nelson's brother Gunnar, a mathematician of note, had flown all the way from Dayton, Ohio, to welcome him, and a quiet Englishman came up who turned out to be none other than the British World Flier, Major Stuart MacLaren. In addition to thanking us for sending his spare plane from the Kurile Islands to Burma by destroyer, he told us that he was on his way home to outfit another round-the-world expedition. That's the English spirit.

'After signing the airport entry book for "Bob" Brown, who had been the chairman of the World Flight Committee and had been partly responsible for it, we were hustled into a fleet of Eddie Rickenbacker's cars and whirled through the streets at a speed that made us pop-eyed. If any of us had thought that Boston was a sleepy town, we were quickly disillusioned. Paul Revere's ride was a doddering jog-trot compared to the hair-stiffening clip at which his descendants took us to Boston Common.

'As we flashed through the streets, the sidewalks were jammed with cheering throngs. It was all totally unexpected. Of course we hadn't seen a paper in Iceland, Greenland, or Labrador. In fact, we had only glanced at a few foreign journals since leaving Seattle, so we hadn't the faintest idea there was going to be all this enthusiasm.

'We pulled up at Boston Common, and there, in addition to addresses of welcome, we were showered with gifts, such as keys to the city, sabers, huge Paul Revere bowls, American flags, silver wings, watches, and even silver mesh-bags for our mothers.

'When we were each presented with a great Stars and Stripes in silk, a dramatic incident occurred. Erik, the only naturalized American among us, bent gracefully over the folds of his country's flag and kissed it.

'Next we were whirled to the Copley-Plaza Hotel, where all the rooms along one floor had been thrown open to us. They wouldn't even allow us to sign the ordinary hotel register, but the manager came up with a special card in a silver frame just as they do when a President visits them.

'Just as we were beginning to wonder in what clothes we should be able to dine with General Patrick, some one called our attention to the closet in each suite. And there, as if by magic, we found dress uniforms neatly pressed, clean shirts, and everything that we needed. Surely Aladdin had nothing on us! Our "slave of the lamp" was none other than Lieutenant Robert J. Brown, who, with Lieutenant St. Clair Streett, had been responsible for so much of the detail work of the Flight. When it comes to detail, or anything else, for that matter, these two are incomparable.

'Dressing that night was quite an undertaking. The telephones in all six rooms were all ringing at once, and they never stopped. So we put a bell-boy on each. Crowds of officials and friends surged in and out. Bell-boys dashed hither and thither. Pandemonium reigned. But we certainly were sitting on top of the world for once in our lives.

'That night we dined quietly with General Patrick, and between courses a radio microphone was served up to us on a platter so we could chat with the world at large. Whenever I get in front of one of these instruments, my gas pump refuses to feed, lung compression drops to zero, my heart starts to knock, and the old think-box freezes!

'Although the hospitable people of Boston seemed to think that the World Flight was over when we reached their glorious old city, which to them is still the "Hub of the Universe," down in our hearts we knew that the time had not yet arrived to do any shouting. We appreciated Boston's welcome; in fact, we reveled in it, having just come down from the bleak Arctic; but it did make us feel uneasy and fidgety, for we still had over three thousand miles to go.'

THE CAPITOL AND THE CONGRESSIONAL LIBRARY AS THEY APPEARED
TO THE WORLD FLIERS

PRESIDENT COOLIDGE AND THE MEMBERS OF HIS CABINET
WAITED FOR THREE HOURS IN THE RAIN AT BOLLING FIELD
TO CONGRATULATE THE CIRCUMNAVIGATORS

LEFT TO RIGHT: LIEUTENANT LOWELL H. SMITH, SECRETARY OF WAR JOHN W. WEEKS, MAJOR GENERAL MASON M. PATRICK, BRIGADIER GENERAL WILLIAM MITCHELL, LIEUTENANT ERIK H. NELSON, LIEUTENANT LEIGH WADE

THE YOUNG LADY WHOSE PICTURE ON CELLULOID FLEW ROUND THE WORLD
ON THE INSTRUMENT BOARD OF THE NEW ORLEANS

CHAPTER XXXIII

THE LAST

'GUESS we'll have to fly around the world again,' said Smith, with that wry smile of his, when he had finally brought the Flight safely to Seattle, — 'just to recover from all these receptions!'

For boys who had undergone six months of nervous and physical strain, during their Flight around the globe, the ordeal by banquets which they passed through while crossing America, came as a severe and unforeseen test of endurance. Hand-shaking and speech-making have exhausted many a celebrity, men whose whole lives are spent in the public eye, but of such things Smith and his companions knew nothing and cared less. They had flown twenty-three thousand miles around the world, and still had more than three thousand miles to go in airplanes that in spite of their sturdiness had long since passed their allotted span. Constant attention to business was therefore necessary by day; while by night they had no rest, for at each and every step between Boston and Seattle they met old friends and new ones, responded to toasts, gave interviews, were the center of civic functions, and lived a life which is known to be perilous to nerves and digestion. All this in addition to the routine of flying across a continent, no mean task in itself.

For these reasons, a living buffer of *bonhomie* and tact was required to stand between the boys and the public. This shield was forthcoming in the person of their social representative, the charming and disarming Lieutenant Burdette Wright.

'"Birdie" is as able a diplomat as he is pilot,' says Smith, ' — and that is saying a whole lot. We were often late in arriving at the various cities on our schedule and committees naturally were peeved about having to arrange new dates for their banquets. But "Birdie's" smile always allayed their annoyance and we owe him a very hearty vote of thanks for the way he looked after us.'

To tell of the triumphal progress of the airmen, over the spires and canyons of Manhattan Island, to meet the President and his Cabinet and all official Washington assembled at Bolling Field, across the Alleghanies to the great air post at Dayton, the fierce welcome of Chicago, the clustering escort planes of the Southwest, the joy at San Diego, the rose-strewn field at Santa Monica, and the final return to Seattle, is to write a very different story from that of the Flight around the World. The Flight is an Odyssey of six men in working clothes who outfaced many deaths in 'silence and unswerving.' The receptions in America, on the other hand, are the record of what a hundred million people thought about that Odyssey; and that is a tale of a different sort, although one that may be told with pride and pleasure.

'On the 7th, we spent the entire day changing from pontoons back to wheels again and at two minutes past twelve on September 8th, we left Boston for New York,' said 'Les' Arnold. 'Ahead of us, in escort planes, flew General Patrick, Assistant Secretary of War Davis, James T. Williams, Jr., the Boston editor and aviation enthusiast, Senator James Wadsworth of New York, and "Billy" Streett. Erik's brother Gunnar was also in one of the leading planes. Behind us, came ten other planes carrying journalists, photographers, and a radio operator who broadcasted as we flew.

'As we passed over Providence, Rhode Island, and other cities, we could see jets of steam coming from every factory whistle, all traffic in the streets had stopped, and the roofs were black with people waving to us. After leaving Providence, we flew over New London, Connecticut, my home town. Now in New London they have a big whistle, which they use as a fire alarm and also in case of serious trouble requiring the summoning of all police. As we roared over my home at ninety miles an hour, I'll be darned if they didn't blow the riot call: I could see they were doing so by the continuous jet of steam. I got a big kick out of this!

'As we passed Bridgeport, and neared New York, ten more planes from Long Island came out to escort us to Mitchel Field. We crossed the East River, and turned south at the Bronx, flying right down the center of Manhattan Island. The sun was shining on Fifth Avenue and Broadway and all the traffic was held up there, where fifteen years ago Erik had been a super in "Ben-Hur." I'll tell the world little old New York looked good to us!

'Every liner, tug, and ferry blew a welcome as we flew on over the lower end of the island and out to salute the Statue of Liberty. Then we cut across Brooklyn and out over Long Island. As we swung past the Meadow Brook Club, we saw a vast acreage of automobile tops, stretching from Garden City to Hempstead. There must have been ten thousand parked there, and Mitchel Field was black with people.

'General Patrick and the two planes accompanying him landed first. The crowd, thinking it was us, mobbed them, and we had to circle round until the police cleared the field. Then we glided down against the wind, and as we were taxiing into position the crowd broke through the police lines again. For ten minutes we had to fight to keep souvenir hunters from pulling the planes to bits. Finally we milled through the mob to the reception stand, where Senator Wadsworth made a speech and presented us with the handsomest green-gold cigarette cases we had ever seen. On one face was a six-inch replica of a Douglas Cruiser cut out of a block of platinum, and on the other an engraved map of the world showing the route of the flight and every place where we had stopped.

'And there was the Prince of Wales, pink with pleasure. He came over and shook hands and said: "Great show, boys. Well done."

'After the usual evening's work of looking the planes over, we attended a reception given by Colonel Hensley,

Commanding Officer at Mitchel Field, and then "hit the hay" as early as possible in order to be in shape for the flight to Washington the next day.

'September 9th was dark and foggy. It was not until nearly ten o'clock that we got off with General Patrick again. General Mitchell, who had flown out from Washington, met us at Aberdeen, Maryland.

'Ten miles beyond Baltimore the motor of the *New Orleans* suddenly stopped dead. But luckily it had picked out the right place to baulk, for at that moment Erik and Jack were directly above a pasture, and it was the only safe field for miles. Nelson made a very skillful landing and several of the smaller escort planes, including General Patrick's, came down beside the *New Orleans*. At the General's request Erik jumped into a De Haviland and took the place of Lieutenant Louis Meister, who had been piloting Gunnar Nelson. Jack stayed with the *New Orleans* and discovered that the timing gears had slipped, thereby causing the motor to register "sudden death."'

Owing to a stiff head wind, that made it necessary for the escort planes to refuel at Aberdeen, the World Cruisers were several hours behind their schedule, but, in spite of the downpour and important engagements, the President and his Cabinet waited patiently to welcome the World Fliers at Bolling Field. This was the first time in history that a President of the United States ever went out from the White House to welcome a citizen to Washington.

For three hours Mr. and Mrs. Coolidge waited in the rain, while work steadily piled up for the President at the White House. Some one suggested that he might like to return. 'Not on your life,' was his answer. 'I'll wait all day if necessary.'

He shook hands with each of the boys in turn, congratulating them individually, and asked them many questions. Then the President and the Secretary of War were shown all over the *Chicago* by Smith. They surprised him, he told the historian, by their technical knowledge of aviation matters.

General Mitchell, who assisted General Patrick in making the Flight possible, was a notable figure on Bolling Field and attracted the attention of newspaper men by stepping from his airplane with spurs and a riding-cane to supplement his flying-clothes. Ever since the World War, General Patrick and General Mitchell had dreamed and planned of the American World Flight. Now their dream had come true.

September 12th had been set aside as Defense Day and Secretary Weeks ordered the World Fliers to remain in Washington and take part in the national demonstration. While they were waiting, the airmen were entertained by General Patrick and made official calls at the White House, the office of the Secretary of War, and the office of General Pershing.

Hundreds of telegrams and cables of congratulations were pouring in from all parts of the world and from people in every walk of life, from the King of England to the Western Union messenger boys of Boston.

The King's cable read:

Will you kindly convey to Lieutenant Smith and the other fliers my hearty congratulations on completion, for the first time in history, of the circling of the world by airplanes? I have followed with interest and admiration the progress of this heroic undertaking.

On Defense Day, the boys flew over Washington to Arlington, where on the tomb of the Unknown Soldier, they dropped flowers which Mrs. Coolidge had sent them from the White House. No other planes were allowed in the air at the same time, so that the people of Washington might have an opportunity of seeing the Cruisers.

Returning to Bolling Field, they motored to the Peace Monument and rode in the parade down Pennsylvania Avenue. Next day they left for their westward flight.

'So far as there may have been any hazard in it,' says Erik Nelson, 'the most dangerous leg of the remaining journey lay directly ahead of us on September 13th when we left Washington and rammed our noses into the fog west of Harper's Ferry. Crossing the Alleghanies in the best of weather has its risks. But Lowell led us through or we should have had to turn back, as did the escort planes.

'Just after leaving Cumberland, Maryland, the weather was so thick you could have cut it with a knife. We tried to climb over the fog, but it reached beyond our ceiling. Then we tried hugging the tree-tops. Smith had never been across this particular section before. When it proved impossible for us to proceed straight ahead without running considerable risk of hitting a mountain, the five escort planes left us; but Smith, with the aid of his map and the uncanny faculty he has for finding his way in any weather, turned to the right until we picked up a canyon, and flying just high enough off a railroad to avoid trains and telegraph poles, he managed to lead us through the pass, single file, to Uniontown, Pennsylvania. The five escort planes, unable to find a way through, returned to Washington and followed us the next day. Twenty planes met us near Columbus, Ohio, and escorted us from there on to Dayton. Lieutenant Harold Harris led them in the largest plane in the world, the Barling Bomber triplane, which has a wing spread of about one hundred and twenty feet, weighs over ten tons, and is propelled by six Liberty engines each of four hundred and fifty horse-power. Hovering beside it was the tiny Sperry Messenger with a small three-cylinder motor — like a hummingbird following an eagle.

'As we passed over Wilbur Wright airdrome, we saw "Welcome World Fliers" painted in huge letters on the ground, and between fifty thousand and a hundred thousand people cheered us a moment later as we came gliding down over McCook Field, the United States Army Air Service experimental station.

'The first men to reach us were the mechanics. They were Jack's pals, men with whom he had worked for years. They said: "Well, Jack, old boy, what have you brought us from China in the way of souvenirs?" to which Jack replied that he had only brought himself. So they turned him upside down, shook all the tools out of his pockets, and kept them as trophies. A moment later, a young lady broke through the crowd and threw her arms around him. From now on, this became a daily feature of our receptions, and in every city Jack was invariably met by one of these "new cousins."

'Here also I met with old "Nome" again, my Siberian sled-dog that I brought from Alaska in the cockpit of my plane on the New York to Nome flight. Our Dayton friends presented us with Liberty bonds, flowers, and traveling-bags. And for the first time on our Flight we allowed some one else to check and service-up the planes. The boys at McCook Field worked on the ships in shifts, for two nights and a day, without stopping, going over every bolt and wire to find out exactly how the Cruisers had stood the strain of the Flight. The result of their investigation was very satisfactory: they were still capable of carrying us another three thousand miles to Seattle. So that we should take no more risks than necessary, we decided to fly the southern route from Chicago, to avoid the higher ranges of the Rockies.

'We ourselves were subjected to tests as well as our Cruisers, for the Air Service doctors insisted on putting each of us through the rigid physical examination given to aviation cadets. This is the stiffest medical test in the world, and we were half afraid that our knee jerks, blood pressure, or breathing, etc., might not satisfy the exacting experts. However, we agreed to undergo the examination only on the condition that no matter what they discovered we were to go on. To our surprise, we were passed as very "paragons of physical fitness." We were very tired, of course, but more in mind than in body.

'Monday morning, September 15th, we continued on across Ohio, Indiana and Illinois,' added Smith. 'Dozens of railway lines pointed to that giant of the prairies, Chicago, with the expanse of Grant Park lying verdant between gray skyscrapers and the scintillating waters of

Lake Michigan. North of the skyscrapers of Michigan Boulevard and the Drake Hotel we turned west and flew across the city to the airmail landing-field in the little Illinois city of Maywood.

'A flying squadron of motor-cycle police escorted us to the Drake. They evidently thought that aviators must have speed on the ground as well as in the air, for they dashed through the streets and across Lincoln Park at fifty miles an hour with shrieking sirens. One "cop," who was a trick rider, let go the handle-bars, and stood up on his saddle with his arms folded. Another poised with his head on the saddle and his feet in the air and steered as though he were right side up.

'At a mammoth banquet that night, we were each presented with an engraved cigarette box crammed with five-dollar gold pieces and a card bearing the following legend: "May this box never be empty. Enclosed is the wherewithal to keep it filled."

'Next morning, when we went out to the field to take off for Omaha, a dense fog had come down. So, after waiting till 1.30 P.M., we returned to the city, spent our second night as the guests of the manager of the Chicago Beach Hotel in elegant suites which we were told were ours for a honeymoon, and made our departure the following morning at 10 A.M.

'At Omaha, four hundred and fifty miles to westward, which was our next stop, the people of Nebraska, led by that prince among hosts, Mr. Gould Dietz, had devised a particularly pleasant form of entertainment for us. Each year they choose a "Queen of Omaha" and five ladies-in-waiting. To these delightful damsels they gave the duty of entertaining us. Instead of shaking hands for hours, we held one hand the whole evening. Instead of returning thanks to a civic welcome in stuttering sentences, we spoke in the more eloquent language of the eyes. The idea met with our unanimous and enthusiastic approval. Next morning, September 17th, we flew down the Missouri River for one hundred and twenty-five miles to St. Joseph,

IF THEY HAD BROUGHT HOME ALL THEIR GIFTS AND SOUVENIRS

Drawing by Franklin Collier for *The Independent*

A PROUD MOTHER AND HER SON

'MISS SAN FRANCISCO' GIVING COMMANDER SMITH THE OFFICIAL KISS OF WELCOME WHILE THE OTHERS NERVOUSLY AWAIT THEIR TURNS

ERIK LEANING AGAINST THE PROP, REMINISCING WITH MARTIN, WHILE LES TELLS A GOOD ONE TO LEIGH AND SMITTY, AND HANK AND JACK LISTEN IN

A WELCOME SIGHT — MOUNT SHASTA AGAIN AFTER
26,000 MILES

'PETIE' AND 'FELIX,' THE STUFFED MONKEY MASCOTS OF THE
CHICAGO, WELCOMED BACK TO LOS ANGELES BY THEIR GOD-
MOTHER, MISS PRISCILLA DEAN

where we attended a civic luncheon, and were presented with gold plaques entitling us to free admission to everything in that city as long as we live. We hope to return before we are too old to enjoy a little Missouri high life.

'A few minutes before 1.30 P.M. we bade *au revoir* to the St. Josephians, and forty minutes later passed over Kansas City before heading for Muskogee. As we approached the Arkansas River, we were met by a large number of planes — privately owned busses that citizens of Oklahoma had flown in from various parts of the State. The air was thick with them, for the cowboys and oil drillers of the great Southwest are taking as naturally to the cavalry of the clouds as they ever did to pinto ponies.

'Although Muskogee is only a small city, fully twenty-five thousand people were waiting at Hat Box Field to give us one of the heartiest receptions that we met with anywhere. As we glided into the wind a salute of twenty-one guns was fired and at a banquet that night we were presented with gold medallions commemorating our visit.

'Next morning, we wanted to push off early for Texas, but a storm had suddenly arisen, of such violence that it blew in the windows of our hotel, and made a lake of the flying-field. Shortly before noon, however, Jupiter Pluvius turned off the faucets and we hopped from the mud into the sky and droned on across Oklahoma and the Red River to Dallas, Texas. "Droned" is right, because a stiff head wind made it possible for a Texas passenger train to get ahead of us till it made one of its usual prolonged stops. After landing at Love Field before a crowd of some forty thousand people, we attended another banquet, accepted more unexpected presents, and hopped off the following day, September 20th, for a 645-mile flight across the desert to El Paso.

'Again we had to face a stiff head wind. We had left Dallas at 9.40 and three hours later broke our journey for an hour by landing at Sweetwater, where we took on more gas and oil and enjoyed a picnic lunch that had been prepared by the thoughtful Texans. From 1.30 P.M. we flew on until, in the soft light of one of the matchless sunsets for which the Painted Desert is famous, we caught sight of El Paso and the silver serpent of the Rio Grande.

'The only incident of that long flight occurred just outside Pecos, when Lieutenants Goddard and Bockhurst in an escort plane had a forced landing. Their "DH" was badly damaged while attempting to insinuate itself into an *arroyo*.

'"Birdie" Wright, our resourceful general manager, who crossed the continent twice with us in a DH-9, which he fondly called his "puddle jumper," landed at Pecos, and rescued pilot and photographer from gila monsters and rattlesnakes, before continuing after us. Goddard and Bockhurst chartered an ancient "flivver," drove all night and caught up with us at the Mexican border where they borrowed another plane. They had accompanied us all the way from Mere Point, Maine, in order to film our crossing of North America.

'Just as night was closing over the desert, we landed at Fort Bliss, with red fire shooting from our exhausts. A crowd of twenty thousand people broke through the guards and surged around us. Disentangling ourselves at last we were rushed to the banquet without which we were beginning to feel our day was not complete and were here presented with beautifully embroidered Mexican *serapes*, a type of Spanish shawl that goes as well with the beauty of a débutante from Dubuque as it does with that of a siren of Seville.

'Next morning, September 22d, at 7.15 A.M. we took-off for Tucson. At one o'clock we passed over the Rincon Mountains and a few minutes later landed at this ancient and picturesque metropolis. As usual, the city fathers had arranged a banquet. We were also presented by the different cities of Arizona, such as Tucson, Phœnix, Bisbee, and others, with the most beautiful Navajo blankets, the finest to be found in all the country of the Rio Grande.

'By now our cockpits, as well as our insides, were laden with the gifts of our countrymen. But still more lavish gifts awaited us.

'We were on the home stretch when we left Tucson for San Diego,' says Commander Smith, 'and had we not made it a practice of never deviating from our course, we should have flown over Phœnix in order to pay tribute to the memory of one of the gamest men that ever held a control stick — Lieutenant Frank Luke. If there lives an American who has never heard of the adventures of daredevil Luke in shooting down German sausage balloons, he has missed a great story.

'With some twenty-five thousand miles of air trail behind us, our motors sang a triumphant chorus as we flew toward the familiar jagged peaks of the Crater and Growler Mountains.

'There isn't much use trying to describe my feelings during this flight. Every minute was bringing us a mile and a half nearer my California home, just over the desert's rim. We had been gone a long time. We had crossed vast continents and distant seas. We had passed through experiences when we lived a lifetime in a day. And now, on this radiant morning, San Diego lay ahead! When our wheels touched the soil of Coronado Island we had been around the world. How can I describe it? Ten years hence, perhaps. But now it seems like a dream.'

For weeks, San Diego had been preparing for the greatest celebration in the history of the city. Special ferries, busses, and strings of street cars were in readiness to take thousands of people to Rockwell Field. Hundreds of soldiers and sailors were in their barracks awaiting the command to 'fall in.' Thirty army and navy airplanes had just been trundled out of their hangars.

But at 9.20 a message flashed across the mountains that the Fliers were ahead of time. A few moments later, thirty propellers were being swung at Rockwell Field, thirty planes leaped into the air, and half the telephones in San Diego began to ring. Where were Mr. and Mrs.

Jasper Smith, and Mrs. Roberta Harding, who had come down from their homes in Los Angeles the night before?

By ten o'clock, some hundreds of spectators had drifted out to North Island. A few minutes later, cars arrived with the parents of the Fliers and the city officials.

Mr. Otis M. Wiles, of Los Angeles, gives us an intimate picture of the scene:

'Three planes, flying abreast and trailed by twenty-five others, loomed through the morning mist to eastward.

'"Oh, my dear — here he comes," said Mrs. Jasper Smith, standing on tiptoe and waving her handkerchief toward the middle plane — for she knew her boy was piloting it. There were tears of joy in her eyes. "I'm proud, and I don't care who knows it!" said the Reverend Jasper Smith.

'At 11.25 A.M. Pacific Coast time, on the morning of September 22d the wheels of Smith's Cruiser touched the ground, and he led the Flight down in such a way that Nelson's and Wade's planes landed at the same instant. As the Fliers jumped out of their cockpits, Smith's friends hoisted him into the air.

'"Let me down, fellows, I want to see my mother first," he shouted. A moment later they were together. The little family of three just stood there, wedged in the throng, speechless, supremely happy, while near by "Smiling Jack" was also in the arms of his mother.

'A hush came over the spectators as an Army chaplain gave thanks to Almighty God:

'"*We thank Thee, our Father, for the safe return of these Magellans of the air, for their bravery, fortitude and daring that caused them to be the first to carry the Stars and Stripes around the world on the wings of the wind. And we thank Thee for hearkening to the prayers of their countrymen for the success of this great undertaking.*"'

Next day the boys were taken out to Balboa Park where they were presented with a silver service set apiece, appropriately inscribed.   Erik Nelson also received an ancient and very valuable copper coin from his brother Swedes, three and a half inches thick and weighing four pounds!

That night Smith's old 'buddies,' men like Paul Richter, 'Gil' Irvin, Vergil Hine, Frank Siefert, and others, gave a banquet for them at the Hotel del Coronado, where they were guests until their departure for Santa Monica the following day.

Three cities were bidding for the honor of being the terminus of the World Flight; San Diego, whither they had gone to have their compasses swung, Santa Monica, where the Cruisers were built, and Seattle, their point of departure. Officially, the latter was the terminus, but the reception next day at Santa Monica was perhaps the most remarkable demonstration of enthusiasm which they encountered in their travels.

'All night long the mechanics at Rockwell Field worked over our planes, installing new engines and tuning them up for our final hop,' says Smith. 'This was the second time during the entire flight that we had allowed any one to touch our planes. At 1 P.M. on the afternoon of September 23d, we circled over North Island, and started on the 125-mile trip from Coronado to Santa Monica.

'Almost before we knew it, we were flying over the palm groves and palaces of Los Angeles. To our right were the mansions of the movie-stars and the minarets of Fairbanks's Baghdad, reminding us how far we had come from the date groves and domes of Haroun-al-Rashid's city by the Tigris. Between Los Angeles and the sea lay one big checker-board of real-estate projects.

'As we approached Santa Monica and looked down to see whether Clover Field, under command of Lieutenant Horace Kenyon, was still there, we noticed that the adjoining fields were packed with automobiles. They were lined fender to fender in rows a half-mile long and a half-mile deep.

'The size of the crowd was variously estimated at from

one hundred thousand to a quarter of a million. As we circled around and came gliding down into the wind at 2.25 P.M. I thought to myself: "Boys, we're in for a wild time." And we were.

'A grandstand had been erected on one side of the field, and in front of that was a fenced enclosure which had been thickly carpeted with roses. All night long, while our mechanics had worked on the engines at San Diego, other mechanics here at Santa Monica had been transporting truckload after truckload of blossoms to our landing-ground. There must have been an acre of flowers and into the midst of this fragrant field we landed, raising a cloud of dust and rose petals as we taxied to the grandstand.

'All around was a heavy line of guards. As we crawled out of our cockpits, the crowd went wild. With a roar, they knocked down the fence. They knocked down the police. They knocked down the soldiers. They knocked us down.

'They tried to pull our ships apart for souvenirs, but somehow we fought them off. Los Angeles had a pot of gold waiting for us in the grandstand, we were told, symbolizing our arrival at the end of the rainbow. But we had as hard a time reaching it as the Forty-Niners had in winning gold from the soil of California.

'Burly policemen helped us on our way. People were tearing bits off our clothes and snipping off buttons for souvenirs. One lady cut a chunk out of my collar with a penknife. And another got hold of my ear — I suppose by mistake. Somebody else took a keepsake out of the seat of my trousers. Luckily I had my old friend "Dutch" Henry for my bodyguard or I might have fared far worse. The last I saw of Jack he was being smothered by a dozen females. Hank was in the arms of another six, and the same number clustered on "Birdie's" neck, having either mistaken him for a Magellan (as they kept calling us) or loving him for himself, which would not be unreasonable. Erik's bald head shone valiantly above the battle. After forty-five minutes of this, we finally arrived at the "end of the rainbow" — much the worse for wear.

'"Where's Donald Douglas?" was the first question that Erik had asked when he jumped out of the cockpit of the *New Orleans* and landed ankle-deep in roses. "I want to congratulate that boy, for he sure does know how to build airplanes."

'More than ten thousand school children were at Clover Field to see us land. They saw that, and a riot as well.'

Owing to the souvenir hunters, it was impossible for the boys to do any work on their planes that night, so they started for Hollywood and the Christie Hotel.

Weeks before the start of the World Flight, when word arrived that a group of pilots and mechanics were coming West to supervise the building of the airplanes, an officer of the Air Service stationed at Santa Monica took it upon himself to ask the managers of the various hotels whether they would not give the airmen a special rate. But to no avail, until a Mr. Christie, proprietor of an hotel in a suburb of Los Angeles, sent word that he would consider it a very great honor to have as his guests the men chosen for such an heroic task. When, six months later, the Fliers arrived at Boston, having achieved world fame, the great hotels of Los Angeles wrote and wired to them, offering to place suites at their disposal. But the Fliers arranged to stay with Mr. Christie, who had been their friend before the Flight. On the way to the hotel they passed through Beverley Hills, where the city had made elaborate preparations, and another throng had assembled to honor them and to present Jack with a loving-cup. Unfortunately, some one had neglected to tell them about it, with the result that all of them were there except Jack!

At Christie's, in Hollywood, the boys found the lobby banked with flowers. They were ushered up to the same rooms they had occupied before the Flight, on each door of which a silver plate was now affixed with an inscription similar to the following:

LIEUTENANT LOWELL H. SMITH

of the United States Army Air Service
occupied this room upon completion of
the World Flight, September 23, 1924.

After the boys had flown on north, a certain Mr. Sam
Perkins presented himself to the room clerk of the Christie
Hotel.

'I want to sleep in a World Flier's room,' he said. Accordingly, the clerk assigned him to the room that had
been occupied by Smith. Two days later, Mr. Perkins left
and an hotel employee found the following message tacked
underneath the memorial plate:

This room occupied by Sam Perkins,
of Sioux City, Iowa. He didn't fly out,
but he's going to have to walk back.

'Our arrival at San Francisco on September 26th was
not like our return to Los Angeles,' says Smith, 'for no one
was trampled under foot by our happy fellow countrymen
at the Presidio as had happened at that dervish dance at
Santa Monica. For this we have to thank General Morton,
the corps commander, and Colonel Lahm, who guarded
Crissey Field with several regiments of soldiers. There was
a big crowd waiting for us here at San Francisco, but at
our urgent request their special entertainment was postponed till our return from Seattle, when we were fairly
overwhelmed with hospitality at the hands of Mayor
Rolf and his fellow citizens who even went so far as to
present each of us with a check for twelve hundred and
fifty dollars. It began to look as though we had indeed
found the end of a rainbow.

'Our next stop was at Eugene — my second home — so
you can imagine how much attention my friends paid to
our requests that they cut the glad-hand business to the
minimum. Governor Pierce came from Salem to welcome
us on behalf of the people of Oregon, and Mayor Parks,
Earl Simmons, Eugene's aviation enthusiast, and thou-

AT THE JOURNEY'S END
Landing at Seattle after winging their way round the world. 26,345 miles

TIMID IN TALK, THOUGH BOLD IN THE AIR, SMITH REPLIES TO
MAYOR BROWN OF SEATTLE

sands of others from all over that part of the State were there.

'The following day, September 28th, at 9.55 A.M. we set out on the last leg of the Flight. Passing over Salem, we stopped for a few minutes at Vancouver Barracks near Portland, crossed the Columbia River into Washington, and headed toward a cloud on the horizon "no bigger than a man's hand." And the cloud turned out to be old Mount Rainier — a cone of shining white. Above the great forest it stood, over which I had so often flown on fire patrol, a friend beckoning us on.

> ' " There was sunshine in the heart of me
>   My blood sang in the breeze,
> That mountain was a part of me,
>   And so were all these trees." '

'As we drew near Lake Washington, for the second time on our journey we broke our V-formation and flew abreast over Sand Point Field just as we had done at San Diego, so that each plane should finish the flight at the same time.

'Beneath us we saw a welcome sign, one hundred and fifty feet long and with letters twenty feet high. According to the official timers the wheels of the *Chicago* touched the field at 1.28 P.M., Pacific time, on September 28th, 1924.

'From Seattle to Seattle we had flown 26,345 miles, in a total of 363 hours and 7 minutes. Our average rate of speed in circling the world had been 72½ miles per hour and our flying time the equivalent of 15 days, 3 hours, and 7 minutes.

'Fifty thousand citizens of Seattle gave us a magnificent reception. More speeches were made and we were presented with platinum and gold rings from Alaska, set with bloodstones.

'The enthusiasm all along the Coast was really remarkable. Couples arranged their marriages to coincide with the termination of the World Flight and there was a fashion for a time of wearing beauty patches cut in the silhouette of a Douglas Cruiser. They were even naming babies for us.

'One of the most gratifying experiences of those great days in Seattle, when we were whirled around so fast that we hardly had time to realize that our flight was really over and that our dreams had come true, was the way in which Major Martin congratulated us. The speech he made in Seattle was one of the finest we have ever heard, and it touched us all very deeply.

'The following afternoon, Seattle friends took us out to Sand Point Field, where "Les" Arnold's sister, Mrs. Francis L. Cole, unveiled a monument commemorating the fact that Seattle had been the starting-point and end of the first World Flight. It was a granite shaft fifteen feet high with a globe at the top surmounted by a pair of bronze wings. On one side was a bronze plate bearing our names and the dates of our departure and return. We had certainly never expected to see our names on a monument until we were under it.

'While we were saying, "Well, where do we go from here?" a telegram arrived from General Patrick instructing us to come at once by train and attend the International Air Races in Dayton. We were delighted, because we thought, oh, well, the Flight's over and to-morrow the country will have forgotten about it and us, so on our way to Dayton we'll just catch up on lost sleep. But we were wrong.

'All along the route of the Chicago, Milwaukee & St. Paul, crowds gathered at the stations, calling for "Smiling Jack," "Leigh-the-Sheik," "Erik-the-Viking," "Hank," and "Les," our aerial Demosthenes.

'On our way across the mountains, we went up to the engine, to see why we were not getting the regulation number of cinders in our eyes, and found there was an electric locomotive pulling the long transcontinental train. So we climbed into the cab and rode away with the engineer. While there, Joe Bahl, a railroad official who was looking after us as far as Chicago, read us a telegram that he had just received from the president of the Chamber of Commerce at Spokane saying that he and a Committee of Six would shortly join the train to greet us, and asking us to stop the *Olympian* for forty-five minutes, instead of the usual fifteen, upon our arrival at Spokane, so that the city could tender us a public reception.

'We were fed-up with receptions. So we begged Mr. Bahl to say that the *Olympian* could wait for no man.

'Well, when the president of the Chamber of Commerce came on board, instead of an escort of aldermen, his Committee consisted of the six snappiest Spokanese that ever wore short skirts. So we at once called Bahl and asked him to delay the *Olympian* until Doomsday, by all means. In fact we were thinking of settling down in Spokane, we said, the progressive spirit of the citizens having struck a sympathetic chord within us. But Bahl confuted us with our own words, saying the C., M. and St. P. could wait for neither man nor woman. But he relented, and we lay over for a whole hour.

'As we were pulling into Miles City, Montana, we were met by cowboys flying in airplanes. They dived down to the train, and waved to us, and they flew alongside all the way into the city. When the train stopped we were hauled out onto the station platform, presented with silk "bandanas," and then loaded into a Deadwood stage-coach of the vintage of Custer's last stand and pulled up and down the platform.

'At nearly every stop Mr. Bahl returned with ducks, grouse, squab, and prairie chickens that local committees had brought down for us. In Aberdeen, I believe it was, a committee presented us with a case of canned corn. Some of the passengers in the car opened it at once to see if it really contained what it claimed to hold, for they were under the impression that we were too near the Canadian border to find undistilled corn in a can!

'On the outskirts of Minneapolis, I was kidnaped from the train, hustled into an auto, and taken through the streets of the city to a radio broadcasting station while crowds of tall Scandinavians yelled: "Where's the Swede? *Show us the big Swede!*" Whereupon Erik would bare his patriarchal pate to the plaudits of his race-fellows.

'By now our mail was becoming a formidable problem. "Birdie" Wright and Mr. Bahl used to bring stacks of it on the train every day. One man wrote and asked us if there was any truth in the story that ice-worms lived in the glaciers of Alaska. Another wanted to know if we had seen any of the tropical fish that climb trees, which he had been reading about in the papers. A third asked us if we could favor him with news of his brother, Ignatz Salmovitz, who was last heard of as a convict working in a Siberian coal mine. But for some unknown reason letters from girls predominated. One that I received upon our return to our after-the-flight headquarters at the Lafayette Hotel in Washington, is a model of the simple, vivid epistolary style, which even the author of a book of etiquette could not better. It read: "*My name is Carmen. I am Spanish.*" Underneath was a telephone number. What a wealth of feeling she packed into a little space!

'To offset that sort of thing, "Les" got one with a mean jab from a co-ed: who said that our achievement was all right, but the newspaper dope about us was the bunk. There were two classes of men who got her nanny, she wrote — clergymen and aviators! And I dare say she was logical, for there are times when both sorts of sky-pilots do a deal of praying.

'At Dayton we were much honored by being met at the train by Orville Wright, co-inventor of the airplane, and many other distinguished men. Following the aeronautical programme in which we took part, General Patrick directed us to return to Seattle and fly our Cruisers back across the continent so that the Government could make proper arrangements for their final disposal.

'So off we went again, with "Birdie" Wright still acting as our flying chaperon. On our way through Los Angeles this time, we fulfilled another obligation. Before we had started on the Flight, the Ambassador Hotel had given a party for us in the Cocoanut Grove, and that evening the manager had taken eight stuffed monkeys down from his palms and presented them to us. The six marmosets which we returned (for "Leigh" and "Hank" had rescued theirs) were auctioned off and the manager handed us the proceeds.

'Here I would like to again express our deep gratitude to the people of all the cities who presented us with gifts. We had expected nothing and were overwhelmed by the generosity that we encountered on every side.

'At El Paso it was necessary that the flight be divided in order that all engagements might be fulfilled. Accordingly the *Boston* and the *New Orleans* went to San Antonio, Houston, and New Orleans, and worked up to St. Louis *via* Dallas and Muskogee; while the *Chicago* went direct to St. Louis *via* Dallas.

'At San Antonio the boys were dined by the Canopus Club at Jim Maverick's Sunshine Ranch, where Toastmaster Hall cracked his quirt, lassoed each in turn, and hauled him to the center of the floor to make a speech.

'In New Orleans "Erik" and "Jack" were made honorary citizens and presented with mammoth loving-cups four feet high.

'Our plane was left at Scott Field near St. Louis, while "Les" and I continued on to Chicago by train, arriving there on the morning of November 8th. We were met at the station by a committee and escorted to the Drake Hotel, where we were the guests of the city of Chicago through the combined city Civic Clubs and the Army and Navy Club. We were swamped with invitations, and even if we could have bade the sun stand still in order to lengthen the days from twenty-four to seventy-two hours we could hardly have accepted them all.

'Among the most notable affairs that we did attend was a reception at the Army and Navy Club. Here the combined Civic Clubs had a luncheon, where Chicago's business men, dropping their work, crowded in for a few hours. We were also the guests of the American Legion at their annual Armistice Ball where we were greeted by each Legionnaire and his lady.

'But the night of nights was that of November 9th,

when at the huge Chicago Auditorium, before a howling crowd, Mayor Dever, on behalf of the citizens of Chicago, presented us each with a Packard straight-eight, we were so overwhelmed that words failed us and about all we could stammer was that "of all the cities in America that our plane could have been named after, we were indeed thankful that Lady Luck had been kind enough to award us the name Chicago" — no longer the "Windy City" to us, but now the city of "sweeping hospitality," and, for "Les" and myself, best of all the cities that we had visited on our way around the world.

'On November 11th, after three days and nights of entertainment, during which time we had had little or no rest, we realized that we must leave this city of perpetual entertainment or collapse from lack of sleep; so we stole away to the station, and boarded a train for St. Louis, determined to sleep all the way. But no sooner had the train started than an official knocked on the door and announced that the President of the Chicago and Alton Railroad desired to extend us the hospitality of his private car. So our "nap" had to be deferred again.

'Several things will always make us remember St. Louis. The first was a farce that just escaped being a tragedy. Mr. Joseph O'Neil, the vice-chairman of the Reception Committee, took the Flight Historian's place in the rear cockpit of Lieutenant Moseley's escort plane in order to throw a huge bouquet of roses at the feet of the Fliers while they were being officially welcomed by the city. But O'Neil had never been in an airplane before, so he was fair game for all of us. Some one brought him a document to sign, in which he agreed not to hold the Government responsible for any accident that might befall him on the flight. A colonel said to him: "Now, Joe, you have no doubt noticed that Moseley's plane is painted black and looks like a coffin. You have your flowers right along with you, so when you get up there if there is an accident all you have to do is to fold your arms."

'When the rest of us had landed at Lambert Field,

Moseley circled around so that O'Neil could throw the flowers. He threw them at the proper moment all right, but in the wrong direction, so that instead of their falling clear of the plane, the air stream carried them back into the tail where they caught in the elevator wires. For several minutes the plane was out of control, and shot up into the air. Just as she was about to stall and fall into a spin, Moseley succeeded in shaking the flowers free, otherwise there might have been a tragedy.

'But the chief reason why we shall remember St. Louis is because of a speech delivered at the Racquet Club banquet on our first evening by a leading criminal lawyer of Missouri, famous also as an after-dinner speaker. His name is Eugene H. Angert. He had sized the situation up and knew that we had listened to orators from Coast to Coast slopping whole bib-fulls of "blah" about our heroism. So he decided to give us a kick in the pants! Here is a specimen:

Colonel Perkins called me up late this afternoon and told me he had discovered why the visit of our distinguished guests was delayed for a whole week under such mysterious circumstances. They have been in a sanitarium. They had broken down under the strain of the dinners, luncheons, and banquets that were forced upon them in almost every city of the country since their return. It was not the food; and, strange to say, it was not even the drink, that did it. It was the speeches that had prostrated them. After-dinner speakers, or in the vernacular, postprandial orators, had fed them on flattery until they became afflicted with acute mental indigestion. Extravagant praise, garnished with a sauce of superlatives, was served to them at each celebration. They were gorged with hero worship and glutted with glorification. They were asphyxiated by adulation.

'Thus spake Perkins. And then he went on to say,

It is up to you to administer an antidote.

Since I must tell the truth about our guests, I want them to know that it hurts me just as much as it does them — as the father always says when he spanks his child.

Long before the guests of the evening were born, fully half a century ago, Jules Verne demonstrated that, even in the era of travel by ox-cart and sailing vessel, it was possible to go Around the World in Eighty Days. Many years later, and within the memory of all of us here, a frail young woman, Nellie Bly, with only such equipment as God and Nature had given her, assisted by no mechanician to keep her propellers in shape and carrying no spare parts to replace those worn out by careless use, steering her solitary course solely by feminine instinct and not by sextant, earth inductor compass, or gyroscopic fore-and-aft inclinometer, Nellie Bly lowered the record established by Jules Verne. Unaccompanied, unequipped, untrained, and unsupported, she made the trip around the world in seventy-two days.

But who among us ever yields a brief tribute to the memory of Henry Frederick? From birth, he was minus a surname and he was blind in one eye; but despite these handicaps, in 1903 he went around the world in fifty-four days and captured from Nellie the Marquis of Queensberry's diamond championship belt.

Eight years later, there entered the lists of world-trippers a Paris newspaper man, André Jaeger Schmidt, of uncertain nationality, but evidently French by his first name, German by his last, and related to a popular brand of underwear by his middle name. History records that Smith had only one leg. With no companion except his crutch, and no equipment except one extra pad for the crotch, he made the trip around the world — and in midwinter at that — in a little less than thirty-nine days, the record up to the present hour.

More in sorrow than in anger, let us compare these trips around the world with the one we are celebrating to-night. Our guests were aided and abetted from the beginning to the end of their journey by an army of mechanics, radio experts, weather forecasters, cheerupidists, mah jongg players, and ouija board mediums — an army greater in numbers than Cornwallis surrendered at Yorktown. They were supported by a fleet of Government ships scattered throughout the navigable and unnavigable waters of both hemispheres as large as the combined fleets which the Five Great Naval Powers, by the Washington Treaty, agreed to scrap and did not. And I tell you in strict confidence, that I have it from a member of the Naval Strategy Board that during the entire flight it was impossible for these aviators to have dropped into the Atlantic or Pacific, the Arctic or Antarctic Oceans, the Dead Sea, Salt Lake, or Cripple Creek, or into any bay, inlet, lagoon, or pond, within the jurisdiction of

'MISS AMERICA' PINS A ROSE ON 'SMILING JACK

AT SEATTLE WE SAID GOOD-BYE TO OUR CRUISERS AND STARTED
EAST, READY FOR OUR NEXT ADVENTURE

ON THEIR WAY EAST THE AIRMEN GOT STILL ANOTHER THRILL CROSSING THE
CASCADE RANGE IN THE SWAYING CAB OF A MILWAUKEE ELECTRIC FLIER

THE LAST PICTURE TAKEN OF THE WORLD FLIERS BEFORE THEY
TURNED THEIR PLANES OVER TO THE GOVERNMENT

Commander Smith is holding on to a strut of his flagship.
Left to right: Standing: Lieutenants Wade, Corliss Moseley, Ogden, Arnold,
Burdette Wright, Nelson. Seated: Lowell Thomas, Sergeant Kennedy,
Lieutenant Harding with 'Frank,' the raccoon mascot. Moseley, Wright,
Thomas, and Kennedy were flying in escort planes.

GOING OVER THE ROUTE WITH THE FLIGHT HISTORIAN

From left to right: — Arnold, Harding, Nelson, Wade, Flight-Commander Smith, Lowell Thomas, Ogden, and Mrs. Corliss Moseley, secretary to the Fliers

the League of Nations, without alighting upon the deck of a United States warship.

At every point where they were expected to hop off, the Government had sent from the Weather Bureau at Washington a bunch of weather experts, whose long association with the Harding administration had taught them just where to look for hot air and whose few months' contact with the Coolidge Administration had made them experts in locating cross-currents of cold air.

Shades of Jules Verne! We know not to what Elysian fields your spirit may have taken flight; but, if you have tuned in tonight, let your imaginative soul take joy from the message we broadcast to you, that, fifty-two years ago, you did the trip around the world in less than half the days that the greatest aviators of the greatest nation on the globe required in this year of grace 1924.

Keep your mind on their number — one hundred and seventy-two! And then think of little Nellie Bly, plodding her weary way over the continents, from one hemisphere to the other; scaling the mountains of Bessarabia, winding in and out the sandy deserts of Hindustan, leaving her tiny foot prints in the trackless forests of Africa, and yet back home to punch the time-clock in the office of the New York 'World' at the end of seventy-two days! A hundred thousand citizens of Boston greeted these World Fliers when they finally reached their own country; but when she got back there was no one 'Seeing Nellie Home.'

Think of Henry Frederick, his one good eye glued to the course, stumbling along with not even a faithful dog on a string to show him the way, retracing two steps every time he took one, unable to see his finish — or at least only half of it — and yet turning in a perfect card of fifty-four on the home tee.

And above all, think of André Jaeger Schmidt, denting the globe with his well-worn crutch, slipping and sliding over Greenland's glassy glaciers or sinking his crutch up to its padded crotch in the muck and mire of the African jungle; but with true Teutonic perseverance, pushing on and on in his self-imposed race and coming under the wire an easy winner, in the record time of thirty-nine days! Then let your manly bosoms contract with humility when you think of these three strong, sturdy Americans comfortably seated behind a Liberty engine capable of doing a hundred miles an hour, each with a mechanician by his side to put cracked ice on his head when he was hot and a hot-water bottle on his back when he was cold, and supported by enough accessories before the fact and accessories after the fact to make a lawyer green with envy, not able to finish the trip in less than one hundred and seventy-two days!

An Irishman went to the races with a sure thing. He bet his entire roll on the horse he was tipped off would win, but when the race was run, all of the other horses were back in the stable before his horse finally came under the wire. Then he walked over on the track, went up to the jockey and whispered in his ear, 'And pray what detained you?'

Well may we here to-night count ourselves fortunate in having lived long enough to see their return. Many men and women who cheered their landing were babes in arms when they started. Thirty thousand happily married couples had been happily divorced and most of them happily remarried; we had turned out 1,862,974 automobiles and two members of the President's Cabinet while they were gone. Much water had gone over the dam and more whiskey over the decks of the rum runners' fleet to find its final rest in the stomachs of prohibitionists and anti-prohibitionists alike. The American Bar Association had gone to London and returned, wiser and wetter men. Most of us were still living beyond our means, and thanks to the Federal Inheritance Tax, many of us were dying beyond our means. Truly, it was a far, far different country they came back to from the one they left.

But, after all, absence makes the heart grow fonder; and so, may I say to the guests of the evening, in all seriousness, that, despite your long absence, we are glad that you are back. We are honored to have you with us to-night. You have written an imperishable chapter in the record of American achievement — a record full of great accomplishments. You have met almost insurmountable difficulties and overcome them by your skill, your bravery, your endurance. It was an uncharted sea you sailed. It was a land of nothingness and space you conquered. The whole world has acclaimed your flight, and we, your fellow citizens, are proud of the glory you have brought to the Nation.

'This was the last function we attended before reporting to General Patrick and returning to our pre-Flight jobs. And we were real glad to have a little fresh air after the "asphyxiation by adulation" to which Mr. Angert referred.

'From St. Louis we flew straight on to Dayton, bade farewell to our planes after turning them over to the Commanding Officer at McCook Field in whose charge they are to be kept for the present, and boarded a train for Washington. We are glad the Flight is over. But if General Patrick ordered us to start around the world again tomorrow we should all be ready to go.'

A few months later, Congress voted the award of the Distinguished Service Medal, never before awarded except for services in war, to the six airmen, gave permission for them to accept decorations from foreign countries, and recommended that they receive promotion. Smith, now a Captain, has been advanced one thousand files and is well on his way to a Majority. Nelson, Wade, and Arnold have been advanced five hundred files each, and both Harding and Ogden were offered commissions as second lieutenants in the regular army. All six have been made Chevaliers of the Legion of Honor by France, and several have already received honorary degrees.

'Do you ask, "What is the practical value of the flight around the world?"' said Josephus Daniels in a recent speech. 'Years and years ago, when I was much younger, I had the pleasure of an interview with General Greely, whose expedition to the North gave him just distinction and honor. I said to him, "After all, General Greely, what was the practical value of your expedition?" The minute the words were out of my mouth, I would have given anything to have recalled them, for they could be construed as minimizing the value of his epochal cruise.

'But the General, with his unfailing courtesy, at once put me at my ease by saying: "That is the exact question a member of the British Parliament asked me when I visited London. I told him that whenever the time should come when men of our race would not be ready to discover new countries and to lead in explorations — if that day should ever come, our race would retrograde." And as I do honor to the world-girdlers and congratulate them, I feel proud,

as an American, that these youths have given fresh proof
that "Onward" is the motto of the forward-looking
pioneers of our race to-day.'

C. G. Gray, editor of 'The Aeroplane,' and one of
Britain's foremost aeronautical authorities, wrote of the
Flight:

It was the Americans, Wilbur and Orville Wright, who were
the first to fly an aeroplane under proper control. It was an
American crew under Commander Read in a Curtiss-built
flying-boat who first flew the Atlantic. And it is in accord with
precedent that an American team should be the first to circle the
globe by air.

What could be more natural? Such feats are achieved by
grit, energy, pertinacity, determination, endurance, and faith.
Such human qualities, and especially faith in one's future, are
precisely those which inspired the ancestors of these men to pull
themselves up by the roots and press ever Westward to the
promised land.

Always the wave of conquest has flowed Westward, and perhaps there is a significance in the fact that this flight should en-
circle the earth in the direction in which all our ancestors have
traveled.

Captain Nungesser, the French Ace, who met the boys
in New York, sent them this fine and characteristic letter:

To my Glorious Comrades
Lowell Smith, Erik Nelson, Leigh Wade,
Henry Ogden, John Harding, and Leslie Arnold:

I have rarely witnessed a more heart-stirring home-coming
than that at which I have the pleasure to assist at Mitchel
Field upon this impressive termination of your flight around the
world — for this voyage which you have just accomplished as-
suredly marks an epoch in the history of aviation, and all those
who have so enthusiastically welcomed the appearance of your
wings in the sky of New York, have most certainly been associated with a new page in history.

In memory of the close and affectionate comradeship which
united the French and American Aviation Services during the
War, I am indeed happy to be present at your triumphant return
and to bring you an expression of admiration which I am sure is
shared by all the aviators of France.

At this moment, so glorious for you and American aviation, I cannot but recall with emotion the shadows of all my departed French comrades, who, hallowed in flames, their wings broken or their brows pierced by steel, fell from the skies, leaving their famous names to history. Heroes such as Guynemer, Navarre, Garros, Vedrines, Pegoud, and many others among our brothers in arms come to my mind at this great moment — and I have only to follow the impulse of my own sentiment to know with what warm admiration these great knights of the air would open their arms to you in fraternal greeting.

For you are worthy of them, dear comrades. Even as they, you have given to history names which will be among those we call the aces of aviation. You have won the right to take your place among the greatest of those whose names will never be forgotten. You have been the first to accomplish a voyage around our planet, and thanks to your endurance, your energy, your splendid technical abilities, you have won a victory which is the more brilliant since it is a peaceful one. This victory will be a fertile one — never doubt it — and one day all humanity will enjoy its fruitful promise.

In the name of all my French comrades, in the name of our glorious dead, in the name of all the French aviators who, by their daily exploits are ever working for the progress of aviation, I am most happy to be here to-day, to salute you upon your arrival on American soil and to express to you my personal sentiments of profound admiration. I know what great difficulties must be overcome to accomplish such a voyage as you have just completed, and I extend to you my heartiest congratulations for having so brilliantly conquered them.

My dear comrades, your Country can well be proud of you.

NUNGESSER

These compliments to the Fliers are true and well said, but history will forget both the plaudits of foreign contemporaries and the enthusiasm of their own countrymen. It will forget even the long labor, American in its thoroughness, that made the World Flight possible. It will forget that these dauntless lads faced death a hundred times on their long journey and that their assistants achieved miracles. We shall remember rather that Erik, a knightly figure, carried his sweetheart's picture as an oriflamme on his instrument board, that Leigh's touch on the controls was that of a master evoking the melody of motion, and that the strange, shy Smith, who navigates as well as he speaks badly and is as modest as he is brave, possesses one of the rarest combinations of the human mind — selflessness and strength.

The boys won through because they thought of the day's work and of that alone. They took few photographs, kept few notes of their high adventure: and when it was over they did not talk, but chucked caps in air and danced for glee. The gesture was typical of the spirit in which they approached their task and laid it down when it was very well done. 'Other men will fly around the earth,' as Admiral Robinson said at San Diego, 'but never again will anybody fly around it for the first time.'

THE END